BURY PUBLIC LIBRARIES

THE
Art
of
Murder

*Other books by Jonathan Goodman
published by Piatkus*

**Murder in High Places
Murder in Low Places
The Lady Killers
The Passing of Starr Faithfull**

THE
Art
of
Murder

Edited by
JONATHAN GOODMAN

PIATKUS

For Ronald Settle,
musical artist,
and his wife Margaret

© 1990 Jonathan Goodman

First published in 1990 by
Judy Piatkus (Publishers) Ltd of
5 Windmill Street, London W1P 1HF

British Library Cataloguing in Publication Data
The Art of murder.
1. Murder, history
I. Goodman, Jonathan 1931–
364.152309

ISBN 0–7499–1020–8

Typeset by Phoenix Photosetting, Chatham, Kent
Printed and bound in Great Britain by
Butler & Tanner Ltd, Frome

Contents

Stilled Lifes – an Introduction   Jonathan Goodman   *page*   1
Pen, Pencil, and Poison   Oscar Wilde   5
The Immortal Trooper   Jonathan Goodman   23
The Murderous Brush-Work of William Hepper
   Richard Whittington-Egan   27
The Sportsman and the Scholar: A Family Secret
   Jeffrey Bloomfield   61
Salieri and the 'Murder' of Mozart   Albert Borowitz   78
Bloody and Bowed: The Brief Life of a Playwright
   Joan Lock   100
Architect of a Murder   *New York Times* and
   Jonathan Goodman   109
A Literate Killer   Rayner Heppenstall   158
Revenge in Rome   Benvenuto Cellini   192
In the Name of Love   Kenneth G. Weinberg   198
Artist With a Razor   Molly Tibbs   208
A Reader's Revenge   Albert Borowitz   219
Lamb and a Slaughter   Jonathan Goodman   228
Acknowledgments and Sources   232

Stilled Lifes

Jonathan Goodman

IT IS HARD nowadays to make out what some people, not all lacking dictionaries, mean by Art. In a few pages' time, you will come across Oscar Wilde's declaration, incidentally circa the autumn of the Whitechapel Rippings, that 'Life itself is an art, and has its modes of style no less than the arts that seek to express it' – but as the declaration, *because* it was made by Wilde, was not taken too, if at all, seriously, he cannot be blamed for the decay of the word 'Art'. Its rotting seems to have set in some ten years later, around the start of this century, when music-hall performers (all of them, even the escapologists, the fire-eaters, the muscle men) took to calling themselves variety *artists*: in 1910, Dr Crippen's come-uppance for the murder of his wife, stage-named Belle Elmore, was set in train by female members of the Music Hall Artists' Railway Association. But at least the illegitimate performers had the genteel temerity to pronounce themselves arTEESTS. In the 1950s, only partly as a consequence of practically-free-for-all TV, Variety died, and those music-halls that were not then Mecca-nized for bingo or demolished to make car parks were taken over by pop singers and, quite as dependent on electronics, guitarists, producing a multitude of dins. And before long, the pop stars insisted that they were ARtists, that the noises they made were art; and their raving fans went along with those insistences; and *soi-disant* music critics wrote articles on The Art of Recording Artists like Gary Glitter, Alvin Stardust and, I shouldn't be surprised, Elvis Tinsel.

I

Meanwhile, a much-publicised novelist contended that graffiti on tube trains and high-rise blocks of council flats (the latter designed by architects, they too speaking of Their Art, who hadn't even grasped the basics of Leggo, let alone of Meccano) were the modern equivalent of primitive works of art – that the aerosol paint-spray was the most art-assisting innovation since the palette. I don't know whether the novelist, having already gone too far, went farther – by contending, for instance, that the competitive chorusing of obscenities at football matches made contrapuntal oratorios, that the dumping of old bikes and prams in pretty ponds created collages, that traffic-jamming protest processions were as stirring to the soul as the Grand March in *Aida*.

Don't misunderstand me. Art is not bound within genres. For instance, some lyrics by Cole Porter, Ira Gershwin, and Oscar Hammerstein II (whose paternal grandfather's opera house is mentioned on page 115) are superior as poetry to many of the poems written since; some graphic design is more artistic than some old masters; some modern romantic novels entertain the intellect and touch emotions more successfully than some elderly 'classic' novels that have to be read by students of Eng Lit; some mechanical gadgets are better looking than some sculptures.

But, in choosing the contents of this book, I have stuck to arts that are undeniably such – or rather, to artists who definitely were. Not all of the artists herein were great – indeed, a couple were merely competent. Eleven of the thirteen accounts are of murders certainly or suspectedly by or of artists; one of the odd two out is of a murder that had an outcome that was turned into art, and the other – complicated, this – is of a case of unnatural death that seems to have resulted from a foolish attempt to force nature to imitate a detail of a work of art that was itself inspired by nature.

'In choosing the contents,' I said a minute ago – meaning, in one respect, that certain apt cases are left out. Albert Borowitz (a contributor to the body of this book) thinks that

> . . . perhaps the greatest musician to have figured as murderer in a domestic tragedy was the Renaissance madrigal composer, Don Carlo Gesualdo, Prince of Venosa. In 1586 he married a noble Neapolitan lady, Donna Maria d'Avalos. Four years later, having

learned of her love affair with the Duke of Andria, he had her murdered by hired assassins. The story is told by Gesualdo's contemporary, Abbe Brantome, in his *Lives of Fair and Gallant Ladies* . . . The lady's relatives were hot to avenge her murder, but the focus of their anger struck Brantome as distinctly odd. They would not have sought satisfaction from Gesualdo if he had struck the blows with his own hands (for the law of Renaissance Italy recognised the right of a wronged husband to kill his wayward spouse). What annoyed Donna Maria's family was that the prince had had his wife slain by low-born bravos who did not deserve to have their hands stained with noble blood. He wrote: '. . . I make appeal to our great orators and wise lawyers that they tell me this: which act is the more monstrous, for a man to kill his wife with his own hand, the hand which hath so oftentimes loved and caressed her, or by that of a base-born slave?' In any event, like Hamlet, the relatives of Donna Maria were so entranced by their moralising about revenge that Gesualdo escaped unharmed – and lucky for us, because he went on to compose many more beautiful madrigals.

As for omitted murderous artists of the painting kind, the foremost, no doubt about it, was Michelangelo Merisi, better known as Caravaggio. In 1606, after several diverse but always bungled homicide attempts, he managed to stab to death Ranucchio Tommasoni of Terni, who had sided with a man to whom Caravaggio insistently owed a slight gambling debt. Caravaggio fled south from the scene of his crime, which was the Via della Scrofa in Rome – first to Naples, where he stayed troublesomely for a year or so, and then to Malta, where he was imprisoned for another ill-tempered attempt at murder, and then, having broken out of the Maltese gaol, to Sicily, where a posse of Knights of Malta caught up with him and gave him some of his own stabbing back; recovered from his wounds, and pardoned for his crimes, he boarded but was soon taken off a Rome-bound ship, accused of a crime committed by someone else, and when the error was admitted, shambled about the shore, screaming for the return of his belongings from the long-gone ship, and within a short while died from what seems to have been apoplexy aggravated by the heat of the midsummer sun, debilitating even for men younger than he was, which was thirty-nine.

The main reason for the absence hereafter of accounts of the Gesualdo and Caravaggio cases, and of accounts of murders by or of lesser artists, is that I have failed to find decent ones. If you happen to know of any, I wish you would let me know too.

Pen, Pencil, and Poison

Oscar Wilde

IT HAS CONSTANTLY been made a subject of reproach against artists and men of letters that they are lacking in wholeness and completeness of nature. As a rule this must necessarily be so. That very concentration of vision and intensity of purpose which is the characteristic of the artistic temperament is in itself a mode of limitation. To those who are preoccupied with the beauty of form nothing else seems of much importance. Yet there are many exceptions to this rule. Rubens served as ambassador, and Goethe as state councillor, and Milton as Latin secretary to Cromwell. Sophocles held civic office in his own city; the humourists, essayists, and novelists of modern America seem to desire nothing better than to become the diplomatic representatives of their country; and Charles Lamb's friend, Thomas Griffiths Wainewright, the subject of this brief memoir, though of an extremely artistic temperament, followed many masters other than Art, being not merely a poet and a painter, an art-critic, an antiquarian, and a writer of prose, an amateur of beautiful things, and a dilettante of things delightful, but also a forger of no mean or ordinary capabilities, and as a subtle and secret poisoner almost without rival in this or any age.

This remarkable man, so powerful with 'pen, pencil, and poison,' as a great poet of our own day has finely said of him, was born in Chiswick, in 1794. His father was the son of a distinguished solicitor of Gray's Inn and Hatton Garden. His

5

mother was the daughter of the celebrated Dr Griffiths, the editor and founder of the *Monthly Review*, the partner in another literary speculation of Thomas Davies, that famous bookseller of whom Johnson said that he was not a bookseller, but 'a gentleman who dealt in books,' the friend of Goldsmith and Wedgwood, and one of the most well-known men of his day. Mrs Wainewright died, in giving him birth, at the early age of twenty-one, and an obituary notice in the *Gentleman's Magazine* tells us of her 'amiable disposition and numerous accomplishments,' and adds somewhat quaintly that 'she is supposed to have understood the writings of Mr Locke as well as perhaps any person of either sex now living'. His father did not long survive his young wife, and the little child seems to have been brought up by his grandfather, and, on the death of the latter in 1803, by his uncle George Edward Griffiths, whom he subsequently poisoned. His boyhood was passed at Linden House, Turnham Green, one of those many fine Georgian mansions that have unfortunately disappeared before the inroads of the suburban builder, and to its lovely gardens and well-timbered park he owed that simple and impassioned love of nature which never left him all through his life, and which made him so peculiarly susceptible to the spiritual influences of Wordsworth's poetry. He went to school at Charles Burney's academy at Hammersmith. Mr Burney was the son of the historian of music, and the near kinsman of the artistic lad who was destined to turn out his most remarkable pupil. He seems to have been a man of a good deal of culture, and in after years Mr Wainewright often spoke of him with much affection as a philosopher, an archaeologist, and an admirable teacher who, while he valued the intellectual side of education, did not forget the importance of early moral training. It was under Mr Burney that he first developed his talent as an artist, and Mr Hazlitt tells us that a drawing-book which he used at school is still extant, and displays great talent and natural feeling. Indeed, painting was the first art that fascinated him. It was not till much later that he sought to find expression by pen or poison.

Before this, however, he seems to have been carried away by boyish dreams of the romance and chivalry of a soldier's life, and to have become a young guardsman. But the reckless dissipated life of his companions failed to satisfy the refined

artistic temperament of one who was made for other things. In a
short time he wearied of the service. 'Art,' he tells us, in words
that still move many by their ardent sincerity and strange fer-
vour, 'Art touched her renegade; by her pure and high influences the noisome mists were purged; my feelings, parched,
hot, and tarnished, were renovated with cool, fresh bloom,
simple, beautiful to the simple-hearted.' But Art was not the
only cause of the change. 'The writings of Wordsworth,' he
goes on to say, 'did much towards calming the confusing whirl
necessarily incident to sudden mutations. I wept over them
tears of happiness and gratitude.' He accordingly left the army,
with its rough barrack-life and coarse mess-room tittle-tattle,
and returned to Linden House, full of this new-born enthusiasm for culture. A severe illness, in which, to use his own
words, he was 'broken like a vessel of clay,' prostrated him for a
time. His delicately strung organization, however indifferent it
might have been to inflicting pain on others, was itself most
keenly sensitive to pain. He shrank from suffering as a thing
that mars and maims human life, and seems to have wandered
through that terrible valley of melancholia from which so many
great, perhaps greater, spirits have never emerged. But he was
young – only twenty-five years of age – and he soon passed out
of the 'dead black waters,' as he called them, into the larger air
of humanistic culture. As he was recovering from the illness
that had led him almost to the gates of death, he conceived the
idea of taking up literature as an art. 'I said with John
Woodvill,' he cries, 'it were a life of gods to dwell in such an
element,' to see, and hear, and write brave things:

> *These high and gusty relishes of life*
> *Have no allayings of mortality.*

It is impossible not to feel that in this passage we have the
utterance of a man who had a true passion for letters. 'To see,
and hear, and write brave things,' this was his aim.

Scott, the editor of the *London Magazine*, struck by the
young man's genius, or under the influence of the strange
fascination that he exercised on everyone who knew him,
invited him to write a series of articles on artistic subjects, and
under a series of fanciful pseudonyms he began to contribute to

the literature of his day. *Janus Weathercock, Egomet Bonmot*, and *Van Vinkvooms* were some of the grotesque masks under which he chose to hide his seriousness, or to reveal his levity. A mask tell us more than a face. These disguises intensified his personality. In an incredibly short time he seems to have made his mark. Charles Lamb speaks of 'kind, light-hearted Waine-wright,' whose.prose is 'capital'. We hear of him entertaining Macready, John Forster, Maginn, Talfourd, Sir Wentworth Dilke, the poet John Clare, and others, at a *petit-dîner*. Like Disraeli, he determined to startle the town as a dandy, and his beautiful rings, his antique cameo breast-pin, and his pale lemon-coloured kid gloves, were well known, and indeed were regarded by Hazlitt as being the signs of a new manner in literature: while his rich curly hair, fine eyes, and exquisite white hands gave him the dangerous and delightful distinction of being different from others. There was something in him of Balzac's Lucien de Rubempré. At times he reminds us of Julien Sorel. De Quincey saw him once. It was at a dinner at Charles Lamb's. 'Amongst the company, all literary men, sat a mur-derer,' he tells us, and he goes on to describe how on that day he had been ill, and had hated the face of man and woman, and yet found himself looking with intellectual interest across the table at the young writer beneath whose affectations of manner there seemed to him to lie so much unaffected sensibility, and specu-lates on 'what sudden growth of another interest' would have changed his mood, had he known of what terrible sin the guest to whom Lamb paid so much attention was even then guilty.

His life-work falls naturally under the three heads suggested by Mr Swinburne, and it may be partly admitted that, if we set aside his achievements in the sphere of poison, what he has actually left to us hardly justifies his reputation.

But then it is only the Philistine who seeks to estimate a personality by the vulgar test of production. This young dandy sought to be somebody, rather than to do something. He recog-nized that Life itself is an art, and has its modes of style no less than the arts that seek to express it. Nor is his work without interest. We hear of William Blake stopping in the Royal Academy before one of his pictures and pronouncing it to be 'very fine'. His essays are prefiguring of much that has since been realized. He seems to have anticipated some of those accidents of modern culture that are regarded by many as true essentials. He writes about La Gioconda, and early French poets and the Italian Renaissance. He loves Greek gems, and Persian carpets, and Elizabethan translations of *Cupid and Psyche*, and the *Hypnerotomachia*, and book-bindings, and early editions, and wide-margined proofs. He is keenly sensitive to the value of beautiful surroundings, and never wearies of describing to us the rooms in which he lived, or would have liked to live. He had that curious love of green, which in individuals is always the sign of a subtle artistic temperament, and in nations is said to denote a laxity, if not a decadence of morals. Like Baudelaire he was extremely fond of cats, and with Gautier, he was fascinated by that 'sweet marble monster' of both sexes that we can still see at Florence and in the Louvre.

There is of course much in his descriptions, and his suggestions for decoration, that shows that he did not entirely free himself from the false taste of his time. But it is clear that he was one of the first to recognize what is, indeed, the very keynote of aesthetic eclecticism, I mean the true harmony of all really beautiful things irrespective of age or place, of school or manner. He saw that in decorating a room, which is to be, not a room for show, but a room to live in, we should never aim at any archaeological reconstruction of the past, nor burden ourselves with any fanciful necessity for historical accuracy. In this artistic perception he was perfectly right. All beautiful things belong to the same age.

And so, in his own library, as he describes it, we find the delicate fictile vase of the Greek, with its exquisitely painted figures and the faint ΚΑΛΟΣ finely traced upon its side, and behind it hangs an engraving of the 'Delphic Sibyl' of Michael Angelo, or of the 'Pastoral' of Giorgione. Here is a bit of Florentine majolica, and here a rude lamp from some old Roman tomb. On the table lies a Book of Hours, 'cased in a cover of solid silver gilt, wrought with quaint devices and studded with small brilliants and rubies,' and close by it 'squats a little ugly monster, a Lar, perhaps, dug up in the sunny fields of corn-bearing Sicily'. Some dark antique bronzes contrast 'with the pale gleam of two noble *Christi Crucifixi*, one carved in ivory, the other moulded in wax'. He has his trays of Tassie's gems, his tiny Louis-Quatorze *bonbonnière* with a miniature by

Petitot, his highly prized 'brown-biscuit teapots, filagree-worked,' his citron morocco letter-case, and his 'pomona-green' chair.

One can fancy him lying there in the midst of his books and casts and engravings, a true virtuoso, a subtle connoisseur, turning over his fine collection of Marc Antonios; and his Turner's *Liber Studiorum*, of which he was a warm admirer, or examining with a magnifier some of his antique gems and cameos, 'the head of Alexander on an onyx of two strata,' or 'that superb *altissimo relievo* on cornelian, Jupiter Aegiochus'. He was always a great amateur of engravings, and gives some very useful suggestions as to the best means of forming a collection. Indeed, while fully appreciating modern art, he never lost sight of the importance of reproductions of the great masterpieces of the past, and all that he says about the value of plaster casts is quite admirable.

As an art-critic he concerned himself primarily with the complex impressions produced by a work of art, and certainly the first step in aesthetic criticism is to realize one's own impressions. He cared nothing for abstract discussions on the nature of the Beautiful, and the historical method, which has since yielded such rich fruit, did not belong to his day, but he never lost sight of the great truth that Art's first appeal is neither to the intellect nor to the emotions, but purely to the artistic temperament, and he more than once points out that this temperament, this 'taste,' as he calls it, being unconsciously guided and made perfect by frequent contact with the best work, becomes in the end a form of right judgment. Of course there are fashions in art just as there are fashions in dress, and perhaps none of us can ever quite free ourselves from the influence of custom and the influence of novelty. He certainly could not, and he frankly acknowledges how difficult it is to form any fair estimate of contemporary work. But, on the whole, his taste was good and sound. He admired Turner and Constable at a time when they were not so much thought of as they are now, and saw that for the highest landscape art we require more than 'mere industry and accurate transcription'. Of Crome's 'Heath Scene near Norwich', he remarks that it shows 'how much a subtle observation of the elements, in their wild moods, does for a most uninteresting flat,' and of the popular type of landscape of his day he says that it is 'simply an enumeration of hill and dale, stumps of trees, shrubs, water, meadows, cottages, and houses; little more than topography, a kind of pictorial map-work; in which rainbows, showers, mists, haloes, large beams shooting through rifted clouds, storms, starlight, all the most valued materials of the real painter, are not'. He had a thorough dislike of what is obvious or common-place in art, and while he was charmed to entertain Wilkie at dinner, he cared as little for Sir David's pictures as he did for Mr Crabbe's poems. With the imitative and realistic tendencies of his day he had no sympathy, and he tells us frankly that his great admiration for Fuseli was largely due to the fact that the little Swiss did not consider it necessary that an artist should only paint what he sees. The qualities that he sought for in a picture were composition, beauty and dignity of line, richness of colour, and imaginative power. Upon the other hand, he was not a doctrinaire. 'I hold that no work of art can be tried otherwise than by laws deduced from itself: whether or not it be consistent with itself is the question.' This is one of his excellent aphorisms. And in criticizing painters so different as Landseer and Martin, Stothard and Etty, he shows that, to use a phrase now classical, he is trying 'to see the object as in itself it really is'.

However, as I pointed out before, he never feels quite at his ease in his criticisms of contemporary work. 'The present,' he says, 'is about as agreeable a confusion to me as Ariosto on the first perusal . . . Modern things dazzle me. I must look at them through Time's telescope. Elia complains that to him the merit of a MS poem is uncertain; "print," as he excellently says, "settles it." Fifty years' toning does the same thing to a picture.' He is happier when he is writing about Watteau and Lancret, about Rubens and Giorgione, about Rembrandt, Correggio, and Michelangelo; happiest of all when he is writing about Greek things. What is Gothic touched him very little, but classical art and the art of the Renaissance were always dear to him. He saw what our English school could gain from a study of Greek models, and never wearies of pointing out to the young student the artistic possibilities that lie dormant in Hellenic marbles and Hellenic methods of work. In his judgments on the great Italian Masters, says De Quincey, 'There seemed a tone of sincerity and of native sensibility, as in one who spoke for himself, and was not merely a copier from books'. The highest praise that we can give to him is that he tried to revive style as a conscious tradition. But he saw that no amount of art-lectures or art congresses, or 'plans for advancing the fine arts,' will ever produce this result. The people, he says very wisely, and in the true spirit of Toynbee Hall, must always have 'the best models constantly before their eyes'.

As is to be expected from one who was a painter, he is often extremely technical in his art criticisms. Of Tintoret's 'St George delivering the Egyptian Princess from the Dragon' he remarks:

> The robe of Sabra, warmly glazed with Prussian blue, is relieved from the pale greenish background by a vermilion scarf; and the full hues of both are beautifully echoed, as it were, in a lower key by the purple-lake coloured stuffs and bluish iron armour of the saint, besides an ample balance to the vivid azure drapery on the foreground in the indigo shades of the wild wood surrounding the castle.

And elsewhere he talks learnedly of 'a delicate Schiavone, various as a tulip-bed, with rich broken tints,' of 'a glowing portrait, remarkable for *morbidezza*, by the scarce Moroni,' and of another picture being 'pulpy in the carnations'.

But, as a rule, he deals with his impressions of the work as an artistic whole, and tries to translate those impressions into words, to give, as it were, the literary equivalent for the imaginative and mental effect. He was one of the first to develop what has been called the art-literature of the nineteenth century, that form of literature which has found in Mr Ruskin and Mr Browning its two most perfect exponents. His description of Lancret's 'Repas Italien,' in which 'a dark-haired girl, "amorous of mischief," lies on the daisy-powdered grass,' is in some respects very charming . . .

His sympathies were wonderfully varied. In everything connected with the stage, for instance, he was always extremely interested, and strongly upheld the necessity for archaeological accuracy in costume and scene-painting. 'In art,' he says in one of his essays, 'whatever is worth doing at all is worth doing well'; and he points out that once we allow the intrusion of anachronisms, it becomes difficult to say where the line is to be drawn. In literature, again, like Lord Beaconsfield on a famous occasion, he was 'on the side of the angels'. He was one of the first to admire Keats and Shelley – 'the tremulously-sensitive and poetical Shelley,' as he calls him. His admiration for Wordsworth was sincere and profound. He thoroughly appreciated William Blake. One of the best copies of the *Songs of Innocence and Experience* that is now in existence was wrought specially for him. He loved Alain Chartier, and Ronsard, and the Elizabethan dramatists, and Chaucer and Chapman, and Petrarch. And to him all the arts were one. 'Our critics,' he remarks with much wisdom, 'seem hardly aware of the identity of the primal seeds of poetry and painting, nor that any true advancement in the serious study of one art cogenerates a proportionate perfection in the other'; and he says elsewhere that if a man who does not admire Michelangelo talks of his love for Milton, he is deceiving either himself or his listeners. To his fellow-contributors in the *London Magazine* he was always most generous, and praises Barry Cornwall, Allan Cunningham, Hazlitt, Elton, and Leigh Hunt without anything of the malice of a friend. Some of his sketches of Charles Lamb are admirable in their way, and, with the art of the true comedian, borrow their style from their subject:

> What can I say of thee more than all know? that thou hadst the gaiety of a boy with the knowledge of a man: as gentle a heart as ever sent tears to the eyes.
>
> How wittily would he mistake your meaning, and put in a conceit most seasonably out of season. His talk without affectation was compressed, like his beloved Elizabethans, even unto obscurity. Like grains of fine gold, his sentences would beat out into whole sheets. He had small mercy on spurious fame, and a caustic observation on the *fashion for men of genius* was a standing dish. Sir Thomas Browne was a 'bosom cronie' of his; so was Burton, and old Fuller. In his amorous vein he dallied with that peerless Duchess of many-folio odour; and with the heyday comedies of Beaumont and Fletcher he induced light dreams. He would deliver critical touches on these, like one inspired, but it was good to let him choose his own game; if another began even on the acknowledged pets he was liable to

13

interrupt, or rather append, in a mode difficult to define whether as misapprehensive or mischievous. One night at C—'s, the above dramatic partners were the temporary subject of chat. Mr X. commended the passion and haughty style of a tragedy (I don't know which of them), but was instantly taken up by Elia, who told him '*That* was nothing; the lyrics were the high things – the lyrics!

One side of his literary career deserves especial notice. Modern journalism may be said to owe almost as much to him as to any man of the early part of the nineteenth century. He was the pioneer of Asiatic prose, and delighted in pictorial epithets and pompous exaggerations. To have a style so gorgeous that it conceals the subject is one of the highest achievements of an important and much admired school of Fleet Street leader-writers, and this school *Janus Weathercock* may be said to have invented. He also saw that it was quite easy by continued reiteration to make the public interested in his own personality, and in his purely journalistic articles this extraordinary young man tells the world what he had for dinner, where he gets his clothes, what wines he likes, and in what state of health he is, just as if he were writing weekly notes for some popular newspaper of our own time. This, being the least valuable side of his work, is the one that has had the most obvious influence. A publicist, nowadays, is a man who bores the community with the details of the illegalities of his private life.

Like most artificial people he had a great love of nature. 'I hold three things in high estimation,' he says somewhere: 'to sit lazily on an eminence that commands a rich prospect; to be shadowed by thick trees while the sun shines around me; and to enjoy solitude with the consciousness of neighbourhood. The country gives them all to me.' He writes about his wandering over fragrant furze and heath, repeating Collins's 'Ode to Evening', just to catch the fine quality of the moment; about smothering his face 'in a watery bed of cowslips, wet with May dews'; and about the pleasure of seeing the sweet-breathed kine 'pass slowly homeward through the twilight,' and hearing 'the distant clank of the sheep-bell'. One phrase of his, 'the polyanthus glowed in its cold bed of earth, like a solitary picture of Giorgione on a dark oaken panel,' is curiously characteristic of his temperament, and this passage is rather pretty in its way –

The short tender grass was covered with marguerites – 'such that men called *daisies* in our town' – thick as stars on a summer's night. The harsh caw of the busy rooks came pleasantly mellowed from a high dusky grove of elms at some distance off, and at intervals was heard the voice of a boy scaring away birds from the newly-sown seeds. The blue depths were the colour of the darkest ultramarine; not a cloud streaked the calm aether; only round the horizon's edge streamed a light, warm film of misty vapour, against which the near village with its ancient stone church showed sharply out with blinding whiteness. I thought of Wordsworth's 'Lines written in March'.

However, we must not forget that the cultivated young man who penned these lines, and who was so susceptible to Wordsworthian influences, was also, as I said at the beginning of this memoir, one of the most subtle and secret poisoners of this or any age. How he first became fascinated by this strange sin he does not tell us, and the diary in which he carefully noted the results of his terrible experiments and the methods that he adopted, has unfortunately been lost to us. Even in later days, he was always reticent on the matter, and preferred to speak about *The Excursion* and the *Poems Founded on the Affections*. There is no doubt, however, that the poison that he used was strychnine. In one of the beautiful rings of which he was so proud, and which served to show off the fine modelling of his delicate ivory hands, he used to carry crystals of the Indian *nux vomica*, a poison, one of his biographers tells us, 'nearly tasteless, difficult of discovery, and capable of almost infinite dilution'. His murders, says De Quincey, were more than were ever made known judicially. This is no doubt so, and some of them are worthy of mention. His first victim was his uncle, Mr Thomas Griffiths. He poisoned him in 1829 to gain possession of Linden House, a place to which he had always been very much attached. In the August of the next year he poisoned Mrs Abercrombie, his wife's mother, and in the following December he poisoned the lovely Helen Abercrombie, his sister-in-law. Why he murdered Mrs Abercrombie is not ascertained. It may have been for a caprice, or to quicken some hideous sense of power that was in him, or because she suspected something, or for no reason. But the murder of Helen

Abercrombie was carried out by himself and his wife for the sake of a sum of about £18,000 for which they had insured her life in various offices. The circumstances were as follows. On 12 December, he and his wife and child came up to London from Linden House, and took lodgings at No 12 Conduit Street, Regent Street. With them were the two sisters, Helen and Madeleine Abercrombie. On the evening of the 14th they all went to the play, and at supper that night Helen sickened. The next day she was extremely ill, and Dr Locock, of Hanover Square, was called in to attend her. She lived till Monday, the 20th, when, after the doctor's morning visit, Mr and Mrs Wainewright brought her some poisoned jelly, and then went out for a walk. When they returned, Helen Abercrombie was dead. She was about twenty years of age, a tall, graceful girl with fair hair. A very charming red-chalk drawing of her by her brother-in-law is still in existence, and shows how much his style as an artist was influenced by Sir Thomas Lawrence, a painter for whose work he had always entertained a great admiration. De Quincey says that Mrs Wainewright was not really privy to the murder. Let us hope that she was not. Sin should be solitary, and have no accomplices.

The insurance companies, suspecting the real facts of the case, declined to pay the policy on the technical ground of misrepresentation and want of interest, and, with curious courage, the poisoner entered an action in the Court of Chancery against the Imperial, it being agreed that one decision should govern all the cases. The trial, however, did not come on for five years, when, after one disagreement, a verdict was ultimately given in the companies' favour. The judge on the occasion was Lord Abinger. *Egomet Bonmot* was represented by Mr Erle and Sir William Follet, and the Attorney-General and Sir Frederick Pollock appeared for the other side. The plaintiff, unfortunately, was unable to be present at either of the trials. The refusal of the companies to give him the £18,000 had placed him in a position of most painful pecuniary embarrassment. Indeed, a few months after the murder of Helen Abercrombie, he had been actually arrested for debt in the streets of London while he was serenading the pretty daughter of one of his friends. This difficulty was got over at the time, but shortly afterwards he thought it better to go abroad till he could come to some practical arrangement with his creditors. He accordingly went to Boulogne on a visit to the father of the young lady in question, and while he was there induced him to insure his life with the Pelican Company for £3000. As soon as the necessary formalities had been gone through and the policy executed, he dropped some crystals of strychnine into his coffee as they sat together one evening after dinner. He himself did not gain any monetary advantage by doing this. His aim was simply to revenge himself on the first office that had refused to pay him the price of his sin. His friend died the next day in his presence and he left Boulogne at once for a sketching tour through the most picturesque parts of Brittany, and was for some time the guest of an old French gentleman, who had a beautiful country house at St Omer. From this he moved to Paris, where he remained for several years, living in luxury, some say, while others talk of his 'skulking with poison in his pocket, and being dreaded by all who knew him'. In 1837 he returned to England privately. Some strange mad fascination brought him back. He followed a woman whom he loved.

It was the month of June, and he was staying at one of the hotels in Covent Garden. His sitting-room was on the ground floor, and he prudently kept the blinds down for fear of being seen. Thirteen years before, when he was making his fine collection of majolica and Marc Antonios, he had forged the names of his trustees to a power of attorney, which enabled him to get possession of some of the money which he had inherited from his mother, and had brought into marriage settlement. He knew that this forgery had been discovered, and that by returning to England he was imperilling his life. Yet he returned. Should one wonder? It was said that the woman was very beautiful. Besides, she did not love him.

It was by a mere accident that he was discovered. A noise in the street attracted his attention, and, in his artistic interest in modern life, he pushed aside the blind for a moment. Someone outside called out 'That's Wainewright, the Bank-forger.' It was Forrester, the Bow Street Runner.

On 5 July he was brought up at the Old Bailey. The following report of the proceedings appeared in *The Times*:

Before Mr Justice Vaughan and Mr Baron Alderson, Thomas

Griffiths Wainewright, aged forty-two, a man of gentlemanly appearance, wearing mustachios, was indicted for forging and uttering a certain power of attorney for £2259, with intent to defraud the Governor and Company of the Bank of England.

There were five indictments against the prisoner, to all of which he pleaded not guilty, when he was arraigned before Mr Serjeant Arabin in the course of the morning. On being brought before the judges, however, he begged to be allowed to withdraw the former plea, and then pleaded guilty to two of the indictments which were not of a capital nature.

The counsel for the Bank having explained that there were three other indictments, but that the Bank did not desire to shed blood, the plea of guilty on the two minor charges was recorded, and the prisoner at the close of the session sentenced by the Recorder to transportation for life.

He was taken back to Newgate, preparatory to his removal to the colonies. In a fanciful passage in one of his early essays he had fancied himself 'lying in Horsemonger Gaol under sentence of death' for having been unable to resist the temptation of stealing some Marc Antonios from the British Museum in order to complete his collection. The sentence now passed on him was to a man of his culture a form of death. He complained bitterly of it to his friends, and pointed out, with a good deal of reason, some people may fancy, that the money was practically his own, having come to him from his mother, and that the forgery, such as it was, had been committed thirteen years before, which to use his own phrase, was at least a *circonstance atténuante*. The permanence of personality is a very subtle metaphysical problem, and certainly the English law solves the question in an extremely rough-and-ready manner. There is, however, something dramatic in the fact that this heavy punishment was inflicted on him for what, if we remember his fatal influence on the prose of modern journalism, was certainly not the worst of all his sins.

While he was in gaol, Dickens, Macready, and Hablot Browne came across him by chance. They had been going over the prisons of London, searching for artistic effects, and in Newgate they suddenly caught sight of Wainewright. He met them with a defiant stare, Forster tells us, but Macready was 'horrified to recognize a man familiarly known to him in former years, and at whose table he had dined'.

Others had more curiosity, and his cell was for some time a kind of fashionable lounge. Many men of letters went down to visit their old literary comrade. But he was no longer the kind light-hearted Janus whom Charles Lamb admired. He seems to have grown quite cynical.

To the agent of an insurance company who was visiting him one afternoon, and thought he would improve the occasion by pointing out that, after all, crime was a bad speculation, he replied: 'Sir, you City men enter on your speculations and take the chances of them. Some of your speculations succeed, some fail. Mine happen to have failed, yours happen to have succeeded. That is the only difference, sir, between my visitor and me. But, sir, I will tell you one thing in which I have succeeded, to the last. I have been determined through life to hold the position of a gentleman. I have always done so. I do so still. It is the custom of this place that each of the inmates of a cell shall take his morning's turn of sweeping it out. I occupy a cell with a bricklayer and a sweep, but they never offer me the broom!' When a friend reproached him with the murder of Helen Abercrombie, he shrugged his shoulders and said, 'Yes; it was a dreadful thing to do, but she had very thick ankles.'

From Newgate he was brought to the hulks at Portsmouth, and sent from there in the *Susan* to Van Diemen's Land along with three hundred other convicts. The voyage seems to have been most distasteful to him, and in a letter written to a friend he spoke bitterly about the ignominy of 'the companion of poets and artists' being compelled to associate with 'country bumpkins'. The phrase that he applies to his companions need not surprise us. Crime in England is rarely the result of sin. It is nearly always the result of starvation. There was probably no one on board in whom he would have found a sympathetic listener, or even a psychologically interesting nature.

His love of art, however, never deserted him. At Hobart Town he started a studio, and returned to sketching and portrait-painting, and his conversation and manners seem not to have lost their charm. Nor did he give up his habit of poisoning, and there are two cases on record in which he tried to make away with people who had offended him. But his hand seems to have lost its cunning. Both of his attempts were complete failures, and in 1844, being thoroughly dissatisfied with Tasmanian society, he presented a memorial to the governor of the settlement, Sir John Erdley Wilmot, praying for a ticket-of-leave. In it he speaks of himself as being 'tormented by ideas struggling for outward form and realization, barred up from increase of knowledge, and deprived of the exercise of profitable or even of decorous speech'. His request, however, was refused, and the associate of Coleridge consoled himself by making those marvellous *paradis artificiels* whose secret is only known to the eaters of opium. In 1852 he died of apoplexy, his sole living companion being a cat, for which he had evinced an extraordinary affection.

His crimes seem to have had an important effect upon his art. They gave a strong personality to his style, a quality that his early work certainly lacked. In a note to the Life of Dickens, Forster mentions that in 1847 Lady Blessington received from her brother, Major Power, who held a military appointment at Hobart Town, an oil portrait of a young lady from his clever brush; and it is said that 'he had contrived to put the expression of his own wickedness into the portrait of a nice, kind-hearted girl'. Monsieur Zola, in one of his novels, tells us of a young man who, having committed a murder, takes to art, and paints greenish impressionist portraits of perfectly respectable people, all of which bear a curious resemblance to his victim. The development of Mr Wainewright's style seems to me far more subtle and suggestive. One can fancy an intense personality being created out of sin.

This strange and fascinating figure that for a few years dazzled literary London, and made so brilliant a *début* in life and letters, is undoubtedly a most interesting study. Mr W. Carew Hazlitt, his latest biographer, to whom I am indebted for many of the facts in this memoir, and whose little book is, indeed, quite invaluable in its way, is of opinion that his love of Art and Nature was a mere pretence and assumption, and others have denied to him all literary power. This seems to me a shallow, or at least a mistaken, view. The fact of a man being a poisoner is nothing against his prose. The domestic virtues are not the true basis of art, though they may serve as an excellent advertisement for second-rate artists. It is possible that De Quincey exaggerated his critical powers, and I cannot help saying again that there is much in his published works that is too familiar, too common, too journalistic, in the bad sense of that bad word. Here and there he is distinctly vulgar in expression, and he is always lacking in the self-restraint of the true artist. But for some of his faults we must blame the time in which he lived, and, after all, prose that Charles Lamb thought 'capital' has no small historic interest. That he had a sincere love of art and nature seems to me quite certain. There is no essential incongruity between crime and culture. We cannot re-write the whole of history for the purpose of gratifying our moral sense of what should be.

Of course, he is far too close to our own time for us to be able to form any purely artistic judgment about him. It is impossible not to feel a strong prejudice against a man who might have poisoned Lord Tennyson, or Mr Gladstone, or the Master of Balliol. But had the man worn a costume and spoken a language different from our own, had he lived in imperial Rome, or at the time of the Italian Renaissance, or in Spain in the seventeenth century, or in any land or any century but this century and this land, we would be quite able to arrive at a perfectly unprejudiced estimate of his position and value. I know that there are many historians, or at least writers on historical subjects, who still think it necessary to apply moral judgments to history, and who distribute their praise or blame with the solemn complacency of a successful schoolmaster. This, however, is a foolish habit, and merely shows that the moral instinct can be brought to such a pitch of perfection that it will make its appearance wherever it is not required. Nobody with the true historical sense ever dreams of blaming Nero, or scolding Tiberius or censuring Caesar Borgia. These personages have become like the puppets of a play. They may fill us with terror, or horror, or wonder, but they do not harm us. They are not in immediate relation to us. We have nothing to fear from them. They have passed into the sphere of art and science, and neither art nor science knows anything of moral approval or disapproval. And so it may be some day with Charles Lamb's friend. At present I feel that he is just a little too modern to be treated in that fine spirit of disinterested curiosity to which we owe so many charming studies of the great criminals of the Italian

Renaissance from the pens of Mr John Addington Symonds, Miss A. Mary F. Robinson, Miss Vernon Lee, and other distinguished writers. However, Art has not forgotten him. He is the hero of Dickens's *Hunted Down*, the Varney of Bulwer's *Lucretia*; and it is gratifying to note that fiction has paid some homage to one who was so powerful with 'pen, pencil, and poison'. To be suggestive for fiction is to be of more importance than a fact.

The Immortal Trooper

Jonathan Goodman

MOST PEOPLE who, since schooldays, have read anything other than the news will have read some or all of 'The Ballad of Reading Gaol', Oscar Wilde's discursive recollection of when he, serving a two-year sentence as Convict C.3.3. (that title made from his whereabouts: Block C, Landing 3, Cell 3), briefly encountered a prisoner on remand who

> . . . *walked amongst the Trial men*
> *In a suit of shabby grey;*
> *A cricket cap was on his head,*
> *And his step seemed light and gay;*
> *But I never saw a man who looked*
> *So wistfully at the day.*

The poem has this dedication:

> *In memoriam* C.T.W.
> sometime Trooper of the Royal Horse Guards.
> *obit* HM prison, Reading, Berkshire, July 7, 1896.

The trooper of whom Wilde wrote was Charles Thomas Wooldridge, who in the early spring of 1896 was quartered in barracks in Regent's Park, London. He had, immediately previously, been stationed at Windsor, and during that time, as an outcome of his purchases of stamps at the post office in the High

23

Street of the adjacent Eton, had got to know, and then courted, Laura Glendell, a twenty-two-year-old native of Bath who had been an assistant to the Eton post-mistress for a few months; on 9 October 1894, just prior to his transfer to London, he and Laura had been unfussily wed at St Martin's Church in Kentish Town, North London; he had not, as he should have done, obtained his commanding officer's blessing for the marriage – therefore, in the army's eyes, he remained a bachelor.

In the absence of evidence, as opposed to tittle-tattle, I leave it to you to surmise why Laura continued to use her maiden name; why, in virtually all of her business and social dealings, she pretended spinsterhood. So far as I can tell, the only person in or near Windsor who was certainly privy to her marital status was her husband's niece, Alice Cox, who resided with her at 21 Alma Terrace, a diminutive house in Arthur Road, leading from near the Great Western Railway terminus to the village of Clewer.

Laura's reticence about her marriage strangely contrasted with Charlie's eagerness to talk adoringly of her to his comrades: to exhibit a sepia snapshot of her to people he chanced to meet in the Mother Red Cap, a pub that was local to the barracks. His visits to the Mother Red Cap were not frequent, and he usually rationed himself to a single pint of porter, for most of his pay was put aside as soon as he had saluted for it. That was parsimony in the best of causes, he thought – so that he could please Laura with small presents, could travel to Windsor whenever he had a day and a night off duty.

Early in March 1896, he turned up at 21 Alma Terrace without having told Laura to expect him. Though it was a weekday, she was resplendent in her Sunday-best. She was about to go out – for what purpose, she refused to reveal. No, she could not change her plans, she screamed at him: he had 'a pretty good cheek in coming there at all'. Miserably but meekly, he returned to London.

During the following fortnight, he made several trips to Windsor. None was appreciated by Laura. On an occasion in the middle of the month, she so riled him that he slapped her face, so forcefully or surprisingly that she finished up on the floor of the parlour. The commotion caused Alice Cox to come downstairs. Charlie was standing over his untidy wife, who was crying her eyes out. He looked confused. 'What have I done now?' he muttered, seemingly to himself. Lifting his voice, he exclaimed: 'Why does she try my temper so?' With that, he ran from the house. He returned soon afterwards, and handed Laura a note in which he expressed his love and pleaded for forgiveness. Then he asked Alice to walk with him to the station; on the way, he spoke disjointedly of his unhappiness, of his bewilderment at Laura's attitude towards him.

Back at Regent's Park, the soldiers in his billet tried, but vainly, to cheer him up. On 27 March, a Friday, he went down to see Laura again. Before he left, she handed him a document to sign – a pledge that he would stop 'molesting' her. She promised to meet him outside the barracks on the following Sunday afternoon.

She did not keep the promise. Charlie waited till about seven and then left the barracks. In one of his pockets was the document, signed and stamped; in another was a cut-throat razor that he had borrowed from a comrade. He puzzled the sentry by saying: 'I have to go to Windsor. I must go. I'm going to do some damage.'

Laura was upstairs when he arrived at the house. He asked his niece to send her down, explaining that he had 'a little matter of business to discuss'.

Having fulfilled Charlie's request, Alice stayed upstairs. After only a moment or so, she heard a scream – a scuffling noise – the sound of rushing footsteps. She dashed to the front window, and, looking out, saw Laura lying in the road, close to the iron gate to the tiny garden. Charlie was kneeling over her. Already people were running towards them.

One of the people was the beat-policeman, Constable Henry Miles. 'Take me,' Charlie said to him. 'I have killed my wife.' There was no doubt about that: Laura's head, pillowed in a puddle of blood, was almost severed. Before manacling Charlie, Constable Miles picked up a glistening cut-throat razor from beside the body.

The trial was held at Reading Assizes, before Mr Justice Hawkins, on Thursday, 18 June. The counsel assigned to Charlie submitted that, in the light of Laura's unfaithfulness, the jury could find him guilty of manslaughter; but Mr Justice Hawkins, already known as 'the hanging judge', summed up strongly against him. The jury took ten minutes to decide that though he was guilty as charged, he should be recommended to mercy. Ignoring the rider to the verdict, the judge passed sentence of death. Subsequently, Charlie petitioned both the Home Secretary and Queen Victoria for a reprieve, but neither responded sympathetically.

After three clear Sundays in the condemned cell at Reading Gaol, Charlie was marched to the execution shed. There, he stood to attention, as if on parade, while the hangman girdled his neck. He said nothing before the trap opened, dropping him to eternity.

In the following year, Oscar Wilde, released from prison and living in exile in France, ensured that Charles Thomas Wooldridge, sometime Trooper of the Royal Horse Guards, would never be forgotten.

The Murderous Brush-Work of William Hepper

Richard Whittington-Egan

1

THE WICKED OLD *chèr mâitre's* hand of Salvador Dali himself could hardly have bettered the macabre surrealism of the scene.

A dingy one-room flatlet. Centre-canvas an artist's easel, bearing upon it the half-painted portrait, head and shoulders, of a captivatingly pretty young girl – shiny, almost-black hair, dark, straight eyebrows over wide, intelligent eyes, a full, well-shaped mouth. The paint on the canvas still tacky. Beside the easel, a seedy divan-bed. Spiayed upon it the young model. No longer young or lovely. Timeless now, frozen in the ugly moment of sudden, premature death. Naked, save for a pair of rumpled socks. Discoloured. Bruised. Seeping a dried scab run of blood. Decay setting in. Popping eyes. Swollen lips. Jutting tongue. Lank hair. Bloodied face. Empurpled throat. A stilled life. Throttled and raped. A hideous and pitiful reality, drawn, fashioned and finished by that same artistic hand which had created the fantasy, the make-believe beauty of the unfinished pretty, pretty picture.

2
The Crime

Every picture tells a story. Behind this one lies a tale of . . . Well, it is not possible to be quite sure. It may be one of cruelty

27

and cunning, of an evil self-indulgence; or it may be the sad outcome of an action conceived in innocent kindliness, which, touched by the goblins of mischance and madness, went all-unexpectedly and tragically wrong. If one looks to pinpoint the first link in the ill-starred sequence, the juncture of circumstance where it all started would have to be when, on Christmas Eve, 1953, eleven-year-old, royally named Margaret Rose Louise Spevick – Margot as she was generally and affectionately called – tumbled from a wall and broke her arm.

Margot, an only and much-loved child, lived with her father – a civil servant – and mother in Embankment Gardens, Chelsea, and attended a secondary school in nearby Victoria. Her special friend there was twelve-year-old Pearl. She also lived in Chelsea, in a flat in Ormonde Gate, just a few minutes' walk away from Margot's. The two little girls were often in each other's homes, and Margot got to know Pearl's father very well. She liked him as much as he seemed to like her, and she used to call him Uncle William. Both Uncle William and his wife were also on the friendliest of terms with Mr and Mrs Spevick.

Naturally, Uncle William was very sorry to hear of poor Margot's accident, and when, some three weeks later, her arm seemed to be on the mend, he wrote – on Sunday, 17 January 1954 – a little note to Margot's mother, Mrs Elizabeth Spevick, in which he invited Margot to come and spend a fortnight's convalescence beside the seaside with him in the family flat which he owned at Hove, near Brighton, in Sussex. There was, he added, an old nurse sharing the flat, and she would be able to give Margot medical attention should she need it.

He wrote also to Margot, telling her: 'I want to paint a nice canvas of you (16 × 12 inches), which I want to exhibit here together with another portrait of a very pretty Greek Jewish girl. I will pay you three shillings per hour when sitting. If you could sit two hours a day during seven days that will be enough. There is an old nurse sharing this flat who could look after you in case you need medical attention or to replace bandages, etc.'

Mrs Spevick wrote thanking Uncle William for his kind offer, but added that, although Margot's arm was out of plaster, she still had to attend the doctor for exercises.

Back came another letter. No problem. The exercises could be arranged daily at a local Brighton hospital.

And, on Tuesday, 2 February, before the Spevicks had really made up their minds one way or the other, Uncle William turned up in person at Embankment Gardens and, kindly and charming as ever, persuaded them to let Margot return with him to Hove the following day.

So it was that, on Wednesday, 3 February, off the pair went, hand-in-hand, for the much-looked-forward-to seaside holiday.

. On Thursday, 4 February, Margot's mother received a postcard from her daughter. 'Enjoying myself. Having a splendid time. Love.' And that same Thursday, accompanied by a solicitous Uncle William, Margot attended at the Royal Sussex County Hospital, in Brighton, to make arrangements to have her arm looked at.

On Friday, 5 February, the Spevicks were delighted to receive another postcard, this time from Uncle William. 'Dear friends, We are writing sitting on a deck-chair at West Pier Head. It is like a summer day. Margaret is happy about it.'

It had been agreed that Margot's mother would go down to Brighton on the Sunday – 7 February – to collect her daughter and take her back to London. She would catch a train from Victoria. Margot and Uncle William were to be at Brighton station to meet her.

When Betty Spevick arrived, there wasn't a sign of them. Had they got the train time wrong? Had they been delayed? She waited patiently. Half an hour. An hour. An hour and a half. Two hours. Still no sign of them. Some sort of silly mistake. A misunderstanding, no doubt. What was even sillier, she couldn't go off to see what had happened to them because she hadn't brought Uncle William's Hove address with her, and for the life of her she couldn't remember it. There was nothing for it but to trail all the way back to London, check if by chance they had returned to Embankment Gardens or Ormonde Gate, and, if not, ferret out the address of the Hove flat, and catch another train back to the south coast. *What* a stupid muddle!

And that, at this stage, was all that Betty Spevick thought it was – a stupid muddle.

She went round to Ormonde Gate. Knocked. Rang. Waited.

No reply. No one there. Dead quiet. Still as the grave. Totally empty and lifeless.

Down to Embankment Gardens by the riverside. No, they had not put in an appearance there either. But now she had the address. Of course, that was it – Western Road. Flat 14. A bus to Victoria station. Back on the Brighton train. Soon now they'd all be together, laughing over the silly mistake.

Fear, real fear, first fixed its grip on her heart and stomach, set her scalp and spine tingling, when, hammering ever more desperately on the door of Flat 14, she realized that here, too, was only lifeless silence and its echoes which she provoked, bestirred.

Bang. *Bang*. BANG . . .

Disturbed, made curious, by the unusual Sunday evening noise and turmoil, Mrs Holly, tenant of another of the flats, creaked open her door, enquired what was the matter, and could she help?

Pleased and relieved to have at least some human contact, an ear into which to release the overspill of the pent-up torrent of her anxieties, Mrs Spevick told her story. Mrs Holly invited her into her flat, wrote on her behalf a note to the caretaker of the flats, Mr David Bishop. He was out for the evening, but would find it waiting him as soon as he returned.

Over the inevitably offered – and equally inevitably accepted – cup of tea, disquieting things began to emerge. The seaside holiday flat, of which Uncle William had boasted so grandiloquently, turned out to be nothing more than a single-roomed flatlet, with no one but Uncle William living there. Had they known *that*, Margot's parents, who had regarded Uncle William as a reliable and trusted family friend, would never have let their little daughter go to stay with him.

'Another cup of tea, dear?' Time dragged. 'Sugar?' Lead rather than sand draining from the upturned glass. Terrible alternations of bright, hopeful chatter and heavy, aching, hollow spaces of darkness and aridity deep down inside – all under the glaring alien light of the meaningless landscape of Mrs Holly's welcoming alien parlour. The waiting-room, the reception area to . . . what . . . ?

It was getting on for midnight. At last Mr Bishop returned. He read the note. He came up and tapped at the door. Explanations were furnished. He fetched his passkey. Mrs Spevick had missed the last train back to London. Did he think that, in the circumstances, she could stay the night in Uncle William's flat?

Mr Bishop opened the door.

This is where we came in . . .

It is, too, where the police came in.

3
Medical File

Patient:	William Sanchez de Pina Hepper.
Born:	14 August 1891, in Huelva, Huelva Province, Andalusia, South West Spain.
Father:	British. Born in Gibraltar. Died in a mental hospital in Madrid.
Mother:	Spanish.
History:	Patient is married and has five children. Has lived in Gibraltar, Spain, Portugal and England. Representing a Yorkshire woollen firm, built up a successful business in Lisbon as a wool merchant.

In 1928 joined the American Consulate, and for eleven years, until 1939, supplied the Americans with details of airfields, naval bases, and all sorts of background information concerned Portuguese political and economic life.

Patient states: 'One of my achievements at this time was my discovery of a plot to overthrow the Spanish Republic before the Civil War broke out in 1936.'

He further says that once the Civil War had started, he worked full-time for the United States Intelligence Service, spying on General Sanjujo, head of the Spanish Fascist Party, whose headquarters were in Lisbon, and supplying details of his plans.

Patient states: 'My information about all these events was so accurate that the Secretary of State in Washington, Mr Cordell Hull, rated my reports "excellent", but I received no reward for my work other than praise. I was never a politician, simply a socialist pacifist and a champion of human rights. While the Civil War was on, a stream of refugees from Franco's invading forces fled to the frontier hills between Spain and Portugal and, using my official position, I became the key figure in an escape route.'

He also claims to have rescued from a frontier jail, an American political prisoner who was due to be shot. Not long after this incident, he was arrested by the Portuguese authorities, accused of spying, and given ten days to leave the country.

Patient states: 'To go to Spain would have been certain death for me, so I decided to come, with my wife and four children[1], to England, feeling that it was the last free country in Europe. A refugee from Spanish and Portuguese Fascism, I landed at Tilbury, jobless and penniless, in June 1939, on the eve of World War Two.'

He made for London. He was to work there for the London County Council, the American Red Cross and, finally, the BBC. During the London blitz, he found a job looking after bombed-out people in a rest centre. In 1944 he became a 'night translator-typist' in the BBC's Latin-American service.

Patient states: 'I worked at night, and early one morning, as I was being taken home from the BBC to Chelsea, I was in a bad car smash. The car ended up like an accordion. I was thrown out of the vehicle, my skull was

---

1 His fifth child, Pearl, was born in London in 1942.

fractured, and I was in hospital for more than a month. That accident had an important effect on my life. My health became bad. I suffered from severe headaches, and sometimes lost my memory. For a time I returned to the BBC, but after several relapses I had to give up and was never again able to do a full day's work. Fortunately, I had always loved painting. As a child I would sketch from nature at the seaside and I was so enthusiastic that when I was ten years old my mother sent me to evening classes at an art school.'

Family Life: *Patient states:* 'Often I told my mother and sister that I would never marry because it was impossible to find a woman who would live up to my idea of what a wife should be. When I first met Patra, my wife, I tried to dismiss her from my mind. It was impossible. I was too much in love. And within three months of our first meeting she had become my bride. The British Consulate-General in Madrid had just asked me to become secretary at his Consulate, so I was a good catch and our wedding was an important event. But though we had five children, and one of them graduated with highest honours, I cannot pretend that we were happy. Throughout our married life I have been tortured by jealousy. Friends I trust have told me it was all nerves and imagination and that my wife has always been loyal and true.'

Seen by Dr Hugh Gainsborough, Physician, St George's Hospital, London, in November 1951.

Observations: The patient was suffering from asthma. He displayed lung changes possibly due to tuberculosis.
In 1952 patient wrote a letter to me in which he outlined the history of his relationship

33

with his wife. He referred to her confessions
of infidelity and his reactions. I am not
disposed to believe these accusations of his.
Referred him for psychiatric examination.

Seen by Dr Desmond Curran, Consultant Psychiatrist at St
George's Hospital, London, in February 1952.

Observations: Case referred to me by Dr Gainsborough. I
consider this patient presents as a [*sic*] case
of paranoia. It seems, however, impossible
to certify him as insane, since for all I know
patient's wife may have had an affair with a
Spanish marquis who has been murdered.

4

Manhunt

When, that February Sunday night, they arrived at the scene of
the crime, naturally, the first thing that the Hove police wanted
to know was all about the missing Uncle William. It might, of
course, turn out that he was completely innocent, but, for the
time being, he was the obvious, and only, suspect.

His name, they were told, was William Hepper[1]. He was an
artist, earning a living as a painter of flowers and portraits. He
was also, apparently, a drifter. An eccentric. A wanderer,
whose family saw him only at unpredictable intervals. He
would turn up unexpectedly – and leave again abruptly, without a word of warning or farewell; he – and they alike – victims
of the so-called artistic temperament.

Shortly after the police, the doctor arrived. He formed the
opinion that she had been dead at least twenty-four hours.
Noted that her clothes – frock and underwear – lay in a pile,
neatly folded. On top of them, her books and a jigsaw puzzle.
On top of that, Hepper's rent book, paid in full to date.

Preceded by a sudden whirlwind of police movement, local
top brass, Superintendent Joseph Nicholson, in charge of the

1 He spelt his surname variously d'Epina or de Pina. Hepper was the Anglicised form.

Hove Division of the East Sussex Constabulary, and Detective
Inspector Reginald Bidgood, Head of Hove CID, erupted into
the small, and by now overcrowded, room. Under their direction, a number of photographs of Hepper were collected from
walls, shelves and drawers. Interviews were conducted with the
other tenants of the Western Road flatlets and the caretaker,
and from them a description of the man they urgently wanted to
help them with their inquiries was rapidly put together:

> *Aged between 50 and 60. Height: 5 ft 10 in.*
> *Of medium build. Grey hair. Brown eyes.*
> *Sallow complexion. Long angular face.*
> *Of foreign appearance but speaks with a*
> *cultured English accent. Inclines forward*
> *when walking.*

This description was widely circulated.

An instant and immense hunt was launched. Hepper's photograph was shown to railway staff and taxi drivers. Ports, especially the Channel port of Newhaven, were checked to see if the
wanted man had passed through. A watch was put on airfields.
Hepper's description went to Interpol in Paris to be broadcast
throughout European police networks. Sûreté men in Paris
made discreet inquiries among the members of the French
capital's Spanish community, while back at Western Road
detectives were seeking a lead from a cache of old letters from
women friends which they had discovered in a shabby deed box
in the flatlet. Incidentally, the various women were subsequently traced, through several Lonely Hearts' clubs, and interviewed, but the interviews yielded nothing.

On Monday – 8 February – afternoon, a Sussex force
detective made fourteen separate journeys on buses whose
routes lay along Western Road, hoping to jog the memories of
conductors or passengers who might have seen Hepper. Other
detectives in London scoured the various Chelsea clubs and
other haunts of artists, and kept Hepper's home in Ormonde
Gate under round-the-clock surveillance, just in case he should
return there.

That evening's newspapers – describing him, because of his
known habit of peering forward, as the 'Stooping Artist' –

carried Hepper's photograph. It was also shown on cinema screens. More than six thousand police on night patrol in the Metropolitan area were put on alert. They kept a sharp eye on bombed-sites, waste ground, wrecked buildings, empty houses, cinema queues, cafés and amusement arcades. The Flying Squad ran spot-checks on lodging-houses and other, less salubrious, known bolt-holes.

Despite everything, by Tuesday, 9 February, there was still no news of the so eagerly sought artist's whereabouts. That day, two important conferences took place at Scotland Yard as to the desirability of asking for the co-operation of BBC Television to put Hepper's face on the small screen. In fact, the Yard had first requested the help of television in a murder hunt when, in the previous September-October, they had been trying to track down a twenty-seven-year-old labourer from Eltham, south-east London, William Pettit, wanted for the stabbing to death of a woman at Chislehurst, Kent. As was forthrightly pointed out at the first of these two conferences, the results of the television publicity in the Pettit case had hardly been encouraging. However, at the second conference, an urgent request from the Chief Constable of Sussex being accorded due weight, there was a consensus in favour of making an approach to the BBC.

It was not until seven o'clock that evening that a picture of Hepper was delivered to Lime Grove Studios, but, at peak viewing time, immediately following the TV news-reel, for two minutes – from 8.15 to 8.17 pm – there stared out of the screens in the homes of an estimated three-million-plus people, the motionless, glazed and static face, grey-whiskery, sinister, unsmiling, half-averted, of the unspeaking likeness of a possible child-rapist and killer; while the voice of the then-popular television personality, Donald Gray, intoned: 'Here is a special announcement. This is a photograph of William Hepper. Police are anxious to trace this man, who it is believed can assist inquiries in connection with the death of an eleven-year-old girl at Hove.' He then read a description of Hepper, ending: 'He walks quickly and is very active, head usually inclined forward, cultured English speaking voice. When last seen he was wearing a brown overcoat, half-belted, brown brogue shoes, and black or blue socks.'

Within minutes of that grey fox face fading from the screens, telephones began to ring. And went on ringing. Sightings poured in from Hastings and Horsham, Canterbury and Margate, Southend and Southampton, Bristol and Birmingham, Liverpool and London. From, indeed, all points of the compass. All well-intentioned. All false alarms. No better than the Pettit fiasco, nodded the departmental wiseacres.

But there were inchings of progress. Back at Hove, inquiries were revealing that Margaret Spevick had last been seen alive two days previously – Thursday, 4 February – by both Mrs Holly and a Major G. R. K. Davey. Mrs Holly had seen Margot and Hepper together when she called at Hepper's flatlet that evening. Major Davey, who worked on a Brighton newspaper, had also visited Hepper at about 8 pm on the Thursday. Margot, he said, had then been sitting in an armchair reading a book while he and Hepper talked. 'He told me that he was going to Gibraltar and that he had been to a travel agency to enquire about fares.'

Another useful discovery made at the scene of the crime had been the fact that the mantelshelf of the room where the dead girl lay had been laden with a long row of medicine-bottles, pill-boxes and packages of drugs of various kinds. Clearly, Hepper was, hypochondriacally or otherwise, treating himself for quite a variety of conditions. A doctor who, at the police's request, examined this therapeutic haul, declared that Hepper apparently departed with such celerity that he neglected to take with him adequate supplies from his medicinal armoury. It looked, for instance, as if he had no more than three days' supply of sodium amytal – for chronic insomnia – and he would need to procure reinforcements PDQ. Consequently, chemists all over the country were put on red alert.

As the unproductive hours slipped by, the officers of law and order exchanged ever-more dejected glances and depressing views. The suspect held a perfectly valid British passport, didn't he? He could easily 'go Spanish', couldn't he? What guarantee was there that he wasn't already hundreds of miles away, out of the country? A palpable air of gloom descended . . . like an old-fashioned English fog.

5

The Capturing

It was a telephone call that brought the good news from Gibraltar to Hove. William Hepper had been found. Miraculously, the fog of despond evaporated.

The clue that led to his capture had come from The Rock. And it was a kinsman of his who had delivered Hepper into the hands of the law.

Hepper had written to this man, his uncle, as, indeed, he had written to all the rest of his relatives – in both Spain and Gibraltar – asking for money, because, he said, he had lost all he had in the course of a journey from England. In some of the letters Hepper even went so far as to say that if he did not get help he would take his own life. And with many of them the threat worked. A considerable number of letters, containing in all quite a substantial sum of money, subsequently arrived addressed to him. But this uncle of his, living in Gibraltar, was an extremely religious man. He had read of the terrible thing that his nephew was alleged to have done in that Hove flatlet, and decided that he could not be forgiven by his fellow-men. With the distressing picture of the murdered child before his eyes, this man felt that the blood of the child ran thicker than the blood of kinship. Therefore, he did not send the ten pounds requested. Instead, he got in touch with the Chief of Police in Gibraltar. 'Because of my religion, and because of what I feel about what this man has done, I have brought you this,' he said, and handed over the begging letter from Hepper. It bore at its head the name of the Pension España, a small hotel in the little northern Spanish frontier town of Irun.

The news was instantly transmitted to Scotland Yard, and immediate action was taken through Interpol. A 'find and detain' message was flashed to police headquarters at Irun.

At Hove, a local magistrate hurried down to the police station at midnight, to sign a warrant for Hepper's arrest when he was located in Spain.

At around two o'clock on the afternoon of Wednesday, 10 February, Don Federico Inglesias, Chief of Police in Irun, accompanied by three of his detective officers, strolled nonchalantly and inconspicuously into the Pension España. Here, in Hepper's own words, is what happened: 'I was sitting on a seat opposite the post office waiting for my lunch-time when I noticed four men like detectives go into my hotel. I suspected that they were looking for me because they mentioned my name. A minute or two later, I went into the hotel. The owner told me there were four policemen waiting for me. I said: "Let them pass into my room, please." The officers came in and asked me my name. Then they said: "Will you please come to our office for the question of documents?" I went across to the police station with them, and half an hour later I had an attack and fainted on the floor.'

Hepper spent the night there. The following morning, after breakfasting on black coffee and a couple of aspirins, he was whisked, surrounded by detectives and provided with an escort of armed motor-cycle police, the eleven or so miles to the nearest large town, San Sebastian, the seaport and watering-place to the west, on the Bay of Biscay.

While the British vice-consul in San Sebastian was busily trying to make arrangements for the Civil Governor to be requested to issue a warrant for Hepper's extradition to Britain, there was also being delivered, in the sealed diplomatic bag to the British Embassy in Madrid, the warrant signed by the Hove magistrate. Also winging its way to Spain was a second warrant, holding an application for extradition under the terms of the Anglo-Spanish Extradition Treaty 1878, which had been issued by the chief magistrate at Bow Street.

Cheerfully unaware that all this was going on, Signor Hepper was, under questioning in San Sebastian, coming up with a garbled story of how he was a translator for the BBC in London, and how, because he had been ill, they had insisted that he should go away to Spain or Portugal for a holiday. However, he had lost the money they had given him for his vacation. He vaguely remembered someone in London lending him money, but he had left his case, containing all the cash he had, as well as his papers and clothes, in a taxi in Paris. Unimpressed, Spanish police officers asked him straight out if he knew Margaret Spevick. Yes, he told them, as a friend of his daughter's. She was often in his family home in London at week-ends. He said that the child was never with him in Brighton, and added that he had always seen her when she was in company of either her parents or his daughter.

Then, without favour or finesse, they lobbed the big question at him. Did he know of the death by strangulation of little Margaret, discovered as a corpse in the very room and the very bed he occupied?

Hepper, bland-faced, roundly denied having any knowledge of such a dreadful occurrence.

Very well then. Did he know of any person who could possibly have been involved in this dreadful occurrence, which had most certainly taken place? He wrinkled his forehead. He rubbed the side of his temple, gave a half-shrug of the shoulders. Well . . . the room he occupied in Hove was frequented by many artist-friends and neighbours who went to his studio to see his works, and . . . yes . . . the door always remained open.

Was he, they asked, disposed to appear voluntarily before the English courts to make a statement? Slowly, sadly, he shook his head. Regretfully, he felt that his state of health would not permit him to do so.

The due time having passed during which international rules and regulations had been observed, Inspector Bidgood, from Hove, accompanied by Spanish-speaking Sergeant Everard Lane, of Scotland Yard, arrived by air in Madrid, and, having completed the necessary formalities, travelled to San Sebastian to see Hepper.

They asked him for an explanation of the death of Margaret Spevick. 'That is impossible,' he replied. 'I cannot remember since I lost my memory in Brighton, until I came round a few days ago.'

After Bidgood and Lane had returned from Spain with preliminary papers, the same magistrate who had originally signed the midnight warrant for Hepper's arrest sat alone behind a desk in police-guarded Room No 25 in Hove Town Hall. Apart from his clerk, the only others present were a representative of the Director of Public Prosecutions and Superintendent H. J. Nicholson. One by one, seven men and four women were admitted to Room No 25. Each made a statement on oath. Each statement was carefully and laboriously written down by the clerk. Each signed his or her statement. The signed sworn statements were then delivered to the Home Office. After careful scrutiny they were passed on to the Foreign Office. Then, after further examination, they were despatched, via the Spanish authorities in London, to Madrid.

The remains of the murdered child were lowered into a grave dug from frozen ground.

Hepper sat in his stuffy cell – writing scores of letters.

To the British vice-consul . . . saying that he had been living in an unconscious mental state for a considerable period, and from which he was only now just awakening. 'I hardly remember anything. The last thing that I do remember is that the BBC sent me at home in Brighton the passage-money to spend a holiday in southern Spain, but I remember that I lost the money, possibly while sleeping in a cinema.'

To the British consul-general in San Sebastian . . . demanding to know the reasons for his arrest and asking for news of his wife and children.

To his daughter, Maraquita . . . asking for sleeping tablets, because of 'something hot running in my head'; saying that his wife had been to see him at Hove, and that when he opened her purse he found in it a letter from her lover. 'I struck her and she gave me one with a bottle. I hit her again and we fought body to body. I believe I left her unconscious on the bed. I tried to revive her with smelling-salts, then, as I love her with madness, although she was unconscious I caressed her. In the morning I decided to flee to my beloved country.'

To the Spanish Ambassador in London . . . 'First of all, I have to inform your Excellency that I am a Spanish subject one hundred per cent, although I had previously believed, until a few years ago, that I was a British subject because my father was from Gibraltar and had registered me as such in the British Vice-Consulate in Algeciras when we were living there. Exactly two years ago, I was called by a secretary of the Home Office in London to be told they had verified that I was Spanish and that I had no right to use the British passport that I had used all my life. I now desire to legalise my Spanish position and to live in Huelva with my family.'

Plainly, Hepper was now attempting to adopt the only salvatory course open to him; that is, to 'go Spanish'. Albeit, this left him with the awkward fact to explain away of his lifelong carrying of a passport which described him as a British subject; but, according to him, the British Home Office had already provided him with help in that direction, and he hoped still to throw a Spaniard in the works!

Many of the letters which Hepper had written in jail had not been posted. The Spanish police handed them over to the British authorities. Despite the wide variety of people to whom they were addressed, in all of them one statement was repeated. It was the statement which Hepper had made over and over again to anyone who would listen to him in prison. 'I had a horrible nightmare. I cannot get it out of my mind. It was a dream of murdering someone, probably my wife.'

In his letter, already quoted from, to the Spanish Ambassador in London, Hepper verbalised unequivocally his position. 'What I now desire is to be put at liberty and to be sent to Huelva, close to my relatives, in order to live there tranquilly and to establish myself with a studio, and be able to paint, which is the only thing I am able to do without causing damage to my brain.' This, without doubt, had been Hepper's plan all along. When, in response to his begging letters, his relatives had sent him, as he was sure they would and as they in fact did, money to Irun, he would flee to Huelva and over the border into Portugal. Hepper, it seems, still thought that he was in with a chance of making a successful break for it. What he did not, could not, know, was that almost a month before he sat down in his San Sebastian prison cell in mid-March to scribe that lengthy epistle – ten foolscap sheets of it – to the Spanish Ambassador, the machinery of Fate had already been set in motion against him.

The Hove police and Scotland Yard had been anxiously consulting between each other and with the Home Office, who, in turn, consulted with the Foreign Office. The upshot was the recognition by one and all that there was an undeniable snag as regards the matter of Hepper's Spanish nationality. In the minds of the police and senior civil servants considering the case for extradition, there was little doubt that he could make a valid claim to be Spanish. But would Spain let him go?

Protracted high-level discussions both in and between London and Madrid proliferated. A lot of this diplomatic chitchat was really no more than that. Mere formality – on the Spanish side. What had tipped the scales – perhaps slightly out of kilter – was Hepper's record. Not the single conviction for larceny against him in 1916, but the much more heinous offence of being on the politically losing side. The Spanish authorities, appreciating from the outset that they were certain to be met with a request for Hepper to be extradited, had made it their business as a matter of priority to take an extremely careful look into his previous history in relation to Spain. What they saw did not please them at all. Namely, that from an office in Portugal he had, during the Civil War, established an escape route for anti-Franco Spaniards. Indeed, so embarrassing to the Portuguese Government had his activities become, that he was eventually arrested, kept for a week in a political prison, and then given ten days to get out of the country.

In frank terms, his record of anti-Franco plottings of nearly twenty years before were about to settle his hash. Franco's Spain would not, and did not, forget. However, as befitted so truly great a country for the outward show, the demonstrated nicety of going through all the legally required forms and formalities, the ritual fire dance, the imprimatured flamenco, the Spanish hierarchy moved with measured and dignified tread towards the reaching of the foregone, and long fore-decided, conclusion. Then . . . protocol having been fastidiously observed, Spain felt not the slightest hesitation in releasing Signor Hepper into the hands that would bear him away to stand his trial. Britain was welcome to him. England have his bones!

Considerable delay resulted from Hepper's refusal to be flown back to Britain – a course to which the Spanish officials were perfectly amenable. But, playing for every moment of time in the hope that the longer that passed the more was the likelihood that he might be permitted to stay in Spain, Hepper adamantly would not fly.

But it was no use. When you've got to go, you've got to go, as they say. And Hepper had to go.

It was in the third week of March 1954 that Spanish police officers escorted William Hepper to the western Spanish seaport of Vigo, where the liner *Alcantara* lay in waiting, and, at the top of the gangway, handed him over to Bidgood and Lane. Passengers and crew members watched him stumble aboard and saw him led below to the sick-bay quarters which had been allocated to the prisoner and his two escorts.

During the voyage to England Hepper proved himself a better sailor than the detectives. With the ship rolling pretty badly and Bidgood and Lane feeling somewhat sorry for themselves, Hepper sat merrily down and wolfed all three of their dinners, complaining the while to the nauseated policemen that he had not been properly fed in the Spanish prison. The part of the voyage that Hepper definitely did not enjoy was having to be locked up at night in a padded cell. He was always very anxious to be let out again when morning came.

The *Alcantara* docked at Southampton on Tuesday, 23 March. Police cars were waiting. At the wheel of one of them sat Superintendent Nicholson. Hepper, with his escorting officers, was first off the ship. He was wearing a battered Panama hat and a crumpled suit. A seedy, pathetic-looking figure, he was led over to Nicholson's car, and, with the Superintendent driving, they set off at a cracking pace for Hove.

A large crowd, composed largely of women and girls, was waiting outside the police station there to see him arrive. Inside was one of his daughters and her husband, a well-known West End pathologist. They were allowed to talk briefly with him. That night Hepper was formally charged with the murder of Margaret Spevick.

He appeared at Hove Magistrates' Court on Wednesday, 24 March. Asked by Mr Arthur Jolly, the chairman of the magistrates, the purely formal question, 'Have you anything to say?' he replied, 'Well, all I can say at this stage is that I didn't do it.' It was noticed that his usually impeccable English pronunciation was now heavily accented.

'You do not want to ask any questions?' enquired Mr Jolly.

Hepper lifted his head. 'I have no questions to ask. The only thing I say is . . .'

The clerk of the court, Mr A. E. Thompson, interrupted him quickly with a cautionary word of advice. 'I shouldn't say too much at this stage.'

But, in a husky voice, Hepper persisted, '. . . I lost my memory and I lost my consciousness.'

The only evidence given was that of his arrest as he boarded the liner at Vigo.

Charged with the murder of Margaret Rose Louise Spevick, he was remanded in custody until the following Wednesday (30 March).

His appearance had been brief – no longer than eight minutes.

After being given lunch at Hove police station, he was driven to Brixton Prison, where he was to be held during the remand.

Back in Hove for the third time before the Magistrates' Court on 5 April, Hepper was asked if he could account for the body of Margaret having been found in his flat. He said he could not.

He was then committed for trial to the coming Sussex Assizes.

6
Called To His Assize

Hepper appeared at Lewes Assizes before Mr Justice Austin Jones on Monday, 19 July 1954.

He pleaded not guilty to the charge of murdering Margaret Rose Louise Spevick between 3 February and 7 February, 1954.

He was defended by Mr Derek Curtis-Bennett, QC. Prosecuting was Mr R. F. Levy, QC.

Inspector Reginald Bidgood, after giving evidence of the finding of Margaret Spevick's body at the Hove flat, was cross-examined by Mr Curtis-Bennett. He agreed that, with the exception of the single conviction for larceny thirty-eight years before, Hepper was a man of good character. He agreed, too, that when Hepper returned to England in 1939 after eleven years abroad, he was recommended by the American Ambassador to the court of St James as suitable for work with the London County Council and the Red Cross. Mr Curtis-Bennett asked Bidgood if, when working in the American Consulate in Oporto from 1928 to 1939, Hepper was 'doing very dangerous investigations in Portugal?' Bidgood replied: 'I know he was assisting the Spanish refugees.'

Letters which Hepper had written were read out in court.

In one to his son he wrote: 'I dream that I left your mother unconscious in a struggle on account of matters of jealousy.' In the same letter he complained of having been held in Spain 'for no apparent reason'.

45

Mr Maxwell Turner, for the prosecution, read a further extract from the mammoth letter which Hepper had addressed to the Spanish Ambassador in London in mid-March. 'When I entered here [San Sebastian Prison], I was in a serious condition, and since I left London I was no more than an automaton that did not know what it was doing, nor what it was saying and writing. Consequently, I am going to make a confession in writing to your Excellency that, with the help of God, will clearly reveal, so all may understand, the motives which incurred [*sic*] in my transforming myself from a cultured and mild, as well as industrious, youth into almost a madman. On the night of my wedding I bore an enormous disillusion. She [his bride] was not what I believed before. I continued to love my wife madly as on the first day, but she treated me coldly.'

The letter went on to say that when he was injured in a car-crash and was 'near to death', his wife, believing he was about to die, revealed to him that she had never loved him. He said that she had told him: 'My heart always belonged to a man whom I loved with passion. I always hated you.' He said that she admitted that she had not always been faithful, adding: 'I have not always received from you the consolations necessary for a young and beautiful woman.' Hepper wrote: 'This put my head in a whirl. She had waited to tell me it for thirty years, believing that I was about to die.'

Commenting on the suggestion, arising from the letters which the prosecution had read out, that the prisoner thought that it was his unfaithful wife he was attacking in the Hove flat, Mr Levy told the jury, 'You may come to the conclusion that he, under some curious sort of delusion, thought that he was attacking his wife and not this little girl. He appeared to be saying that he thought the person he left on the bed was his wife. It may be he was inventing this for the purpose of trying to cover up the consequences of what he knew he had done.'

Referring to Hepper's claim in his letter to the British vice-consul in San Sebastian that he was in a confused state from which he was just awakening, Mr Levy said, 'You may well think that by this time Hepper was taking the view that it would be safer to claim complete loss of memory for everything that had occurred.' Medical evidence attested that the child had been strangled, and that she had been sexually interfered with, but, Mr Levy added, this may have taken place during a period of unconsciousness.

In his opening speech for the defence, Mr Curtis-Bennett told the jury that the defence had 'two fangs'. He said: 'You will see that my defence is quite plain – "I never did this". We say that whether this man did it or not, you are looking at a man who, certainly between 3 February and 7 February, probably long ago, and probably now, is mad in the eyes of the law.' Hepper, he continued, had never at any time made any confession. He had always said, 'I did not do it', or 'It is impossible', or 'I cannot remember'.

It was, said Mr Curtis-Bennett, the submission of the defence that his client was suffering from a disease of the mind known as paranoia. That is a form of chronic insanity which often presents delusions of grandeur or fantasies of being the subject of persecution. It frequently manifests promptings in the sufferer to write letters to grand or important people.

On the second day of the trial, before Hepper gave evidence, his counsel emphasised that in his submission the accused was insane and had harboured prolonged delusions against his wife.

In the witness-box, Hepper effectively confirmed this, telling the Court of a Spanish marquis who was killed by a cuckolding of husbands, of whom he was one, because of the attentions he paid to their wives.

Mr Curtis-Bennett asked him: 'Are you fond of children?'

Hepper: 'Yes, very fond.'

Mr Curtis-Bennett: 'Have you ever had any desire to do anything wrong with one?'

Hepper: 'No, sir, it is inconsistent with my qualities.'

Mr Curtis-Bennett: 'Did you kill this little girl Margaret?'

Hepper: 'Not at all. I could never do it.'

Mr Curtis-Bennett: 'You have heard the evidence that someone had interfered with the little girl?'

Hepper: 'I couldn't do it. It is inconsistent with me in every way. I am impotent since about eleven or twelve months. It is inconsistent with my capabilities, and God knows it is impossible.'

47

Hepper went on to say that he had taken the child, with her parents' permission, to Hove. When they reached his flat, he had found a letter awaiting him there. It was from his sister. In it, she asked him to go to Spain as quickly as possible because his brother was dying. He translated the letter and he and Margot both cried because it had spoilt their stay at Hove for the painting of the picture. 'I gave the girl a spare key to come into the room and leave when she liked. I gave her a ten-shilling note to go home, as I was going to Spain.'

He had had a bad attack of asthma the following night (Thursday, 4 February) and went to the sea-front, leaving Margaret reading a book. He did not remember seeing her after that. When he returned to his room, he went straight to an armchair, had some tablets and a glass of brandy, and fell asleep.

'Then I had a terrible dream. I saw my wife coming into the room with a man I know very well, and I got up from the chair and followed almost in the dark to the corridor outside my room.'

> *The Judge* (Interrupting): 'Whom did you follow?'
> *Hepper:*   'The man. My wife stayed in the room. The man
>   disappeared in the dark. I went back into the room
>   and had a discussion with my wife and accused her
>   of infidelity.'
> *The Judge:*   'This is still a dream, isn't it?'
> *Hepper:*   'Yes, my lord.'

Hepper went on to say that in his dream his wife struck him on the head with a bottle. 'Then we had like a fighting, and she fell on the floor, suffering from pain because we had a fight. Later, I woke up and found nobody in the room. It was about six o'clock in the morning (Friday, 5 February). I took the first train to Victoria, where I buy a ticket as far as Paris. I don't remember reaching Spain.'

As he was entering the dock on the third day of his trial, Hepper suddenly collapsed and fell to the floor. He was attended by a doctor, who told the Judge, 'I can't find any physical cause for his collapse. His pulse is normal. He's just lying down and won't speak to me, and won't even co-operate to the extent of taking smelling-salts.'

Mr Curtis-Bennett went across and spoke to his client, who, after about twenty minutes, took his place in the dock, and sat holding the back of his head.

The previous day, Hepper had spent nearly three hours in the witness-box. Now he was recalled for cross-examination by Mr Levy.

Counsel began by trying to clarify the arrangements which had been made for the little girl to stay with him. Hepper denied that he had told her mother that there was a nurse available, even when a somewhat surprised Mr Levy told him that a nurse who lived in the flats at Hove agreed that she had made arrangements to take in the child.

Mr Levy:	'Do you know why she should tell falsehoods about you?'
Hepper:	'No.'
Mr Levy:	'You knew that Mrs Spevick would never have agreed to let her child go if she knew she had to sleep in that room with you?'
Hepper:	'The child never did.'

Asked why he had not notified Margaret's parents that he was going abroad, Hepper replied: 'I did not do things properly because I was not in a normal condition.'

He also said that the reason that he was at the sea-front for a long time on the Thursday (4 February) night was because he had lost his memory.

Mr Levy:	'When you went off at six o'clock on the Friday (5 February) morning you had still lost your memory?'
Hepper:	'Yes, but I remembered the letter about my brother because it was in my suit-case.'

Seven doctors were called for the defence.

Dr Hugh Gainsborough, of St George's Hospital, told of first examining Hepper at the hospital in November 1951, and of his decision that he ought to be seen by a psychiatrist.

Dr Desmond Curran said that he was in private practice at 6 Devonshire Place, London, W1, and Psychiatrist at St George's Hospital. He told the Court of seeing Hepper in February 1952, and submitting a report of that interview to Dr

49

Gainsborough. Dr Curran said that when he saw the accused in 1952, 'I believed he was in a paranoiac state, but not certifiably insane.'

The Judge:	'You think such a person suffering from paranoia may be mentally responsible?'
Dr Curran:	'Yes, for certain things.'
The Judge:	'You take the view they are better treated in hospital rather than prison?'
Dr Curran:	'Yes, my lord.'

Dr Curran, incidentally, was the specialist who had, the previous year, given expert testimony in *Rex v Christie* – in which case, interestingly enough, Mr Derek Curtis-Bennett, KC, also led for the defence and Mr Maxwell Turner appeared as one of the Crown Counsel.

Dr Alexander Wilson Watt, a mental specialist at the Royal Sussex County Hospital, said that he did not believe the story that Hepper had told him about his wife. He said that he was quite prepared for him to 'deny tomorrow what he said yesterday'. Nevertheless, two examinations had confirmed that Hepper was suffering from paranoia. 'Hepper just left that room and that child, dead or alive, as you would leave an article of furniture, a chair or a table. He had no more thought for it in his mind than an inanimate object of furniture. It is my belief that on the night of 4 February and the morning of 5 February, he was the prey of his delusions.'

Mr Levy suggested that Hepper might have fled from a sense of guilt.

Dr Watt:	'Not a sense, but a feeling, of guilt.'
Mr Levy:	'You are making rather a fine distinction.'
The Judge:	'If he dreamt he strangled his wife, and awoke and found she was not there, why should he go away with a feeling of guilt?'
Dr Watt:	'I cannot give you or myself an explanation of this.'
Mr Levy:	'There is one simple explanation: that he knew he had murdered a little child and wanted to escape when nobody was about.'

Hepper was shaking his head violently. 'No, no,' he exclaimed, 'I had to go to Spain to see my brother.'

The precise itinerary of that alleged flight from justice had by now been established. And it seemed a very rational escape route for an 'insane' man to have planned. The first train to Victoria. The earliest available train thence to Newhaven. The 10.39 am boat to Dieppe, connecting with the Paris train. From there, a third train, four hundred miles south-west to the town of Hendaye on the French-Spanish border. Arriving in the early morning of Saturday, 6 February, he had immediately applied for an entry-visa to Spain. He then took a tram to Irun, where, at around noon, he booked into the modest Pension España. He had spent five days there – 6-10 February – waiting for the solicited donations from his relatives to arrive, passing himself off as an ordinary tourist. On the Wednesday of his capture, he had been out, blue-suited and carrying an umbrella, on a sightseeing tour.

Small wonder that, with such impressive evidence of rational planning capacity manifest, Mr Levy felt that he must put it to Dr Watt whether it had never struck him that Hepper's memory defects might have been simulated.

> *Dr Watt:* 'I think a man would have to be much more clever than that man to keep up such a simulation consistently. I cannot think that he was acting.'

Called on the fourth and final day of the trial – 22 July – Dr John Matheson, Principal Medical Officer at Brixton Prison, was, perhaps predictably, to rebut evidence of insanity. He stated that he had had Hepper under close observation for more than three months while he was in the prison hospital awaiting trial. Not only had he interviewed him six or eight times, but he had also interviewed members of his family, and he had formed the opinion that Hepper was not, at the time of the crime or at the present time, insane in law. Neither had he found any evidence of paranoia.

> *Mr Curtis-Bennett:* 'You heard the doctors I called and it was pretty plain from them that in 1952 this man was abnormal?'

51

Dr Matheson:	'Certainly. I think he is still abnormal, but paranoia gives a defect of reason because of a disease of the mind.'

Detective Sergeant Richard Arnold, of Hove, was questioned by Mr Levy regarding a statement which he had taken on 17 March 1954, from a Miss Lines, who had a flatlet in the same building in Western Road as Hepper. Arnold testified that he was absolutely positive that Miss Lines was mistaken in saying that she had seen Margaret Spevick on Friday, 5 February. He agreed with Mr Curtis-Bennett that if anybody *had* seen Margaret alive on that Friday, it would mean that Hepper could not have committed the murder.

In his closing speech for the defence, Mr Curtis-Bennett was careful to re-emphasize that if the statement made by Miss Lines was true, it meant the end of the case. The fact that Hepper made a journey to Spain to see his dying brother was not evidence that he fled. Doubt after doubt had, he said, been stirred up, and it would not in this case be safe to convict: what, at worst, the jury should do, was to say that his client was guilty but insane. But the main defence was that it was not true that Hepper did the act at all.

In the final speech for the Crown, Mr Levy said that it was an inescapable conclusion that the child was violated and murdered by Hepper and by no one else, and in going to Spain he was fleeing from justice. On the question of insanity, only one doctor had said that Hepper was suffering from a mental disease, and he had based his conclusions on what the accused had told him.

Mr Justice Jones's summing-up lasted for two hours. He told the jury that it was necessary to consider the circumstances in which the girl went to Brighton with Hepper and lived alone with him. In view of the fact that she was violated, they might think that the person who murdered her was the person who had intercourse with her. As regards Hepper's evidence about the letter from Spain relating to the dangerous illness of his brother, the Judge observed: 'I think it is a fact that in none of his letters or written statements does he refer to that letter, which has never been found. I think you will be wise to check the evidence against his statement in the witness-box. You may think he made it up and that no such letter was received. If so, you may derive some assistance in coming to a conclusion as to whether the rest of his evidence was accurate.'

Referring to the postcard which Hepper sent to the Spevicks from Brighton on Thursday (4 February), the Judge remarked: 'When he wrote that postcard . . . he never said a word about going to Spain. That is an important matter.' And he went on to point out that the time of about half-past eight on the Thursday night was a very material period. Hepper had said that he went to the sea-front, leaving Margaret reading, and that he never saw her again, inviting the conclusion that the girl went out on her own somewhere. 'Do you believe,' he asked, 'that this man travelled in a sort of dream all the way from this country to the Spanish border?'

The jury – ten men and two women – pondering all the circumstances of the crime, which included the fact that Hepper had received severe head injuries in a motor-car accident, and the expert medical witness's testimony that he was 'the prey of his delusions', had an anxious time and were obviously worried.

Outside County Hall, holiday-makers in bright summer clothes waited for the verdict. Inside, the court was oppressively packed.

After an absence of one hour and twenty-five minutes, the jury returned.

They found Hepper guilty.

Standing in that same dock where Field and Gray, Patrick Mahon, Norman Thorne, Sidney Fox, and John George Haigh had stood before him, and likewise listened to the pronouncement of their doom, Hepper was asked if he had anything to say.

'I think,' he said, 'it is quite unfaithful – I mean, incorrect. I did not do it.'

Sentence of death was passed.

7
Retribution

There was no appeal.

But it is known now that the Home Secretary of the day, Sir David Maxwell Fyfe (subsequently the Earl of Kilmuir), carefully considered a mass of medical testimony relating to Hepper's mental state. One piece of evidence to which he gave most particular attention was the report, written almost two years to the day before the murder, in which Dr Curran had written: 'I consider this patient presents as a case of paranoia. It seems, however, impossible to certify him as insane.'

On 9 August it was officially announced that there would not be a reprieve.

8

Fiat Justitia?

The case of William Hepper is a disturbing one. Once the natural anger provoked by its grossness and brutality – directed as it was against, and claiming the life of, an innocent and helpless child – has abated, it sits a little uneasily upon the conscience. Did we, not for the first time, in our revulsion judicially murder a madman? Was Hepper a paranoid schizophrenic? Should a padded, rather than a condemned, cell have been his just portion?

Certainly, many of those who actually saw him in court husbanded grievous misgivings as to his sanity. Moreover, a number of doctors unequivocally pronounced him a psychotic. Even so notoriously unsympathetic and cynical an observer as a prison medical officer described him as 'abnormal' – whatever, scientifically, that can be taken to mean.

Those who knew him – and they were not many, for he was essentially, as one would expect, a loner – described him as having always been a compulsive liar, exhibiting a Braggadocio which compelled him to make everything connected with himself much grander than it was. To disentangle the cats' cradles fabricated by involuntary liars is difficult. To distinguish them from the delusional constructs of the diseased mind is equally taxing. Undoubtedly he had plenty of scope to exaggerate and embroider upon his adventures and achievements as a spy, suave master-outwitter of Generalissimo Franco's ferrety minions. Yet the evidence is that he did not gild the lily. The dangers he risked, the good work of rescue he accomplished, were, and were presented as, plain facts.

It is not easy to derive any significant data from his mode of living – because information concerning it is sparse. There is no doubt that he was of a genuinely artistic turn of mind and talent. Painting was the main and absorbing interest of his later years. He exhibited his works at open-air shows on the Thames Embankment and at Brighton. A psychological glimpse is afforded by the reported[1] testimony of a fellow-artist at Brighton who attained to a mild degree of friendship with Hepper. He states that, 'apart from painting, he seemed to have no other interest in life and never joined in the social life of the art set. He specialised in flower studies and would spend hours arranging single specimens of different flowers until he had the exact composition he wanted. Some of his fellow-artists thought his tones were too hard and too brilliant, but his work always sold well. During a discussion on art, he said: "You will never find my paintings in the Royal Academy or in any of the Bond Street galleries. It is the pavement and the seashore for me, because there you will find the greatest painters; you don't find them in fashionable salons."'

Joanna Gomez, of Hove, posed for her portrait by Hepper. He had, she said, started to paint the portrait from 'a photograph, but said that he could not finish it without seeing her in the nude, because he could not paint skin tones from a photograph. 'I agreed to pose and, accompanied by a woman friend, I sat three times for him. He was always very nice to me.'

Was Hepper sexually abnormal? Certainly the raping of a child is not a normal channel of sexual satisfaction, but there was no police record of his having previously committed any type of sexual offence. It may be that he had long fantasized over the commission of such an act, and coolly and deliberately, of lust aforethought, engineered the circumstances for the translation of the fantasy into fact in that sordid little flatlet at Hove. It could equally well be that he had had no such plan or intention in mind when he invited Margaret Spevick to stay with him, and that it was an 'impulse rape' brought about by proximity and opportunity, and that the murder, rather than

1 In *The Child Killers* by Norman Lucas, Arthur Barker Ltd, London, 1970.

being an integral part of a perverted sexual scenario, was the *result* of it: the method of silencing the potential accuser, the betrayer of his rich secret.

Going towards the theory that the impulse came over him is the fact that the child was found naked, with her clothes neatly folded, which could indicate that he was painting her in the nude at the time. (The neat folding of the clothes might, of course, mean no more than that the girl, on her best behaviour as taught, had first undressed and then folded them herself, before going to bed. Or, probably less likely, because he panicked afterwards, it could suggest that Hepper stripped her and, at some stage subsequent to his act, himself obsessively, as with flowers, either to imply natural sleep, or finding work for idle neurotic hands to do, had so imparted neatness and order to them – and the post-coital shambles). Although the portrait was a head-and-shoulders, we have the previous testimony of Joanna Gomez that, even when contemplating what was surely not in her case a nude portrait, he found nudity a prerequisite. All one's instincts, reinforced by the circumstance that the child when found was still wearing a pair of socks, tell one that the little girl was required to stand – foot-warming socks apart – defenceless in the nude. However, tempting as this construct may be, it can be argued that the timing is wrong, in that he must have killed in the late evening or night, after the visit of Major Davey, when the 'painter's light' would not have been right. Conversely, against the sudden-impulse presumption, he might have planned to pounce upon the child *while she was posing* – an exciting situation for him – in which event the fact that the light was inadequate would have been immaterial, as painting was not the object of the exercise. Too much must not be made of the socks 'clue' in this context. One must resist the temptation to read into their retention anything more, per- haps, than a straw indicative of the rapist's impatience to fulfil his purpose.

Norman Lucas offers a psychological explanation which is, and can be, only descriptive. He says of Hepper:

It might be thought that his keenness to paint flowers suggested that he had an admiration for things that were beautiful, delicate and, in his peculiar case, pure with a sexual connotation, virginal. Almost like the convergence of two main highways, Hepper's strange inclinations could be said to come together at the point where, while he still retained pleasure in flower paintings, he derived satisfaction from painting portraits and more particularly from painting Joanna Gomez. As she stated, he began her portrait from a photograph. It is not unreasonable to suppose that he received some minor sexual excitement from copying the picture that promoted within him an urge to see and paint her in the nude . . . One might deduce that Hepper devoured his models with the eyes and then tried to recreate them himself by painting the portraits. This situation must have reached a great point of intensity in the case of Margaret Spevick. Hepper might well have made little Margaret into some kind of Galatea – herself . . . the personification of the bright calm sea. Here, once again, one sees the tranquil beauty of the flowers in line with the virginal and unspoilt Margaret. It would have been quite feasible for Hepper, who stated that he had been impotent for a year before Margaret's murder, suddenly to find that he was far from impotent and become overwhelmed with sexual desire . . . It is also possible that he was overcome by a greedy desire to own her, and with a madness that compelled him to rape her and kill her so that she would never 'belong' to anyone else.

Although it was not raised in his defence, one ought undoubtedly to take into account Hepper's own description of his condition as that of an automaton. There is – or was – a specific and not much used defence of automatism. It did not apply only to murder. From the lawyer's point of view, it was a notoriously difficult defence to run. At the best of times there is, like the presumption of innocence, a presumption of sanity; the difference is that the burden of proof of insanity is placed squarely on the accused. There is, moreover, a wide gulf between medical and legal concepts of insanity.

The definition of legal insanity was laid down in 1843, when Daniel M'Naghten, intending to shoot Sir Robert Peel, mistakenly killed his secretary, and was acquitted of murder on the grounds of insanity. The judges, at the request of the House of Lords, supplied answers to a number of questions submitted to them, and it was those answers which provided what came to be known as the M'Naghten Rules governing the legal concept of insanity. The nub of them was that a defence of insanity could only be established if

> at the time of committing the act, the party accused was labouring under such a defect of reason, from disease of the mind, as not to know the nature and quality of the act he was doing, or, if he did know it, that he did not know he was doing what was wrong.

Did a defence of automatism imply insanity? In the past, two types of automatism were distinguished. Automatism caused by a disease of the mind; that is insane automatism. And automatism due to some other cause, such as a blow on the head or somnambulism; that is non-insane automatism. Normally, an accused wishing to plead automatism would be reluctant to claim that it was of the insane variety. That would be to risk incarceration for an indefinite period. Since Hepper pleaded not guilty, it may be safely assumed that had automatism been offered, it would have been non-insane automatism.

The vexing question to be considered is: when a plea of non-insane automatism is made, can the Court or the prosecution raise the issue of insanity, even though insanity is not pleaded by the defence?

No, it cannot, said Mr Justice Barry in *Regina v Charlson* (1955). In this case, the accused, a devoted father, had suddenly struck his ten-year-old son on the head with a mallet and thrown him from a window. Evidence was given that there was a possibility that the defendant was suffering from a cerebral tumour. Medical testimony affirmed that a person so afflicted would be liable to an outburst of impulsive violence over which he would have no control. Barry, J. directed entire acquittal because the defendant was not guilty if he was 'acting as an automaton without any real knowledge of what he was doing'. The judge did not go into the question of the distinction between diseases of the mind (mental) and diseases of the brain (physical).

Two years later, in *Regina v Kemp* (1957), Mr Justice Devlin reached a very different conclusion. The facts of this case were that the accused made a completely motiveless and irrational attack on his wife with a hammer. It appeared that he was suffering from arteriosclerosis, which was causing a congestion

The Immortal Trooper

TERRIBLE TRAGEDIES AT WINDSOR AND NOTTINGHAM
FULLY ILLUSTRATED.

THE ILLUSTRATED POLICE BUDGET

THE LEADING ILLUSTRATED POLICE JOURNAL IN ENGLAND

No. 148.   SATURDAY, APRIL 4, 1896.   ONE PENNY

HORRIBLE TRAGEDY AT WINDSOR.
A YOUNG WOMAN'S THROAT CUT—AS ALLEGED—BY HER SOLDIER HUSBAND, AND WHO IS NOW IN CUSTODY.

The Murderous Brush-Work of William Hepper

Hepper exhibiting his paintings on the front at Brighton

Hepper having Spanish handcuffs removed before his extradition

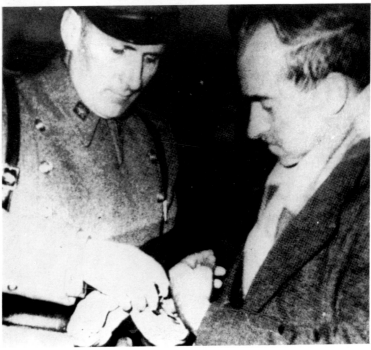

of blood in his brain. As a result, it was claimed, he sustained a temporary lapse of consciousness, during which he made the attack. Relying upon the decision in *Charlson*, it was urged that the defendant was suffering from a non-insane automatism, arising not from any mental disease but, as in the instance of the cerebral tumour, from a purely physical one. But Devlin, J. rejected the argument, holding that the defendant was suffering from a disease of the mind. The law, he said, was not concerned with the brain, but with the mind – in the sense that 'mind' is ordinarily used, that is the mental faculties of reason, memory, and understanding. He said that whereas the doctors were agreed that the defendant in *Charlson* was not suffering from a mental disease, in *Kemp* they disagreed.

Lord Denning, in *Bratty v Attorney-General for Northern Ireland* (1963), doubted *Charlson*, and, upholding the decision in *Kemp*, said that the old notion that only the defence can raise the issue of insanity had gone.

In fact, Hepper's bad luck held. Had he come to trial a bare three years later, his neck might well have been saved under Section 2 of the Homicide Act 1957, which allowed the defence of diminished responsibility

> where a person kills or is a party to the killing of another, he shall not be convicted of murder if he was suffering from such abnormality of mind (whether arising from a condition of arrested or retarded development of mind or any inherent causes or induced by disease or injury) as substantially impaired his mental responsibility for his acts or omissions in doing or being a party to the killing.

In *Byrne* (1960), the so-called Birmingham YWCA Hostel Murder, in which Patrick Byrne, a sexual psychopath, strangled a girl, and decapitated and mutilated her body, Lord Chief Justice Parker said in his Judgment of the Court of Criminal Appeal: '"Abnormality of mind", which has to be contrasted with the time-honoured expression of the M'Naghten Rules of "defect of reason", means a state of mind so different from that of ordinary human beings that the reasonable man would term it abnormal. It appears to us to be wide enough to cover the mind's activities in all its aspects, not only the perception of physical acts and matters and the ability to form a rational judgment whether an act is right or wrong, but also the ability to exercise will-power to control physical acts in accordance with that rational judgment.'

Thus was the defence of irresistible impulse made legally possible.

At eight o'clock on the morning of Wednesday, 11 August 1954, three days before his sixty-third birthday, maintaining to the last that he knew nothing about the murder, Hepper was hanged at Wandsworth Prison.

There were only forty or so people outside to keep the death vigil and watch the posting of the execution notice. But someone left a large bunch of pink gladioli on a ledge at the main entrance to the jail. Attached was a card. On it was written:

In memory of Sanchez de Pina Hepper.
Judge not that ye be not judged.

It was Game, Set, and Match for the spy who came in from the Francine reign in Spain, lost his memory, and got his cover-story lethally wrong.

The Sportsman and the Scholar: A Family Secret

Jeffrey Bloomfield

BACK IN THE FALL of 1975, when I began attending New York Law School, I decided to investigate its library. Among the periodicals was an almost complete run of *The Journal of the American Historical Association*. Tipped into its first volume, 1896–1897, were various documents addressed to the original owner of the book. These recorded how this man was invited to join the newly-created Association, the letterhead of which boasted such pre-eminent historians of the period as Senator Henry Cabot Lodge of Massachusetts, James Ford Rhodes, and the great Henry Adams. But the name of the recipient of these documents held my attention most of all. That name was Paul Leicester Ford. He is only of interest to scholars now; as his works have few readers. Yet, at the time of his death, in 1902, it was different: his entry in the *National Cyclopaedia of American Biography* says that '[h]e gave promise of taking high rank among the few who enriched American history and literature in its broadest field'. Why he did not do so will be explained in this essay.

We begin on 16 December 1823. On that day, Gordon Ford was born in the town of Lebanon, in New London County, Connecticut. The town's biblical name is in keeping with the Puritan heritage of New England. It has always had a small population; in 1960 it had two thousand residents. Gordon Ford was of old New England stock, the family coming over to Massachusetts in the *Fortune*, the first ship to arrive after the *Mayflower*. In 1834, Gordon left Lebanon and went to New York City to work for an uncle. He became a bookkeeper, studied law, and developed a fine legal career. He became a railroad president and a real estate investor. As he prospered, he moved to Brooklyn, which was then a city separate from New York. He became a political figure there. In 1869, he was appointed collector of internal revenue for the third district, but he refused to take political contributions from the salaries of his staff and was removed. Although President Ulysses Grant seems to have been honest, his administration (1869–73) was corrupt. Gordon supported the 'Liberal Republican' revolt against Grant, and aided the campaign of Horace Greeley for President. Unfortunately, Grant won re-election; his second administration was, if possible, worse than his first. Although Horace Greeley died shortly after the election, Gordon was rewarded for his support. Greeley's newspaper, the *New York Tribune*, hired him as its business manager.

This was the period in American history called the 'Gilded Age', when great fortunes were made in railroads, banking, steel and copper and other commodities. The tycoons, the 'Robber Barons' like Vanderbilt and Morgan, are more important than the political figures of this period; for all their flaws (greed being a large one), they were responsible for the economic muscle of America that lasted until the decade we have just gone through. Gordon was never on the same level of power as Morgan, Rockefeller, or Carnegie, but he was rich. He was also cultured. He was a founder of the Brooklyn Art Association and the Academy of Music; like J. Pierpont Morgan, but unlike Commodore Vanderbilt or Jim Fisk, he was a bibliophile. Specializing in the colonial and revolutionary history of the United States, he amassed a hundred thousand manuscripts and fifty thousand volumes. Gordon let scholars use his collection.

As in his book-collecting, Gordon was discriminating in choosing a wife. On 16 December 1853, his thirtieth birthday, he married Emily Ellsworth Fowler, the daughter of the Reverend William Chauncey Fowler and Harriet Webster Fowler. Emily's maternal grandfather was Noah Webster, who created the first American dictionary, and she too was literary; her poetry and essays appeared in *The Atlantic Monthly* and *Harper's Weekly*. She was also civic-minded, trying to reform poorhouses.

The Fords had seven children: Katherine, Worthington Chauncey, Rosalie, Malcolm Webster, Mabel, Paul Leicester and Emily. Worthington Chauncey Ford was born on 16 February 1858. He was to become very prominent in the field of American historical biography, working with such prestigious institutions as the Library of Congress. He died in 1941. Of the sisters, only Mabel will concern us as an individual. She was born in 1864. Twenty years later, she married Richmond Mayo-Smith, an economics professor and statistician at Columbia University, Manhattan. He too will concern us. Mabel died in 1938.

Malcolm Ford was born on 2 February 1862; Paul on 23 March 1865. Paul had a sickly body. His medical problems are hard for us to diagnose. The entry in the *National Cyclopaedia* describes him as 'too delicate'; the historian, Allen Nevins, who wrote the entry for Paul in *The Dictionary of American Biography*, says that it was an injury to Paul's spine that stunted his growth, but gives no particulars; an article in the November 1898 issue of the literary magazine, *The Critic*, mentions that Paul's physical constitution was strong enough to save him during infant illness. This same article suggests that Paul may have forced himself to become an over-achiever, because he feared that his life would end prematurely. It sounds plausible, but we cannot be sure. We can say that he was a hunchback and almost a dwarf, but that is about all. One of the difficulties in the case of Paul Leicester Ford is the scarcity of material on it. It is enough to say that the Ford family did everything to limit and control the information on the case. The minimal attention that has been paid to it is a monument to their stone-walling around the truth – or their cover-up.

Gordon and Emily encouraged all their children to excel in the intellectual sphere. The result was a whole family of bookworms except for one member of it. Malcolm did not care for a purely intellectual life. The *New York Tribune* of 9 May 1902 ran several columns on the family, from an openly biased position regarding Malcolm, and stressing that 'PAUL BORE THE BURDENS'. Malcolm was a believer in first building a healthy body, then a healthy mind. He picked up this devilish idea at the YMCA. Despite a number of arguments with Gordon, he kept up his athletic regimen. He turned increasingly to his mother for affection.

Gordon became closer to Paul. This was a mixed blessing for Paul, who was under unfair pressures from his father, ignoring the boy's physical infirmities. According to an anecdote in the *Tribune*, Gordon would take Paul to the Post Office to pick up books he had ordered for his library. Paul had to lug the books back home, never minding his handicaps. When a postal employee suggested that the books should be sent to the Ford home in a collection wagon, Gordon insisted, 'Give him the books! Give him the books!' If Gordon could be so pig-headed as to treat Paul like that, the wonder is that they remained close. I have no doubt, however, that Paul deeply resented the Adonis-like Malcolm for unwittingly putting him into such a peculiar position.

As the years passed, Malcolm sank lower and lower in his father's esteem. In 1877, when he was fifteen, he was taken out of school, as his grades were poor and he spent virtually all of the recess periods in the gym or on the athletics field. A definite split occurred in 1882 or thereabouts. Malcolm's parents and siblings tried to persuade him to give up sports and plan for a sensible (read 'respectable') career. He refused. Depending on who told the story, Malcolm left or was thrown out of his home.

If this was a Victorian novel, Malcolm Ford would have either returned home chastened by his experiences or died in poverty, bemoaning his failure to heed his family's warnings. But this is not a tale of fiction, and Malcolm, in his own way, was as much a perfectionist as his siblings. In 1883, he won the amateur American running broad jump, running high jump, and Canadian running high jump. In 1884, he won the American broad jump and 100-yard dash, and only lost the Individual All-Round Championship of America to W. R. Thompson of Montreal, Canada, by a whisker. In 1885, he again won the broad jump and 100-yard dash, as well as the 220-yard dash, and the 220 yards and quarter-mile at the Canadian championships; he capped off that year by becoming the Individual All-Round Champion of America – International Amateur Champion as well. To sum up: for some ten years from 1883, Malcolm

Ford was the greatest amateur athlete in the United States (possibly in North America). The pity was that the first modern Olympics were not held until 1896, for he was of that calibre.

At the time of the final tragedy, these achievements were attacked. While the *New York Tribune* of 9 May 1902 acknowledged his sporting prowess under the headline 'MURDERER AS AN ATHLETE', it had to add: 'Unlike "Lon" Meyers, of his club, Ford made enemies out of the men he defeated, while Meyers won friends by his cheery nature on the track', and 'His old clubmates never forgave him for deserting Brooklyn and joining forces with the Manhattan Athletic Club'. Adding acid to the lemon, the *Tribune* went on: 'He had been successful for a time in winning the empty praise of the multitude for his strength and skill, but he had been left behind by other men in the race . . . In disposition there was [an] unlikeness. Paul was sweet tempered and sympathetic, while Malcolm was surly and unforgiving.' If the *Tribune* felt that sports led to empty praise from the multitude, why did it bother printing any sports news at all? Apparently he had that special type of unforgiving, surly nature that newspapers can turn on and off when it suits them.

The *New York Times* made no snobbish comments regarding the value of sports. But it did mention, in its account of the tragedy of 9 May 1902, that Malcolm had undesirable friends: one was Fred Burns, who was the father of a defendant in a murder case; another was Roland B. Molineux, who had been the defendant in the Katherine Adams poisoning case in 1898 (although Molineux had been found guilty, the decision had been reversed, and a second trial was under way – Molineux was acquitted.[1]) The friendship – if it existed at all – between Malcolm and Roland would probably have been based on their enthusiasm for sports, together with the fact that they were from upper-class families in Brooklyn. I cannot help doubting that Roland ever discussed with Malcolm the homicidal efficacy of doctored bromo-seltzer as opposed to that of a loaded revolver.

Normally, any family in their right mind would cheer on and celebrate such a series of triumphs as Malcolm's. But this is

1 See *The Molineux Affair* by Jane Pejsa (Kenwood, Minneapolis, 1983; Piatkus, London, 1988).

BROTHER SLAYS PAUL L. FORD.

MALCOLM W., THE ATHLETE, SHOOTS THE AUTHOR, IN HIS HOME, AND THEN KILLS HIMSELF.

BITTERNESS OVER THE FATHER'S WILL THE CAUSE

A shocking double tragedy was enacted in the ... 27 East Seventy-seventh-st. yester... Jealousy, ...thers, who were wrong and desperation due ...

tary. She was working at her desk at the other side of the room when Malcolm Ford was admitted into the library at about 10:30 a. m. The conversation which took place between the two ... and carried on in low tones, ... dis-
... was ... and along the same lines ... turned my back toward them, and then ... a pistol shot. I looked around. I saw Malcolm Ford coming toward me with a revolver

PAUL LEICESTER FORD.
Well known author, who was killed by his brother, Malcolm W. Ford.

led to the terrible deeds of the once popular and widely known athlete. He had been successful for a time in winning the empty praise of the multitude for his strength and skill, but he had been left behind by other men in the race, and he was jealous of his brother's growing reputation in the field of literature. He had been disinherited on account of his prominence in athletic sports, and had been unsuccessful in trying to get, with the aid of the courts, a share of the estate of his father, Gordon L. Ford. He had accused his brother of unfairness in refusing to share with him. He had wasted his substance and had sought to borrow from his successful brother.

MALCOLM W. FORD,
The well known athlete, who killed his brother and then himself.

in his hand. I was frightened. I ran to the

From the front page of the *New York Tribune*, Friday, 9 May 1902.

not a normal story. The Fords did not glow with pride in Malcolm's triumphs: on the contrary, there was hostility towards him because of the poor fellow's temerity to be a great athlete. Twice in the early 1890s, rumours spread that Malcolm was going professional. This led to a full investigation by the Amateur Athletic Union, thereby endangering his records and awards. The charges were disproved by Malcolm, who acted like a gentleman during the proceedings. But, according to the *Tribune*, 'the indignity . . . embittered him towards the officials of the union for many years afterwards, and he was not on speaking terms with some of the old-time officials at the time of the present tragedy'. One wonders how the reporter would have felt if his journalistic standing had been endangered by a vicious rumour. Would he have felt kindly towards the investigating officials? Malcolm's anger at the inquisition was understandable. So was his disappointment with his family, none of whom supported him in his hour of need.

Why the Fords refused to change their minds about Malcolm has never been explained. I hazard to suggest that the reason was a mixture of snobbery and jealousy. At that time, equestrianism and fencing were about the only sports not considered lower-class pastimes. The common man attended baseball games and boxing matches: people like Gordon Ford (that is, wealthy people) sought entertainment at musical soirées and poetry readings. The image of the sportsman as an uncouth type, probably with underworld connections, was true to an extent (John L. Sullivan was a bouncer in a bar before he became the world heavyweight champion), but only in regard to *professionals*. The fact that Malcolm was an amateur made no difference to his family; the fact that his success was so great probably worsened the situation, by adding jealousy to disdain.

In 1883 Paul and Worthington began their careers by publishing *Websteriana*, a catalogue of all the material pertaining to Noah Webster in the Ford Library. They followed this with a series of detailed bibliographies: on Alexander Hamilton, the Constitutional Debates, Benjamin Franklin, and Eighteenth Century American magazines. The high standard of these works had never been met before; and they are still important. Paul was willing to write on quite scandalous historical matters: in 1889 he published *Who Was The Mother of*

Franklin's Son? The Historical Society of Pennsylvania invited him to edit the writings of John Dickinson. (If you saw the movie or musical *1776*, Dickinson is the character who leads the fight *against* the signing of the Declaration of Independence. Subsequently, Dickinson helped to get Congress to pass the first ten amendments to the Federal Constitution, known as the 'Bill of Rights', to protect free speech, freedom of religion, etc). In 1892, Paul published a ten-volume edition of *The Writings of Thomas Jefferson.*

The year before, a series of events had occurred that made the final tragedy inevitable. Perhaps as a result of Emily's efforts over the years to work out a reconciliation between Gordon and Malcolm, the latter moved back into the house in Brooklyn on 26 May 1891. Malcolm took a trip to Europe, and when he returned, fell ill with typhoid fever. His parents nursed him, and he recovered – but on 14 November Gordon died. Later on, Paul would insist that Gordon caught typhoid from Malcolm, but the obituary in the *New York Times* attributed his death to a heart attack caused by worry over Malcolm's condition. The *Tribune* of 9 May 1902 would opt for gastric fever.

Malcolm insisted that his father had planned to rewrite his will. But the will – dated 8 August 1891 – that was filed for probate on 30 November made no mention of Malcolm. Gordon's estate was set up so that Emily would enjoy a life interest in its income, and then be divided between the other six children. According to Malcolm, at the reading of the will his brothers took him aside and assured him that if he did not contest the will, he would get one-seventh of a share from each of his siblings. Paul and Worthington would deny this, but there is some evidence that Malcolm was telling the truth. He did sign a waiver to contest, and the witnessing notary later testified that Paul and Worthington said that Malcolm would receive a full share; but they were not disposed to put that statement in writing. Malcolm insisted that Emily knew of the arrangement – but that was a moot point when the will was finally contested in 1894, for Emily had died on 23 November 1893. By that time, Malcolm had married Jeanette Wilhelmina Graves, the daughter of a Brooklyn manufacturer of wall-paper; she had a fortune of $400,000. Malcolm would claim that his siblings envied him for having a rich wife, and therefore reneged on their promise. He and Jeanette moved into a large house called 'My Fancy' at Babylon, Long Island.

He brought a lawsuit against his siblings in New York State Supreme Court in Brooklyn in May 1894. The trial was during the special term, and the judge was a very able one: William J. Gaynor – best remembered non-forensically as the Mayor of New York from 1909 to 1913. His career was cut short from the after-effects of an assassination attempt in 1910. The only negative aspect of his term was his confidence in his stupid Police Commissoner, Rhinelander Waldo, which led to the police scandal associated with the murder of the gambler Herman Rosenthal in 1912. Aside from that bad error, Gaynor was one of New York's better mayors.

Paul presented the arguments for the defence: (*a*) Malcolm could only share in the estate if he showed 'a future life that commanded respect', (*b*) as Malcolm's typhoid killed Gordon Ford, the father gave a 'worthy' life for Malcolm's 'unworthy' one; (*c*) there was never any agreement to give Malcolm a share. The report of the trial in the *New York Times* is skimpy, and does not explain how Paul managed the trick of arguing the first and third arguments (which appear contradictory): if there was never an agreement to give a share to Malcolm, how was he entitled to a future share in the estate? Gaynor's decision says it all. He told Malcolm that, because there was no written proof of the agreement, the will had to stand as it was – but added that he regretted this because he believed his story. A subsequent event suggests that Gaynor was right about Malcolm's truthfulness. One of his sisters, Mabel Mayo-Smith, presented him with a seventh of her share of Gordon's estate. No reason for this was ever given.

During this period, the relative public fortunes of Paul and Malcolm began to change. Up to 1894, Paul was a historian and scholar, pure and simple. Now he became a 'real' literary figure, with the publication of his first novel, *The Honorable Peter Stirling*, which is still a good book to read. It was not successful until people began believing that its hero was based on the then pre-eminent American political hero, President Stephen Grover Cleveland. Paul commented: 'I don't blame people for thinking that Peter Stirling is Grover Cleveland, for, really, there are many points of resemblance. But the fact is that

Peter Stirling is a composite of four great American statesmen: Washington, Lincoln, and two others. It is an attempt to show how a man of the noblest aims can get close to the people and rule them. Paul's involvement in Brooklyn politics coloured out the book. That few people now read the novel can be explained. Arthur Bartlett Maurice, writing in *The Bookman* (February 1900) said: '*The Honorable Peter Stirling* was in no sense a work of art. It was totally without symmetry. It had little or no style. Much of its dialogue and some of its characters were meaningless and impossible.' Yet Maurice speaks of Ford's spontaneity, which enlivens his best passages, dealing with the political world. This is reiterated in the entry for Ford in *American Authors: 1600–1900*, edited by Stanley Kunitz and Howard Haycroft: 'The semi-realistic *Peter Stirling* is of value as a picture of petty politics in the 90s, but is open to the charges of lack of form and artificiality of sentiment.'

After *Peter Stirling*, Paul returned to history – but with an eye to the general public: *The Real George Washington* (1896) was the first literary attempt to make the first President a realistic human being. Paul wrote for the stage as well, beginning with *Honors Are Easy*, which was produced by Charles Frohman in 1896. Returning to bibliographic work, in the following year he published a study of the first textbook used in the United States, *The New England Primer*. That year, while on a trip with some friends, he amused them with a detective story about socialites who commit a crime; this he expanded and published as *The Great K and A Train Robbery*. His *Tattle Tales of Cupid* appeared in 1898. A year later, he produced the novel upon which his literary reputation stands or falls: *Janice Meredith: A Story of the American Revolution*. It is a love story painted against the backdrop of the Revolution, but it is only the backdrop which is now of interest. Paul was at home in this area, as all his historical and bibliographical work attests: his pictures of men like George Washington and Alexander Hamilton ring true. In the opinion of Allen Nevins, 'the wealth of semi-realistic details makes it an enlightening study of the social life of the time . . . even if considered merely as the diversion of a historian, this book has more than ephemeral value'. *Janice Meredith* became the first American novel to sell 200,000 copies within three months of its publication. Paul dramatized it for

Frohman, who did well by and from it. Even fashion was affected by the tale, for the 'Janice Meredith curl' became a popular hairstyle.

Paul published *The Many-Sided Franklin* in 1899. This was a companion volume to his book on George Washington, and was the first attempt to show Franklin with warts and all. His final works of fiction, *Wanted: A Matchmaker* (1900) and *Wanted: A Chaperone* (1902) have not stood up like *Meredith* or *Stirling*. He could never amend the gooey love-story conventions of his time, and could not even handle that material well. Only when he dealt with history and politics, materials that he knew something about, did his writing come alive. Perhaps he would have improved in time, developing his strong points, if – but I'm getting ahead of myself.

Just as Paul's literary career was taking off, Malcolm's life went on the skids. In 1895 Malcolm and Jeanette had a son, Malcolm Webster Jr. However, on 19 March 1898, Jeanette obtained a divorce on statutory grounds. The details of her claim were not reported (newspapers tried to avoid such painful matters in turn-of-the-century America), but it could not have been cruelty, for she allowed Malcolm to retain custody of their son. In the *Tribune*'s coverage of the 1902 tragedy, there is mention of a mysterious woman who would come to the divorced Malcolm's apartment when he was away, to see the little boy, who would run over to kiss her while she ran her fingers through his curly hair; she once went to see him when he had a slight fever, the manager of the apartment house allowing her in. These titbits appear in the *Tribune* of 9 May 1902. I suspect they are untrue. If it was Jeanette who sneaked over to see her son, why did the paper coyly refrain from saying so? The paper could hardly have been afraid of a libel suit. I think they knew the stories were unverifiable, and printed them to get some more digs in against Malcolm. As we will see, Jeanette showed that she still sympathized with him apropos of his troubles with his family.

As Malcolm's home-life collapsed, Paul's improved. In 1900 he met Mary Grace Kidder, whose father appears to have been an architect in Brooklyn, and married her in December. During the ceremony (which Malcolm did not attend), Paul showed a side of his nature that was not usually seen. Not liking visual records of his physical condition, he attacked and beat up a photographer who had taken a shot of the bridal party. He was not the only short, crippled man who ever reacted like this, but the other instance that springs to mind is hardly flattering to him. The example is Dr Joseph Goebbels.

According to subsequent testimony of the Ford family, throughout this period Malcolm kept visiting Paul to cadge money from him; Malcolm, they said, was a hopeless spendthrift. There are some problems in accepting this as totally true. First, Malcolm was a hard-working man; even the *Tribune* admitted that he wrote for many magazines and newspapers on sporting topics. He had begun taking an interest in automobiles, and was the first secretary of the Automobile Club of America; also he was the editor of two periodicals, one being an automobile magazine called *The New Centaur*. That magazine folded in April 1902, owing several thousand dollars to the Trow Publishing Company. The *Tribune* could not find out if Malcolm had a financial stake in the magazine. The formal date of receivership was 2 May 1902, which means that Malcolm's financial problems had six days in which to get out of control. At that time, he had the expenses of his apartment (rent of $1000 a year, or less than $83 a month), which were fairly moderate for a single-parent, middle-class man in 1902; and he had to spend money on raising his son, and to employ a housekeeper to watch little Malcolm. None of this strikes one as spendthrift. The only ostensible extravagance that I found was that Malcolm purchased an automobile, which was a rich man's toy in 1902; but as he was the editor of an automobile magazine, and an official in the Automobile Club, he could hardly have stuck with shank's pony.

An incident occurred in this period which may have had some bearing on later events. There were three executors of Gordon's will: Paul and Worthington Ford, and their sister Mabel's husband, the academic Richmond Mayo-Smith. On 11 November 1901, while recovering from a nervous breakdown, Mayo-Smith fell out of a fourth-storey window to his death. Details of his breakdown are sparse: the entry in *The Dictionary of American Biography* says that a boating accident a few months earlier led to his collapse. According to the *New York Times*'s account of his death, it was either an accident while sleep-walking or suicide on impulse; there is no mention of anyone in the house at the time who should not have been there. In none of the accounts of the tragedy of the following May is anything suspicious read into this earlier event.

In 1902, the position of the two brothers was as follows: Paul and Mary Ford (who was pregnant) had moved to 37 East Seventy-Seventh Street, Manhattan. Mary's father had designed this home, which had a library, lit by a skylight, for Paul's collection – still huge, although Paul and Worthington had presented most of Gordon's literary acquisitions to the New York Public Library. Paul worked in his library with his secretary, Miss Elizabeth Hall. Shortly before the tragedy, Paul and his father-in-law purchased a thousand acres of land in Dublin, New Hampshire. Paul had ample spare cash for this purchase, because on 25 January 1902 he and Worthington had sold some of Gordon's remaining property in Brooklyn for $55,000. Paul was very wealthy indeed: his estate was probated at $205,000 after expenses; before the deductions, it amounted to $314,000.

Yet the *Tribune* would report that when Malcolm visited Paul a week before the murder, pleading for financial help, Paul said that his funds were tied-up in building a summer-house. Even with the expense of the summer-house, I find it hard to understand why Paul could not help Malcolm out.

How serious was Malcolm's financial position in the spring of 1902? The failure of *The New Centaur* should not have prevented him from writing for or editing other magazines. The *New York Times* subsequently interviewed his landlord, who mentioned that Malcolm seemed gloomy, but did not say anything about overdue rent. Malcolm's housekeeper left a week before the tragedy, but he straightaway hired a replacement.

On Thursday, 8 May 1902, Malcolm got up, dressed, woke his son, made breakfast. He also loaded a .38 calibre Smith & Wesson revolver, and put it in his coat pocket. The new housekeeper arrived. Malcolm left at half-past nine, promising to buy his son a toy. He returned almost at once, kissed his son again, and told him never to think ill of him. He went downstairs, and said good morning to the elevator man, Thomas Connell, remarking: 'The better the day, the better the deed.' He reached Paul's mansion at half-past ten. One of the five servants opened the door. Malcolm repeated his comment about the day and the deed, and walked into the library unannounced. Paul and his secretary were there. On one of the walls was a painting of a wealthy woman rescuing a street urchin. If, as Malcolm's traducers would suggest, he was there to borrow from Paul, he may have noticed the picture and thought it ironic.

The only witness to the following incidents was the secretarial Miss Hall. Much of her testimony is unhelpful; one comment is somewhat hard to believe. The *Times* and the *Tribune* reported that she refused to say what Paul was working on, but the latter organ stated that it was part of a draft of a novel. Miss Hall said hello to Malcolm as he walked to the desk, which was about ten feet from where she was sitting or standing. She saw Malcolm walk behind Paul. She heard Paul say, 'Just a minute, Malcolm.' Malcolm walked around in front of Paul and glared at him as he finished writing. Then some words passed between them. Miss Hall said that by now her back was turned towards them, and she did not hear the words. If that was true, then it is a pity, for if she had heard them we might know the reason for what happened next.

Malcolm pulled his gun from his pocket and fired into the upper left side of Paul's chest. The frightened Miss Hall ran out of the library. She would later tell a *Tribune* reporter that she soon pulled herself together and went back towards the library. Both the *Tribune* and the *Times* mention that she heard a voice, which she believed was Malcolm's, call her back in. She entered. Malcolm supposedly said to her, 'Come on and see me take my life.' Turning the gun towards his heart, he steadied the barrel with his left hand and fired a single shot. Sufficient. He fell dead upon the rich carpet.

By that time, other members of the staff had come into the room. Paul was still alive, slumped in his swivel-chair. He ordered a maid to go upstairs to reassure his wife. The family physician, Emmanuel Baruch, was called from his office a few doors along East Seventy-Seventh Street. When he realized how serious the injuries were, he sent for another local doctor, Julius Rosenberg. Paul was moved to a couch in a room on the second floor. It was apparent that he could not survive, as the bullet had passed near the left lung, cutting off blood vessels to the heart. He died within thirty minutes of the shooting.

Now strange things began to happen.

Perhaps because Dr Baruch was a family friend as well as the family physician, he made curious statements. He told a *Tribune* reporter: 'It will be of great comfort to his friends to know that Paul met his death calmly and heroically. He went off without a pain or an ache, for he did not know he was going to die.' But in the next breath, the doctor said that Paul's last words were, 'I want to die bravely.' The doctor then expressed a psychiatric opinion: 'I think it was a case of mental aberration on the part of Malcolm Ford. . . . I do not think a man not criminally inclined would shoot his brother unless he was temporarily insane, and unless he knew he was going to commit suicide himself. Malcolm Ford intended to commit suicide. Moreover, he did so before his brother died.' The good doctor seemed to be searching for some quick, pat solution to the killing. The *Tribune* also reported, without any show of shock or surprise, that Dr Baruch had to be persuaded to report the tragedy as a murder-suicide, and not an accident. The doctor insisted, to the same reporter, that he called the coroner's office three times, and was told they were too busy to attend. He finally got through to Coroner Scholer at his home at half-past one in the afternoon.

Police Captain Brown of the East Sixty-Seventh Street Station arrived soon after the shooting. He too talked to the *Tribune* reporter, saying that Malcolm's behaviour had made his family uneasy for a long time, that that was evidence of an unsound mind, and that the murder was committed in a period of temporary insanity. Normally it takes quite a while to determine the exact cause of a domestic murder. Captain Brown had the answer in this case by the evening of the first day.

The family announced that the funerals of both brothers would be held in Irvington, far to the north of Manhattan, on Saturday, 10 May. It was decided that the Episcopal ceremony would be a full one for Paul, a partial one for Malcolm. The fact that the latter was of unsound mind meant that, despite his suicide, he could be buried in consecrated ground.

Worthington Ford had not been in Manhattan on 8 May; learning of the tragedy from reporters, he had told a man from the *Times* that the most friendly relations had existed between

75

Paul and Malcolm, though they had hardly ever seen each other in two or three years. It was as if the contest over the will had never occurred.

The day before the funeral, Worthington went to Malcolm's home to discuss the future of his nephew. The Fords were prepared to take care of the boy. He met Jeanette Graves Ford there, and left empty-handed. Soon afterwards, Jeanette announced:

> 'Now that the boy's father is dead, my boy is mine, more than anyone else's. I shall take him, and care for him, for he belongs to his mother.'
>
> When asked about the tragedy in 77th Street, she said: 'Mr Ford must have been insane. It does seem that he was treated unjustly by his family.'

As with so many other comments that seemed at all unkind to the victim or his siblings, Jeanette's was tucked away in the middle of an article. (She did take good care of Malcolm Jr, who married the daughter of a judge in 1934.)

New York City has had many sensational murders associated with the rich and/or celebrated. I do not know of any that vanished as suddenly, as totally, from the press as the Ford Case. Every newspaper in the city talked of it for three days, from 9 to 11 May 1902. But on the first of those days, Mount Pelée, on Martinique, erupted, killing forty thousand people. That tragedy helped to bury the case. And so, it appears, did a cover-up by the Ford family.

I realize that there was no real excuse for the shooting of Paul Leicester Ford by his brother. But still, I cannot help sympathizing with the criminal. Malcolm's sole former 'crime' was that he, refusing to follow the cultural road his family had mapped out for him, proved that he could make his way as an athlete. That was not a justifiable reason for his father to disown him or for his siblings to cheat him. Paul's assertion that Malcolm's typhoid led to Gordon's death was disgraceful: it was one of the excuses for an act of greed by those siblings. I believe, too, that it was symptomatic of a problem arising from the sins of a father: Paul, crippled and physically weak, had spent his youth under unfair pressure from Gordon; his brother, determined and physically powerful, had refused to knuckle down to Gordon. Paul deeply resented that, as he believed, Malcolm' actions had focused pressures on himself. Paul usually led the siblings against Malcolm. I think his leadership was provoked by sheer hate.

The issue of Malcolm's mental condition is questionable. His actions on Thursday, 8 May 1902, could have been those of a man at the end of his tether – but were they those of a man who was mentally ill? Emmanuel Baruch, no matter how qualified as a physician, had no business diagnosing that Malcolm was crazy; Captain Brown's snap conclusion of insanity was either guesswork or a quote. An attempt was made to show that financial difficulties were behind Malcolm's 'insanity', but aside from rumours concerning a magazine that had folded, an expensive automobile, and unspecified expenses, nothing was produced to show that Malcolm was strapped for cash.

It remains an unsatisfactory case, with too many unanswered questions. It became a family secret, buried with its two victims. It leaves an unpleasant taste in one's mouth, for Malcolm had not deserved the smug ostracism and mistreatment by his family. Though I cannot condone the murder, I will say this for Malcolm:

He did not kill slowly but with a single shot, and a minute later he executed his brother's murderer.

Salieri and
the 'Murder' of Mozart

Albert Borowitz

ON 14 OCTOBER 1791, in his last surviving letter, Mozart wrote to his wife, Constanze, at Baden that he had taken the Italian composer Antonio Salieri and the singer Madame Cavalieri to a performance of *The Magic Flute*, and that Salieri had been most complimentary: 'from the overture to the last chorus there was not a single number that did not call forth from him a bravo! or bello!' Less than two months later, Mozart was dead. The *Musikalisches Wochenblatt*, in a report from Prague written within a week of the composer's death, mentioned rumours of poisoning, based on the swollen condition of his body. Suspicion was gradually to focus on Salieri, who, despite his recently professed delight over *The Magic Flute*, had for a decade been an implacable rival of Mozart in Vienna. In the years prior to Salieri's death in 1825, the rumours of his recourse to poison as a final weapon of rivalry were fed by reports that Salieri, while in failing health, had confessed his guilt and, in remorse, had attempted suicide.

The Mozart-Salieri murder legend has spawned perennial controversies and traditions in the fields of medicine, musicology, history and literature. Beginning in 1970, with the appearance of a novel by David Weiss, entitled *The Assassination of Mozart*, the poisoning hypothesis acquired a new popularity that was enormously broadened by the production of Peter Shaffer's *Amadeus* a decade later. The success of Shaffer's work has overshadowed the continuing medical and historical dispute over Mozart's untimely demise. The writings on this fascinating subject differ widely in quality and point of view, and many of the authors seem unaware of the sources on which others have drawn. It therefore remains tempting to return to this classic historical mystery with a view to providing a 'confrontation' among the various contending parties, including those who blame Mozart's death, respectively, on natural causes, poisoning, professional jealousy, Viennese politics, the Masons, and the Jews. In this centuries-long debate, no possible suspect is spared. Virtually no organ of Mozart's body is regarded as above the suspicion of having failed in its appointed function, and with the exception of the composer's wife, no group or individual is cleared of complicity in his death.

The story of Mozart's last days must begin with the mysterious commissioning of the Requiem, which apparently caused his sensitive spirits to brood upon death. Around July of 1791, when Mozart's work on *The Magic Flute* was virtually complete and rehearsals has already begun, he received a visit from a tall, grave-looking stranger dressed completely in grey. The stranger presented an anonymous letter commissioning Mozart to compose a Requiem as quickly as possible at whatever price the composer wished to name. It is now accepted that the commission had a very prosaic explanation. The patron of the uncanny-looking messenger was Count Franz von Walsegg, who wanted the Requiem composed in memory of his late wife, and intended to pass himself off as the composer. Mozart accepted the commission, but put aside his work on the Requiem when he received an offer to write an opera, *La Clemenza di Tito*, for the coronation of Emperor Leopold in Prague. Just as Mozart and his wife were getting into the coach to leave for Prague, the messenger appeared, it is said, 'like a ghost' and pulled at Constanze's coat, asking her, 'What about the Requiem?' Mozart explained his reason for the journey, but promised to turn to the Requiem as soon as he came back to Vienna.

Franz Niemetschek, Mozart's first biographer, reports that Mozart became ill in Prague and required continuous medical attention while he was there. He states that Mozart 'was pale and his expression was sad, although his good humour was often shown in merry jest with his friends'.

On Mozart's return to Vienna, he started work on the Requiem with great energy and interest; but his family and friends noted that his illness was becoming worse and that he was depressed. To cheer him up, Constanze went driving with him one day in the Prater. According to her account, which she gave to Niemetschek, 'Mozart began to speak of death, and declared that he was writing the Requiem for himself. Tears came to the eyes of this sensitive man. "I feel definitely," he continued, "that I will not last much longer; I am sure I have been poisoned. I cannot rid myself of this idea."'

This conversation, which is one of the cornerstones of the poisoning legend, Constanze later repeated to her second husband, Georg Nikolaus von Nissen, who recorded it in his biography of Mozart in much the same terms as the Niemetschek version. Constanze was still recounting the episode as late as 1829, according to the journal of Vincent and Mary Novello, who paid her a visit in Salzburg that year. In fact, the Novellos' journal records that Constanze told them that Mozart had clearly identified the poison that he thought had been administered to him as *aqua toffana*. This poison, whose principal active ingredient is supposed to have been arsenic, was introduced by a Neapolitan woman named Toffana in seventeenth-century Italy, with startling effect on the statistics of sudden death. It is perhaps regrettable that history has not seen fit to choose the most sublime of her various nicknames for the potion, the 'manna of St Nicholas di Bari'.

One of the most dependable accounts of Mozart's terminal illness is provided by Constanze's sister, Sophie Haibel, in a report sent in 1825 to Nissen at his request for use in his biography. Most of the symptoms with which the medical historians have dealt we owe to her account: the painful swelling of his body, which made it difficult for him to move in bed; his complaint that he had 'the taste of death' on his tongue; his high fever. Despite his suffering, he continued to work on the Requiem. On the last day of the composer's life, when Sophie came to see him, Süssmayr was at his bedside and Mozart was explaining to him how he ought to finish the Requiem. (It is reported by a newspaper article contemporaneous with Sophie's memoir that earlier on this day Mozart was singing the alto part of the Requiem with three friends, who supplied falsetto, tenor and bass.) Mozart retained his worldly concerns to the point of advising Constanze to keep his death secret until his friend Albrechtsberger could be informed, so that his friend could make prompt arrangements to succeed to Mozart's recently granted rights as colleague and heir-apparent of the Kapellmeister of St Stephen's Cathedral. When Mozart appeared to be sinking, one of his doctors, Nikolaus Closset, was sent for and was finally located at the theatre. However, according to Sophie's account, that drama-lover 'had to wait till the piece was over'. When he arrived, he ordered cold compresses put on Mozart's feverish brow; but these 'provided such a shock that he did not regain consciousness again before he died'. The last thing Mozart did, according to Sophie, was to imitate the kettledrums in the Requiem. She wrote that, thirty-four years later, she could still hear that last music of his.

Nissen, in his biography, states that Mozart's fatal illness lasted for fifteen days, terminating with his death around midnight (probably the early morning) of 5 December 1791. The illness began with swellings of his hands and feet and an almost complete immobility, and sudden attacks of vomiting followed. Nissen describes the illness as 'high miliary fever'. He writes that Mozart retained consciousness until two hours before his death.

Neither Dr Closset nor Mozart's other attending physician prepared a death certificate with the cause of death stated. No autopsy was performed. From the very beginning, doctors and other commentators have differed widely as to the cause of death. Nissen's identification of the fatal illness as 'miliary fever' accords with the cause of death as set forth in the registers of deaths of St Stephen's Cathedral and Parish in Vienna. Although that nomenclature does not fit any precise modern medical definition, it is surmised that the term as used in the medicine of the eighteenth century denoted a fever accompanied by a rash. However, a number of other illnesses have been put forward as the cause of death, including grippe, tuberculosis, dropsy, meningitis, rheumatic fever, heart failure, and Graves' disease. The hypotheses of some of these diseases, such as tuberculosis, appear to have been based not so much on any of the observable medical phenomena as on a biographical conclusion that Mozart in his last years was killing himself with overwork and irregular living. The hypothesis of Graves' disease, a hyperthyroidism, is based on facial characteristics of Joseph Lange's unfinished 1782 portrait of the composer, which include, in the words of an imaginative medical observer, 'the wide angle of the eye, the staring, rather frightened look, the swelling of the upper eyelid and the moist glaze of the eyes'. The art historian Kenneth Clark had quite a different interpretation of Mozart's intent gaze in the Lange portrait. The painting conveyed to Lord Clark, not the sign of death nine years off, but 'the single-mindedness of genius'.

Probably the prevailing theory of modern medical authorities who believe Mozart to have died a natural death is that he suffered from a chronic kidney disease, which passed in its final stages into a failure of kidney function, oedema (swelling due to excessive retention of liquid in the body tissues) and uremic poisoning. This theory was advanced as early as 1905 by a French physician, Dr Barraud. It is argued that this diagnosis is most in keeping with the recorded phenomena of Mozart's last sufferings, including the swelling of his body and the poisonous taste of which he complained. Modern medicine has established that certain chronic diseases of the kidneys are commonly caused by streptococcal infections suffered long before the effect on the kidney function becomes noticeable.

Medical commentators on Mozart's death have implicated a number of childhood illnesses as likely contributors to his chronic kidney disease. They are aided in their researches by detailed descriptions of the illnesses of the Mozart children in the letters of their father, Leopold. Certainly their recurring health problems were a proper subject of parental concern, but the pains Leopold takes to describe his children's symptoms and the course of their illnesses and recoveries stamp him as an amateur of medicine. In fact, he often administered remedies to the children, his favourites being a cathartic and an antiperspirant he refers to as 'black powder' and 'margrave powder', respectively. It is fortunate that the children survived both a series of diseases and their father's cures.

In 1762, when Wolfgang was six years old, he was ill with what a doctor consulted by Leopold Mozart declared to be a type of scarlet fever, an infection capable of causing kidney injury. In the following year, 1763, Mozart suffered an illness marked by painful joints and fever, which have led some observers to postulate rheumatic fever, which could also lead to adverse effects on the kidney. When Mozart was nine, he suffered from what Leopold called a 'very bad cold,' and later the same year both his sister and he were more seriously ill. Nannerl was thought to be in such serious condition that the administration of extreme unction was begun. No sooner had she recovered than Wolfgang was struck by the illness, which in his father's words reduced him in a period of four weeks to such a wretched state that 'he is not only absolutely unrecognizable, but has nothing left but his tender skin and little bones'. Some modern commentators identify this severe illness as an attack of abdominal typhus. Two years later, in 1767, Wolfgang contracted smallpox, which left him quite ill and caused severe swelling of his eyes and nose. He also suffered throughout his childhod from a number of bad toothaches, which have led some supporters of the kidney-disease theory to invoke the possibility of a 'focal' infection, contributing to kidney damage. The last reference to an illness of Mozart's prior to his final days is in a letter from Leopold Mozart to his daughter Nannerl in 1784, when her brother was twenty-eight. This letter reported that Wolfgang had become violently ill with colic in Vienna and had a doctor in almost daily attendance. Leopold added that not only his son, 'but a number of other people caught rheumatic fever, which became septic when not taken in hand at once'. There is no other evidence of a serious illness of Mozart's until the period of a few months preceding his death. Dr Louis Carp attempts to demonstrate the presence of severe symptoms of kidney disease as early as 1787 by quoting from a letter by Mozart to his father in April of that year: 'I never lie down at night without reflecting that – young as I am – I may not live to see another day.' This letter, written to console Mozart's dying father, gives us an important insight into the composer's philosophical speculations. However, it does not provide any clue to his own physical condition or to his feelings about his health.

Locked in combat with the medical authorities attributing Mozart's death to disease is a substantial body of modern physicians who would support Mozart's own suspicion by declaring that he was indeed poisoned. These doctors, including Dieter Kerner and Gunther Duda of Germany, believe that the poison administered was mercury, which attacks the kidneys and produces much the same diagnostic picture as that presented by the final stages of a natural kidney failure. Both Kerner and Duda minimize much of the evidence that has been cited in support of the theory that Mozart suffered from a chronic kidney disease stemming from streptococcal infection. Dr Duda believes that the severity and nature of Mozart's childhood illnesses have been mis-stated. He is convinced that the so-called scarlet fever identified as such by the physician whom Wolfgang's father consulted was, in fact, erythema nodosum, a disorder of uncertain origin resulting in raised eruptions of the skin, and of far less severity than scarlet fever. Moreover, Duda is not at all certain that other illnesses of Mozart's, which have been identified as rheumatic fever, were not, instead, common cases of the grippe. He is unimpressed by the speculation that Mozart's toothaches may have involved harmful focal infections. He points out that Mozart's sister, who was exposed to and suffered most of the same childhood illnesses as Wolfgang, lived to the age of seventy-eight, and finds no evidence that Mozart himself had any substantial illness between 1784 and the last year of his life.

Dr Kerner believes that the phenomena of Mozart's final illness more closely resemble those of mercury poisoning than of the terminal phase of a chronic kidney illness. He notes the absence of any evidence that Mozart complained of thirst, which Dr Kerner associates with chronic nephritis. He also observes that Mozart was working actively to the last and was fully conscious, composing, during the last few months of his life, some of his greatest masterpieces. In contrast with this spectacular creative activity, it is Dr Kerner's experience that 'uremics are always for weeks and usually months before their death unable to work and for days before their death are unconscious'. Dr Kerner accepts the contemporary report that Mozart first became ill in Prague, and assumes that small doses of mercury were given to him in the summer of 1791, followed by a lethal dose shortly before his death. Dr Kerner alludes to the fact that in the Vienna of Mozart's time mercury was in limited use as a remedy for syphilis, and states that such use was introduced by Dr Gerhard van Swieten, whose son Mozart knew. From such observations a commentator has erroneously read Dr Kerner as arguing that Mozart poisoned himself in an effort to cure himself of syphilis.

It is hard for a modern reader of these arguments to rid himself of the prejudice against regarding a poisoning as anything but an exotic possibility. Unfortunately, it was for good experiential reasons not so regarded in the eighteenth century. Duda, in an effort to prepare his readers to accept his thesis, begins his book with the reminder that before firearms became generally available, poison was an extremely common weapon, and the subtle arts of its use well known. It is remarkable how many of Mozart's contemporaries who figure in some manner in the controversies over his death regarded poisoning or suspicion of poisoning as risks to be taken quite seriously.

Even if the medical evidence and eighteenth-century experience do not exclude the poisoning of Mozart as a possibility, there has always been difficulty in identifying a murderer and finding an appropriate murder motive. Salieri has always been the prime candidate for the unhappy role of Mozart's murderer. He fits this assignment imperfectly at best. Although (in large part due to the effect of the murder legend) time has not been kind to Salieri's musical reputation, he was undoubtedly one of the leading composers of his period and an important teacher of composition, counting among his pupils Beethoven, Schubert, Liszt, and Meyerbeer. He was also a famous teacher of singing. All his students loved and respected him. Friends remembered him as generous, warm and kind-hearted, and he even had the ability to laugh at himself (at least at his difficulties with the German language). He must have had a way with people, since he established a close personal relationship with the difficult Beethoven.

However, the musicians whose careers Salieri helped to forward shared an advantage that Mozart lacked – they all had the good fortune not to be competitors of Salieri in the composition of Italian opera. There seems little question but that he was a formidable professional opponent of Mozart, although they appear to have been able to sustain correct and even superficially friendly social relationships. Salieri enjoyed a competitive supremacy over Mozart and many other aspiring composers in Vienna, and only partly because of the undoubtedly high regard in which his contemporaries held his own operatic works. Of far greater importance in his ascendancy was the fact that, because of his favour with Joseph II until the emperor's death in 1790 and of his successive roles as court composer, director of the Italian Opera and court conductor, Salieri was able to wield powerful influence over the availability of theatres and patronage. Mozart, his father, and many of their contemporaries believed that Salieri had caused the emperor to be unfavourably disposed towards *The Abduction from the Seraglio*, and had also been responsible for the later plot (fortunately unsuccessful) to induce the court to hamper the opening of *The Marriage of Figaro*. In his letters to his father, Mozart also accused Salieri of having prevented him from obtaining as a piano pupil the Princess of Württemberg. In December 1789, Mozart wrote to his fellow Freemason and benefactor, Puchberg, that next time they met, he would tell him about Salieri's plots 'which, however, have completely failed'.

Although Mozart was undoubtedly very sensitive about barriers to his career, his feeling that Salieri used court influence to frustrate his musical competitors is borne out in the memoirs of Michael Kelly and Lorenzo da Ponte, who worked with both Mozart and Salieri and were on friendly terms with each. Kelly refers to Salieri as 'a clever, shrewd man, possessed of what Bacon called crooked wisdom,' and adds that Salieri's effort to have one of his operas selected for performance instead of *The Marriage of Figaro* was 'backed by three of the principal performers, who formed a cabal not easily put down'. Da Ponte blames attempts to disrupt rehearsals of *Figaro* on the opera impresario, Count Orsini-Rosenberg, and a rival librettist, Casti, rather than directly on Salieri, although both men appear to have been in Salieri's camp. He also remarks that before he came to the rescue, 'Mozart had, thanks to the intrigues of his rivals, never been able to exercise his divine genius in Vienna'. Da Ponte was a slippery man with an elastic memory; it is probably fair to attribute to him the assessment of Salieri that he claimed to have heard from the lips of Emperor Leopold: 'I know all his intrigues . . . Salieri is an insufferable egoist. He wants successes in my theatre only for his own operas and his own women. . . . He is an enemy of all composers, all singers, all Italians – and above all, *my* enemy, because he knows that I know him.'

Nevertheless, there is much to suggest that Salieri's hostility to Mozart did not extend to the sphere of personal relations. He was one of the small group of mourners who followed Mozart's coffin as it was carried from the funeral service at St Stephen's Cathedral towards the cemetery, making a greater display of public grief over Mozart's death than Constanze, who stayed at home, supposedly still overcome by her husband's death. Moreover, Salieri later became the teacher of Mozart's son Franz Xaver Wolfgang, and in 1807 gave him a written testimonial which procured him his first musical appointment.

It is difficult to decide whether Constanze or the Mozart family gave any credence to the rumours against Salieri. Would Constanze have entrusted the musical education of her son to a man she believed to be the murderer of his father? Nissen's biography contains an allusion to Salieri's rivalry, but rejects the poisoning charges. Nissen reports that Constanze attributed Mozart's suspicion of poisoning to illness and over-work. Moreover, he included in his biography an anonymous account of Mozart's early death which had been published in 1803. The quoted article dismisses the possibility of poisoning, and attributes Mozart's fears to 'pure imagination'.

Nissen's biography was undoubtedly written and compiled with Constanze's blessing. However, as witnessed by her con-versations with the Novellos, which took place at approxi-mately the same time as the appearance of the biography, Constanze never put Mozart's suspicions out of her mind. Her preoccupation with this subject reappears a decade later in a letter written to a Munich official (and quoted by Kerner in his study) to the effect that 'her son Wolfgang Xaver knew that he would not, like his father, have to fear envious men who had designs on his life'. Her other son, Karl, on his death in 1858, left behind, according to Kerner, a handwritten commentary, in which there is further discussion of the poisoning of Mozart – this time with a 'vegetable poison'.

The views of Mozart's contemporaries as to Salieri's guilt doubtlessly divided along lines of personal or musical loyalties. In the years 1823 to 1825, partisans of Salieri rallied to the defence of his reputation in the face of widely circulated reports that he had confessed the murder and attempted suicide by cutting his throat. When Kapellmeister Schwanenberg, a friend of Salieri's, was read a newspaper account of the rumour that Mozart had fallen victim of Salieri's envy, he shouted, 'Crazy people! He [Mozart] did nothing to deserve such an honour.' But believers in the poisoning rumours were tireless and ingenious in spreading their gospel. At a performance of Beethoven's Ninth Symphony in Vienna on 23 May 1824, concertgoers were distributed a leaflet containing a poem that pictured Salieri as Mozart's rival 'standing by his side with the poisoned cup'. Giuseppe Carpani, a friend of Salieri and an early biographer of Haydn, responded with an effective public relations campaign on behalf of his maligned compatriot. He published a letter he had received in June 1824 from Dr Guldener, whe had not attended Mozart but had spoken to Mozart's physician, Dr Closset. The latter had advised him, Guldener wrote, that Mozart's fatal illness had been a rheumatic and inflammatory fever which had attacked many people in Vienna in 1791. Dr Guldener had added that in view of the large number of people who had seen Mozart during his illness, and the experience and industry of Dr Closset, 'it could not have escaped their notice then if even the slightest trace of poisoning had manifested itself'. (Presumably Dr Closset was quite industrious after theatre hours.) Carpani appended the text of Guldener's letter to his own article defending Salieri's innocence. The Salieri press campaign also included a statement by the two men who served as the composer's keepers in his last years of declining health. They attested that they had been with him day and night and had never heard him confess the murder.

The views of Beethoven on the poisoning rumours have always been an intriguing subject because of his love of Mozart's music and his friendship with Salieri. We know from the entries in his conversation books that Beethoven's callers gossiped about the case with him. In late 1823 the publisher Johann Schickh referred to Salieri's unsuccessful suicide attempt. In the following year Beethoven's nephew Karl and his friend and future biographer, Anton Schindler, mentioned the reports of Salieri's confession of the poisoning, and Karl, in May 1825, the month of Salieri's death, alluded to the persistence of the rumours. It is generally agreed that Beethoven did not believe Salieri guilty. He was fond of referring to himself as Salieri's pupil, and after Mozart's death he dedicated the violin sonatas Opus 12 to Salieri (1797) and wrote a set of ten piano variations on a duet from Salieri's charming opera *Falstaff* (1798). Nevertheless, wagging tongues delighted in passing along a spurious anecdote that Rossini, when he had induced Salieri to take him to visit Beethoven at his Vienna home, was angrily turned away at the door with the words: 'How dare you come to my house with Mozart's poisoner?'

The irony of the Beethoven-Rossini anecdote lies in the fact that the lives of both men were touched by fears and rumours of poisoning. Beethoven believed that his hated sister-in-law Johanna had poisoned his brother and intended to poison his nephew. Rossini's mourning for the early death of his friend Vincenzo Bellini in Paris was followed, as was Salieri's attendance at Mozart's funeral, by rumours of poisoning. But the Bellini poisoning legend was cut down in its infancy as a result of decisive action on the part of Rossini. Francis Toye writes that 'Rossini, unwilling, perhaps, to figure as a second Salieri, insisted on an autopsy, which put an end to the rumour once and for all'.

It almost appears that Salieri was the only musical protagonist in the case who is not reported to have been subject to fears of poisoning. However, we have the intriguing biographical note that Salieri, though from a land of wine, drank only water. His modest drink, unlike headier beverages, would have given his taste buds early warning should an enemy have surreptitiously added a splash of *aqua toffana*.

Most of Mozart's principal biographers have either held aloof from the poisoning theory or rejected it outright. Franz Niemetschek, the first biographer (1798), appears to straddle the issue. Although he purported to blame lack of exercise and overwork for Mozart's death, he left room for a more sinister possibility: 'These were probably the chief causes of his untimely death (if, in fact, it was not hastened unnaturally).' He also attributed Emperor Joseph's critical remarks about *The Abduction from the Seraglio* to 'the cunning Italians', and added towards the conclusion of his work that 'Mozart had enemies too, numerous, irreconcilable enemies, who pursued him even after his death'. These enemies, including Salieri, were still alive, and Niemetschek, whatever his suspicions, could not very well have gone much further in pointing a finger.

Edward Holmes (1845) was the first to exonerate Salieri expressly. He relegated the poisoning legend to a footnote and concluded that 'Salieri, the known inveterate foe of Mozart, was fixed upon as the imaginary criminal'. Otto Jahn, in his great study of Mozart (1856–1859), continued to keep the charges of poisoning imprisoned in a footnote, and referred to the suspicions of Salieri's guilt as 'shameful'. Hermann Abert preserves Jahn's fleeting reference to the murder legend, and observes that Mozart's suspicion of poisoning evidenced his 'morbidly overstimulated emotional state'. Arthur Schurig blames Mozart's death on a severe grippe. Alfred Einstein not only fails to dignify the poisoning tradition by any mention, but even finds the only explanation for Salieri's animosity in Mozart's 'wicked tongue'. Eric Blom and Nicholas Slonimsky have rejected the possibility of murder, but have fortunately taken the trouble to chronicle some of the excesses of the various murder theories. However, both Russia and Germany have since the Second World War produced writers who claim to have found 'historical' evidence that not only supports the murder thesis but reveals a political motive for the crime and for the prevention of its detection.

The Soviet musicologist, Igor Boelza, in his brochure *Mozart and Salieri*, published in Moscow in 1953, exhibits a chain of hearsay evidence to the effect that Salieri's priest made a written report of Salieri's confession of the murder. He claims that the late Soviet academician Boris Asafiev told him that he had been shown the report by Guido Adler, also deceased. Boelza states that Adler had also spoken of the document to 'colleagues and numerous scholars,' none of whom is named in the brochure. According to Boelza, Adler engaged in a detailed study of the dates and circumstances of the meetings of Mozart and Salieri and established that they bore out the facts of the confession and satisfied the classic element of 'opportunity'. But Adler apparently was no more ready to publish his Inspector French-style timetable than he was willing to publish the Salieri confession itself. It is small wonder that Alexander Werth, in commenting on Boelza's book, remarks: 'It looks as if the Adler mystery has taken the place of the Salieri mystery.'

Boelza also seeks support for the murder case in the mysterious circumstances of Mozart's funeral and burial, which

Salieri and the 'Murder' of Mozart

An unfinished oil
painting of Mozart by
his brother-in-law
Joseph Lange

Salieri, aged 71

Bloody and Bowed

Joe Orton

Kenneth Halliwell

German writers like to refer to as *die Grabfrage* (the burial question). Posterity has always been puzzled by the fact that only a few friends (including Salieri) accompanied the funeral procession, and that even they turned back before arriving at the cemetery. The burial was that of a poor man and Mozart's body was placed in an unmarked grave. These bitter facts, so inappropriate to memorializing the passing of a great genius and a man who had loving friends and family, have been variously explained, and even the explanation least flattering to Mozart's circle usually falls short of implication of criminal conduct. Constanze's absence and the mourners' desertion before the cemetery gates have traditionally been blamed on a wintry storm, but this explanation is belied both by a contemporary diary and by an intelligent modern inquiry made by Nicholas Slonimsky in the Viennese weather archives. Nissen does not mention the weather in his biography and attributes Constanze's absence to her overpowering grief. The poverty of the burial has sometimes been taken to reflect the stinginess of Mozart's friends and patrons, notably of Baron van Swieten, though others have claimed that the burial was in keeping with the surviving spirit of decrees of Emperor Joseph II enacted in 1784 and repealed in the following year. These decrees, inspired by the reforming emperor's dislike for the pomp of burial, had provided that the dead not be buried in coffins but merely sewn in sacks and covered with quicklime, and had also abolished most of the funeral ceremonies.

In Boelza's version, all the events of Mozart's interment take on a more sinister significance. He conjures up a plot, headed by Baron van Swieten, and joined by all of the composer's acquaintances and relatives (with the exception of Constanze). On van Swieten's orders, all the mourners departed on the way to the grave and the body was intentionally interred in unmarked ground. In supplying a motive for this strange plot to suppress traces of the murder, Boelza brings the case into the political arena and adds a Marxist twist. It seems that van Swieten was afraid that 'nationalist upheavals' would result if the working masses of imperialist Vienna learned of the report that Mozart had been poisoned by a court musician and, what was worse, by a foreigner.

German writers have produced a rival tradition that Mozart

was murdered by his Freemason brethren. The Masonic murder theory was apparently originated in 1861 by Georg Friedrich Daumer, a researcher of antiquities and a religious polemicist. Daumer's work was elaborated in the Nazi period, notably by General Erich Ludendorff and his wife, Mathilde, who were so fired by enthusiasm for their revelations that they devoted the family press to the propagation of their indictment of the Freemasons.

The case against the Freemasons takes a number of lines. Daumer claimed that Mozart had not fully carried out Masonry's 'party line' in *The Magic Flute*. Mozart, in his view, had offended the Masons by his excessive attachment to the figure of the Queen of the Night and by his use of Christian religious music in the chorale of the Men of Armour. Daumer also believed that the murder thwarted Mozart's plan to establish his own secret lodge, to be called 'The Grotto'. Mathilde Ludendorff built upon Daumer's imaginings. She preferred, however, another explanation of the Masons' outrage at *The Magic Flute*. She believed that Mozart had hidden under the pro-Masonic surface of the opera a secret counterplot which depicted Mozart (Tamino) seeking the release of Marie Antoinette (Pamina) from her Masonic captors. Mathilde Ludendorff, like Igor Boelza, added an element of nationalism. She claimed that the murder was also motivated by the opposition of the Freemasons to Mozart's hope of establishing a German opera theatre in Vienna. Both Daumer and Mathilde Ludendorff relate Mozart's death to other murders of famous men in which they likewise see the Masonic hand at work. Daumer's conviction of the correctness of his view of Mozart's death was reinforced by his belief that the Freemasons had also murdered Lessing, Leopold II, and Gustav III of Sweden (who was assassinated at the famous masked ball only a few months after Mozart's death). Mathilde Ludendorff expanded this list of victims to include Schiller and, in a virtuoso display of freedom from chronology, Martin Luther as well.

It is not surprising that the Ludendorff writings have a heavy overlay of anti-Semitism. General Ludendorff claimed that the secret of Masonry was the Jew and that its aim was to rob the Germans of their national pride and to assure the 'glorious future of the Jewish people'. He attempted to establish a Jewish role in Mozart's murder by the mysterious comment that Mozart had died 'on the Day of Jehovah'. The combination of anti-Semitic and anti-Masonic prejudices had been common since the nineteenth century and was intensified at the turn of the century in the heat of passions generated by the Dreyfus affair. It is ironic to observe this marriage of hates in retroactive operation in the Mozart case, since Masonic lodges of the eighteenth century generally excluded Jews from membership. There is reason to speculate, at least, that Mozart himself did not develop the racist insanity which so many of his country-men have shown in later periods of history. Paul Nettl observes that if he had done so, the world would have lost the fruits of his collaboration with the talented Jewish librettist Lorenzo da Ponte. To be regarded as further evidence of Mozart's recep-tivity to the ideas of Jewish writers is the catalogue of his library of books left at his death, which lists a work on the immortality of the soul by Moses Mendelssohn.

The anti-Masons murder theory, like the Boelza 'solution', assumes a conspiracy of Mozart's friends and family. Mathilde Ludendorff incriminates Salieri, van Swieten, and even the mysterious messenger who commissioned the Requiem. She accuses this oddly assorted group of slowly poisoning Mozart and of employing Nissen to cover up the crime in his bio-graphy. Constanze is, as a good and loyal housewife, spared any suggestion of complicity. However, as in Boelza's theory, her absence from the burial and its strange character are removed from the plane of personal and financial circumstance and explained by the conscious design of the conspirators. Frau Ludendorff even supplies the ghoulish hypothesis that the interment conformed to requirements of Masonry that the body of a transgressor against its laws must be denied decent burial.

Strangely enough, the Masonic murder legend has also been denied burial. Dr Gunther Duda, whose medical views of the case have already been cited, is a 'true believer' in the researches of Daumer and the Ludendorffs. His book *Gewiss, man hat mir Gift gegeben* ('I am sure I have been poisoned'), a compre-hensive study of Mozart's death written in 1950, is prefaced with a quotation from Mathilde Ludendorff. He views the charges against the Masons as having been established with the same compelling force as a mathematical or logical formula. He supports the condemnation of the Masons by the following syllogism, all of the links in which he accepts as fact: (*1*) Mozart was a Mason; (*2*) the Masonic lodges claimed the right to sentence disobedient members to death; (*3*) Mozart was a disobedient member; and (*4*) the execution of the Masonic death sentence is evidenced by Mozart's death, the manner in which he died and the circumstances of his burial. However, Duda's zeal for his cause carries him well beyond the bounds of medical history or even plain logic. Faced with the question of why the Masons would not have punished not only Mozart but the librettists of *The Magic Flute* as well, he notes with suspicion the sudden deaths of the two men who may have collaborated on the libretto. The principal librettist, Emanuel Schikaneder, died in 1812 (twenty-one years after the opera's première), and Karl Ludwig Gieseke, who may also have had some role in shaping the libretto, died in 1833. Dr Duda must surely be suggesting that the Freemasons had at their disposal the slowest poison in the annals of crime.

Dr Kerner, in the 1967 edition of his study of Mozart's death, does not expressly join in the accusations against Free-masonry. However, his sober medical discussion passes at the end of his work into a vapour of astrology and symbolism which may enshroud suggestions of conspiracy. He points out that a 'Hermes stele' pictured on the left side of an engraving on the frontispiece of the first libretto of *The Magic Flute* contains eight allegories of Mercury, the god who gave his name to the poison that Kerner believes killed Mozart. The engraving was made by the Freemason Ignaz Alberti. The allusion to Mercury in Alberti's frontispiece indicates to Kerner that more people were 'in the know' about the murder than is generally assumed. He demonstrates the continuity of this secret knowledge over the centuries by observing that the special Mozart postage stamp issued by Austria in 1956 shows eight Mercury allegories in its frame. Dr Kerner passes from icono-graphy to alchemy and then to sinister hints. He states that, in the symbolism of the alchemists, the number 8 as well as the colour grey represented the planet Mercury, 'which reawakens lively associations of thought with the "Grey Messenger", who often put Mozart in fear in his last days'.

Neither Dr Duda nor Dr Kerner attempts to reconcile with the Masonic murder theory their shared medical assumption that Mozart's poisoning began in the summer of 1791, before *The Magic Flute* was first performed. Moreover, if Mozart was out of favour with his Masonic brethren, a mind disinclined to conspiratorial thinking would find it hard to explain the commission he received shortly before his death to compose a Masonic cantata or the emotional oration that was delivered to a Masonic lodge in memory of Mozart and was printed in 1792 by the very same Freemason Alberti whose 'Hermes stele' struck Kerner as suspicious.

The elements of conspiratorial thinking and exoticism have recently been supplied in abundant measure. Since the publication of their separate researches Drs Kerner and Duda have, in collaboration with Dr Johannes Dalchow, written two books which make more explicit their incrimination of the Masons as the murderers of Mozart. As elaborated in *Mozarts Tod* (1971), Masonry's involvement in Mozart's death was complex and premeditated. According to the authors (who in this respect as in many others parrot the writings of Mathilde Ludendorff), the 'grey messenger' ordering the Requiem was not the agent of Count von Walsegg, but an emissary of the Masons announcing their death sentence. What was the reason for Mozart's murder? The authors provide two possibilities and like them both so well that they do not choose between them: (*1*) a 'ritual murder' in which Mozart was offered as a sacrifice to the Masonic deities; and (*2*) a punishment of Mozart by the masons, with the participation of Salieri, for the crime of having revealed Masonic secrets in *The Magic Flute*. The authors engage in an extended numerological exegesis of *The Magic Flute* which is believed by them to prove the Masonic murder (and presumably also Mozart's acceptance of his execution). The authors assert that the number 18 is paramount in the music and libretto of the opera, by intentional association with the eighteenth 'Rosicrucian' degree of Masonry, and that Mozart's death was also scheduled to give prominence to this number. It is observed with triumph by Dr Kerner and his colleagues that Mozart's Masonic cantata was performed on 18 November 1791, exactly eighteen days before his death! Amid all this mystification, the medical researches of the authors have come to play a minor role, and the bigoted spirit of Mathilde Ludendorff lives again.

An English writer, Francis Carr, has recently joined the funeral-conspiracy game. In his *Mozart & Constanze* (1983), Carr asserts that 'had Mozart died a natural death, there would have been no reason for the ignominious burial in an unmarked grave'. To explain the crime, however, Carr posits a theory that 'clears' both Salieri and the Freemasons: Mozart was murdered by Franz Hofdemel, the wronged husband of Magdalena, a beautiful piano pupil of Mozart. On the day of Mozart's funeral, Hofdemel cut his own throat after a savage razor assault on his pregnant wife; Magdalena survived to give birth to a son. It is Carr's argument that Hofdemel had long known of Mozart's affair with Magdalena and had poisoned him in revenge. On Mozart's death, his murderer, 'overcome by guilt, remorse and terror [and] fearing imminent discovery of his crime', had been driven to 'terminate the whole ghastly tragedy by attempting to kill Magdalena, her unborn child and finally himself'. This version by Mr Carr (who, by the way, is also a biographer of Ivan the Terrible) may strike some readers as being overwrought with blood and passion.

The novelists have, since the very year of Salieri's death, had a field day with the theme of the poisoning. The succession of bad novels that stress the poisoning has continued unabated to our own day; certainly in the running for honours as the worst novel on the poisoning is David Weiss's *The Assassination of Mozart*, which summons up a vision (straight out of John Le Carré and Len Deighton) of a reactionary Austrian regime giving tacit approval to Salieri's murder of Mozart and ruthlessly suppressing every attempt to investigate the crime.

However, the poisoning tradition has produced one authentic masterpiece, Pushkin's short dramatic dialogue *Mozart and Salieri*, conceived in 1826, only one year after Salieri's death, when the rumours of his confession were still in the air, and completed in 1830. In the Pushkin play (later set by Rimsky-Korsakov as an opera), Salieri poisons Mozart both because Mozart's superior gifts have made Salieri's lifelong devotion to music meaningless and because Mozart has introduced Salieri's soul to the bitterness of envy. Unlike many of Mozart's later admirers, Pushkin does not depict Salieri as a mediocre hack but rather as a dedicated musician who was intent on the perfection of his craft and was able to appreciate innovative genius (as in the case of his master, Gluck) and to assimilate it into his own development. However, Salieri refers to himself as a 'priest' of music to whom his art is holy and serious. He is enraged by Mozart's free, creative spirit and by what he sees as his rival's light-hearted, almost negligent, relation to the products of his genius. Salieri's assessment of his competitor is confirmed for him by the joy Mozart takes in a dreadful performance of an air from *Figaro* by a blind fiddler. As was true in their real lives, both Salieri and Mozart in Pushkin's pages inhabit a world where poisoning is assumed to be a possible event even in the lives of famous and civilized men. Mozart refers to the rumour that 'Beaumarchais once poisoned someone,' and Salieri alludes to a tradition that Michelangelo murdered to provide a dead model for a Crucifixion. In Pushkin's version (to which *Amadeus* appears to be heavily indebted), the murder of Mozart provides no relief for Salieri's torment, but only furnishes final proof of his inferiority. At the close of the play, Salieri is haunted by Mozart's observation immediately before being poisoned that 'genius and crime are two incompatible things'.

Even if we suspect that the play has attributed to Salieri more subtlety as a criminal than he displayed in years of crude plotting against Mozart's musical career, Pushkin possibly comes closer to explaining how Salieri could have made a confession of guilt than does the inconclusive medical evidence or the reference to Viennese court intrigue or Masonic plots. Salieri might have recognized the depth of the animosity he had harboured. He might have come to the understanding that, if the essential life of a divinely gifted composer is in his art, he and others who had stood again and again between Mozart and his public had, with malice aforethought, set out to 'murder' Mozart. Pushkin's view of the criminality of selfish opposition to artistic greatness is incisively stated in a brief note written in 1832 on the origin of the poisoning legend. Pushkin writes that, at the première of *Don Giovanni*, the enthralled audience was shocked to hear hissing and to see Salieri leaving the hall 'in a frenzy and consumed by envy'. The note concludes: 'The envious man who was capable of hissing at *Don Giovanni* was capable of poisoning its creator.'

There is more reason to attribute to Salieri the symbolic crime of attempted 'murder' of a brother artist's work than to speculate that Salieri was a poisoner. This judgment would be supported by the testimony of Ignaz Moscheles. Moscheles, who was a former pupil of Salieri's and loved him dearly, visited the old man in the hospital shortly before his death. According to Moscheles's account, Salieri hinted at the poisoning rumours and tearfully protested his innocence. Although Moscheles wrote that he was greatly moved by the interview and that he had never given the rumours the slightest credence, he added the following comment: 'Morally speaking, he [Salieri] had no doubt by his intrigues poisoned many an hour of Mozart's existence.' In his fictional account of the Salieri protestation, Bernard Grun attributes Moscheles's comment about moral guilt to Salieri himself, thus harmonizing the interview with the rumours of Salieri's 'confession'. According to the Novellos' journal, Mozart's son Franz Xaver Wolfgang expressed a similar view – namely, that Salieri had not murdered his father, but that 'he may truly be said to have poisoned his life, and this thought . . . pressed upon the wretched man when dying'.

If Moscheles's narrative is accepted, many events become easier to explain. Salieri's delight over *The Magic Flute* may have been genuine. It is possible that even in Mozart's lifetime Salieri finally acknowledged Mozart's genius and tempered his own feeling of rivalry. Tardy recognition of Mozart's greatness (and, perhaps, regret for their estrangement) may also account for Salieri's attendance at the funeral and his kindness to Mozart's son.

If Salieri was guilty of hostility to Mozart's art but not of poisoning, his punishment can only be called 'cruel and unusual'. After all, Salieri's plots against Mozart's fame ultimately failed, and yet he has been punished, by reason of the evil legend that clings to his name, with almost total obscurity for his own works. Has not the time arrived to turn from the documentation of Mozart's death to an investigation of the music of Salieri? Perhaps such a study will provide evidence that, even without his adroitness in Viennese opera politics and his prestigious positions, Salieri would have afforded substantial musical competition to Mozart.

Note:
In the autumn of 1990, the following recordings of works by Salieri were available in Great Britain on disc and cassette (★) and/or compact disc (†):

Axur, Re d'Ormus (opera) ★†
Concerto for Flute, Oboe and Orchestra in C ★†
Concerto for Keyboard and Orchestra in B flat †
Concerto for Piano and Orchestra in B flat †
Concerto for Piano and Orchestra in D †
Concerto for Violin, Oboe, Cello and Orchestra in D ★†
Falstaff (opera comica) †
Prima la musica, poi la parole (operetta) ★†
Tarare (opera) †

Bloody and Bowed:
The Brief Life of a Playwright

Joan Lock

THE CHAUFFEUR KNOCKED on the door of the tiny, top-floor flat. No answer. He knocked again, still no answer. This was odd. Joe Orton, the current rave playwright he had come to collect on behalf of producer Oscar Lewenstein, might be known for shocking the public with his provocative and anarchical work, but his manners were considered charming and his attitude to his work always professional. What was more, Joe had been looking forward to the meeting with Lewenstein and film director Richard Lester to discuss a script. Quite excited by the prospect, in fact.

Checking back with the producer's office, the chauffeur was instructed to try again; so he trudged back up the linoed staircase flanked by damp and peeling striped wallpaper. 25 Noel Road was an oddly unappealing residence for such a successful person. The Islington of 1967 was not the trendy media ghetto of today. Nonetheless, it was getting 'too posh' for Orton, who had complained to a *Daily Sketch* reporter about people 'singing out "Goodnight darling"' as they banged car-doors in the early hours. He was going to have to move soon.

This time, the chauffeur knocked louder and longer, but there was still no response from Orton or his long-time companion, Kenneth Halliwell. Orton had met Halliwell fifteen years earlier at the Royal Academy of Dramatic Art – an end-of-the-rainbow spot for both of them. Orton had arrived there by a sustained act of will and determination against the odds – which included no outstanding acting talent. Instead, he had a total conviction that he was not ordinary and did not belong in a conventional job, living on a dreary council estate in Leicester, and that one day people would realize that.

This feeling of being exceptional, despite evidence to the contrary, was one that he had in common with his mother, Elsie. Convinced that she had a remarkable voice, Elsie tended to burst into full-blooded, operatic arias at bus-stops, much to the embarrassment of her four children. But the invitation to appear at Covent Garden never materialized and she had been forced to settle for work as an underwear machinist – until her eyes gave up the struggle and she became a cleaner. Later, Elsie was recalled as being pathetically pretentious and, though out-rageous in dress and given to sudden rages, oddly prudish. 'That's my mum!' Orton's sister Leonie exclaimed on seeing Beryl Reid's interpretation of the coquettish, overdressed Kath in the 1975 Royal Court revival of *Entertaining Mr Sloane*.

The Orton family's home-life was not a happy one. There was little affection and much bickering, leaving Leonie with the impression that everyone appeared to be happy but them. William, the poorly-paid, cowed father, took the easy way out, using his skittles and job as a council gardener as a refuge. He even biked over to his greenhouse at the posh end of town on Sundays to escape.

Joe (then known by his real name, John) was mum's favourite. She alone sensed that he was talented and did her best to help him by scraping up enough money to send him to a private school. This has been put down as merely further pretentiousness on her part, since it transpired that the commercially-orientated Clark's College was hardly the right place for such a tongue-tied and illiterate boy. He certainly failed to shine, and left to become an extremely bored junior office clerk, his life brightened only by books, records, amateur dramatics, and Charles Atlas work-outs designed to improve his frail and puny body.

Joe's enthusiasm for dramatics took off, and soon he was living from role to role – and dying a thousand deaths when not selected for a part. He decided that he must at all costs become an actor so as to gain release from the poverty and utter tedious-ness of provincial and family life. He worked out that if he saved at least five shillings a week, he could go to RADA in the remote future.

Instead, the junior office clerk got the sack for all his dreaming, threw himself more and more into his roles, took elocution lessons, and was suddenly buoyed up by discovering that one could not only get a scholarship to the Royal Academy of Dramatic Art but, if exceptionally talented, a maintenance grant as well. Exceptionally talented he certainly wasn't, but, like his mother, he was convinced that he was special; he had his eyes set firmly on the heights.

He arrived at RADA when he was eighteen, after passing the entrance examination, extricating a maintenance grant from Leicester Educational Committee, and, at the last minute, managing to convince the Army Board that he was medically unfit for National Service as he suffered from asthma and deafness. The first was true, the second was not.

'Started at RADA, O bliss,' he exclaimed to his diary on 15 May 1951. Within a few days he was to have more bliss, sexual this time, when he met Kenneth Halliwell and ceased his diary-writing.

It was the top of Halliwell's totally bald head which the chauffeur saw that August day in 1967 when he finally got round to peering through the letter-box of the top-floor flat at 25 Noel Road. Baldness alone was not to blame for the fact that Halliwell had seemed an old man (he was 25) to many of his fellow RADA students fifteen years earlier. His manner had been cold, unrelaxed, and generally weird. At once shy and superior (a combination common in the insecure), it further isolated him from the others – but not from Orton.

Joe appreciated Halliwell's education and greater sophistication. The latter was aided in no small measure by his access to funds denied the others. He even owned his own apartment in Hampstead – though as a result of tragic circumstances.

Halliwell's mother, an ebullient and sociable woman with whom he had been very close, had died suddenly after being stung by a wasp, when the boy was only eleven years old. His father, a chartered accountant, had little affection, humour or even conversation to offer the boy. Small wonder that neighbours remembered Kenneth Halliwell as never having seemed young.

His home-grown horrors had not yet ended. He came home one day to find that his father had committed suicide by putting his head in the gas-oven. There was no note of explanation for the now completely-orphaned boy, but his father's death did release him from money worries. He inherited £4321 – quite a sum in 1949.

Halliwell lost no time in asking the almost virginal and handsome fellow RADA student to become one of his lodgers. Orton had been initiated into sex in the lavatory of a Leicester cinema by a man who had masturbated him; but, that apart, his sexual activities appear to have been both limited and heterosexual.

Joe fell easily into homosexuality (his sister Leonie told *Gay News* that, in her opinion, he was one of those who actively chose to be a homosexual rather than being 'born that way') and the close relationship which developed was a first for both of them. Halliwell and Orton were similar in that they felt at odds with the world while superior to many of the other people in it, and each had something to gain from the relationship. Orton got someone to lean on, the flattery of ardent sexual attention, and home comforts of a standard and style his real home had never provided. He was also treated to theatre and concert outings and was given lessons in life and literature (as actor Kenneth Williams was to point out to Orton's biographer, John Lahr, Halliwell had a good mind).

In Joe, Halliwell acquired a handsome, quick-witted and light-hearted young boyfriend who was also mouldable. The general impression given by their relationship in those days was that Kenneth was the dominant partner but also the more committed and possessive. Joe liked Ken, knew he was on to a good thing by being under his wing, but tended to tease him by flirting with other men.

RADA did not prove the stepping-stone to fame and fortune they had hoped for; their acting careers quickly fizzled out. It is possible that Halliwell's capital encouraged them to give up more easily. Soon they were living on it while they wrote the Great Novel together.

Between times, they read, voraciously and well. As the money dwindled, their lives became increasingly monastic. To save on electricity they got up and went to bed with the sun and saw very few other people. Occasionally, as when they wanted to buy the flat in Noel Road, they did a stint of factory work or sponged off the society they both despised by signing on at the National Assistance Board.

'The oddest pair of people I'd ever met,' was how editor Richard Brain described them. Their novel, *The Last Days of Sodom*, had been passed on to him by Charles Monteith, another editor who, while having taken an interest in their often strange writings, had not accepted them for publication. He had introduced the couple to some influential people who might be of help to them, but soon discovered that socially they were quite hopeless. Having been cut off for so long, they were like wolf children emerging from the forest.

It could have been rage at continual rejection which encouraged them to begin their strange assault on the books in Islington Central Public Library. Orton later declared that his belief that the library failed to carry good literature, such as Gibbons' *Decline and Fall of the Roman Empire*, but had plenty of rubbish on offer had been a strong contributory factor. In any event, it was an extraordinary and weirdly anti-social exercise: stealing books, then re-illustrating their jackets with inappropriate artwork – a monkey-face in the heart of a bloom on *Collins Guide to Roses*, a tattooed man on a volume of John Betjeman's poetry. They also rewrote blurbs, making some of them mildly obscene.

Finally caught by a librarian who out-foxed them, they were staggered by the ferociousness of the penalty of six months' imprisonment. The experience was to prove more lonely and traumatic for the already much-damaged Halliwell than it was for Orton. Later, when it had ceased to be a matter of much shame and had become one of those glamorous formative experiences in a playwright's life, he told the *Leicester Mercury* that being in the nick had brought a much-needed detachment to his writing: 'Suddenly it worked.'

Orton had already begun writing plays; his short play, *The Visit*, about a man dying in hospital to the background prattle of his daughter and the medical staff, gained the interest of – though not the acceptance by – the Royal Court Theatre and BBC Radio. The breakthrough came in the following year, when his adaptation of his and Halliwell's novel, *The Boy*

Hairdresser (later retitled *The Ruffian on the Stair*), was accepted by Radio Three.

The ruffian on the stair is death, as depicted in a poem by W. E. Henley (1849–1903). Ironically, more famous lines in another poem by the same author read:

'My head is bloody, but unbowed . . . I am the master of my fate, I am the captain of my soul.' By attempting to become the master of his fate, Orton's head was to become literally both bloody and bowed.

In *The Ruffian on the Stair*, one man goads another (who has murdered his brother) into killing him as well. Death looms large in Orton's other plays; it is always dealt with irreverently and as something marginal and inconsequential. He even cocks a snook at it in one of his titles, *Funeral Games*.

Hypocritical religion and sexual repression were other elements of our society which Orton fought against, both in his plays and in real life. But, like many other rebels, he seemed to want freedom for himself but, in some respects at least, not to be too worried about the slavery of others. He raged that if he tried to seduce a comely boy he had seen on Brighton beach, he would land up in the dock – yet in Morocco, where he, Halliwell, and hordes of other homosexuals took long leave, he could buy boys almost wholesale. The fact that the easy submission of the boys might result from the oppression of poverty, also the enforced cloistering of the women of that country, seems never to have occurred to him.

Orton's writing quickly won the appreciation of such celebrated playwrights as Pinter, Rattigan and Emlyn Williams. But his artistic progress, though rapid, was nowhere near as smooth as it may appear in retrospect. Scarcely surprising, given his work's deliberately 'shocking' content and the fact that the success of the productions depended so much on the manner in which they were staged. Only by playing the lines straight, as though all the bizarre and disturbing happenings are quite normal, can the right degree of comedy and menace be achieved – and menace is always there to some degree. Murder, for example, is always spoken of and handled as everyday, and carried out for oddly trivial reasons.

As his fame grew, Orton's agent, Peggy Ramsay, suggested that he should start a diary again. He didn't get around to it until December 1966. It proved to be a fatal move. He gave graphic details of his every doing, from wild orgies in the confines of Holloway Road public lavatories to each round in the battle marking the disintegration of his relationship with Halliwell. The entries are no random jottings but well-written, highly explicit narratives, 'to be published long after my death'. They invite the reader to view both Orton's constant and casual sexual gropings and Halliwell's latest cry for help with an equally cool eye. Halliwell was top-dog turned lap-dog, and he hated it. But, by all accounts, Joe was always loyal to him in public, defending his friend's often embarrassing behaviour as he claimed part-authorship of the plays in an effort to gain some of the limelight.

Orton told Kenneth Williams that he would never leave Halliwell – but, eventually, friends got the clear impression that Orton wanted out. He confided that he had another boyfriend and talked of setting up Halliwell in a gay bar somewhere in the West Country. Buying a villa in Morocco or a house in Brighton, where Halliwell could spend some of his time, also figured as part of an escape-plan.

Meanwhile, the warning signs of Halliwell's mental anguish became plainer. During a row while on one of their holidays in Morocco, he attacked Joe, beating him about the head. Back in London, Halliwell appeared increasingly ill, spoke of suicide, and declared that he was close to a nervous breakdown. He got in touch with the Samaritans and even agreed to see a psychiatrist, but the wearied Orton paid little attention, being totally preoccupied with his play, *What the Butler Saw* – and keeping up his diary.

The play was completed in July 1967; but the diary came to an abrupt end, mid-sentence, in the entry for 1 August. Eight days later, there was, in police parlance, 'no answer to repeated knockings' at the door of the stark yet claustrophobic flat in Noel Road: its walls lined with Halliwell's collages – an art on which he had pinned his final, abortive attempts to prove that he, too, was talented.

When the police broke down the door, they found Orton, clad only in a pyjama jacket, lying dead on his single divan-bed in the corner of the room. He had been struck with a hammer at least nine times, forensic pathologist Professor Francis Camps was to tell the inquest jury. But, Camps added, although the injuries appeared to have been inflicted during 'a deliberate form of frenzy', it seemed unlikely that Orton would have known what had hit him.

Halliwell lay naked on the floor beside his own bed on the other side of the room. Next to him was a large tin of grapefruit juice and a glass containing some of the juice and what police called (in terminology worthy of Inspector Truscott in Orton's play, *Loot*), 'a white deposit'. He had taken off his bloodstained pyjamas and put them on his bed before writing a note saying that Orton's diary, particularly the latter part, would explain everything. Then he had swallowed what Professor Camps described as 'an enormous overdose' of sleeping tablets – washed down with the juice. So enormous was the overdose that Halliwell had died quite quickly and suddenly – well ahead of his lover.

What Halliwell meant by saying that the final sections of Orton's diary would make everything clear has never been satisfactorily explained. The abrupt break in the entries several days before his death is felt by some to be at odds with his meticulous attitude towards the task, and has led to speculation that some pages may have been removed. The previous entries went on more or less as before, explicitly recording Joe's constant sexual adventurings, and casting a cool and seemingly unsympathetic eye on Kenneth's carpings and cries for help. Consequently, although there is no doubt about who killed the playwright and his reasons for doing so, the question of whether there was a final incident which drove Halliwell to do it remains a mystery.

Orton's sister Leonie later admitted to *Gay News* that she believed that had there been no Halliwell, there would have been no 'Joe Orton'. Halliwell's cultural nurturing had made the playwright, but when the puppet had not only cut the strings but become what the master himself desperately wanted to be, Halliwell had destroyed him.

The death scene, with its tin of grapefruit juice and the naked bodies surrounded with collages of words and pictures showing the pair's obsession with sex, art and death, was bizarre enough to have been part of one of Joe Orton's plays.

The farce continued at the funeral. 'When we arrived at the

Crematorium', Peter Willes, Head of Drama for Yorkshire TV, told the *Evening Standard*, 'the attendant asked, "Are you the 12.30 or the 12.40?" That's a line Joe himself would have appreciated.'

Changing attitudes to sex and religion had already begun to take some of the sting out of Orton's work. In the month before he died, the Bill permitting homosexual acts between consenting adults had been passed. The following year, Prince Charles played the vicar in a Cambridge production of Orton's play, *Erpingham Camp*.

But the flippant treatment of death was to remain taboo. 'Joe Orton is an economical humorist,' the critic W. A. Darlington wrote in the *Daily Telegraph* when reviewing the Royal Court's June 1967 production of Orton's *Crimes of Passion*. 'He discovered some time in his career that he could get a laugh by being callous about a corpse, and so now he's always doing it.'

Two months later he could do it no longer.

Architect of a Murder

New York Times and Jonathan Goodman

From the *New York Times*, Tuesday, 26 June 1906 (starting at the top of the front page):

THAW MURDERS STANFORD WHITE

Shoots Him on the
Madison Square Garden Roof.

ABOUT EVELYN NESBIT

'He Ruined My Wife,'
Witness Says He Said.

AUDIENCE IN A PANIC

Chairs and Tables are Overturned
in a Wild Scramble for the Exits.

Harry Kendall Thaw [aged 34] of Pittsburg, husband of Florence Evelyn Nesbit, former actress and artist's model, shot and killed Stanford White, the architect, on the roof of Madison Square Garden at 11.05 o'clock last night, just as the first performance of the musical comedy *Mamzelle Champagne* was drawing to a close. Thaw, who is a brother of the Countess of Yarmouth and a member of a well known and wealthy family, left his seat near the stage, passed between a number of tables, and, in full view of the players and of scores of persons, shot White through the head.

Mr White was the designer of the building on the roof of which he was killed. He it was who put Miss Nesbit, now Mrs Thaw, on the stage.

Thaw, who was in evening clothes, had evidently been waiting for Mr White's appearance. The latter entered the Garden at 10.55 and took a seat at a table five rows from the stage. He rested his chin in his right hand and seemed lost in contemplation.

Thaw had a pistol concealed under his coat. His face was deathly white. According to A. L. Belstone, who sat near, White must have seen Thaw approaching. But he made no move. Thaw placed the pistol almost against the head of the sitting man and fired three shots in quick succession.

Body Fell to the Floor.

White's elbow slid from the table, the table crashed over, sending a glass clinking along with the heavier sound. The body then tumbled from the chair.

On the stage one of the characters was singing a song entitled 'I Could Love a Million Girls.' The refrain seemed to freeze upon his lips. There was dead silence for a second, and then Thaw lifted his pistol over his head, the barrel hanging downward, as if to show the audience that he was not going to harm anyone else.

With a firm stride Thaw started for the exit, holding his pistol as if anxious to have some one take it from his hand.

Then came the realization on the part of the audience that the farce had closed with a tragedy. A woman jumped to her feet and screamed. Many persons followed her example, and there was wild excitement.

L[ionel] Lawrence, the manager of the show, jumped on a table and above the uproar commanded the show to go on. 'Go on playing!' he shouted. 'Bring on that chorus!'

Girls Too Terrified to Sing.

The musicians made a feeble effort at gathering their wits and playing the chorus music, but the girls who romped on the stage were paralyzed with horror, and it was impossible to bring the performance to an orderly close.

Then the manager shouted for quiet, and he informed the audience that a serious accident had happened, and begged the people to move out of the place quietly.

In the meanwhile, Thaw had reached the entrance to the elevators. On duty there was Fireman Paul Brodin. He took the pistol from Thaw's hand, but did not attempt to arrest him. Policeman Debes of the Tenderloin[1] Station appeared and seized his arm.

'He deserved it,' Thaw said to the policeman. 'I can prove it. He ruined my life and then deserted the girl.' Another witness said the word was 'wife' instead of 'life'.

1 The area north from Fourteenth Street to Forty-Second Street, and west from Fifth Avenue to Ninth Avenue, which was replete with theatres, brothels, bars, and honky-tonks. The nickname had been unwittingly coined by Police Captain Alexander Williams, who, in 1876, when transferred from the Fourth Precinct to the midtown Twenty-Ninth, had remarked to a cronie: 'I've had nothing but rump steak for a long time, and now I'm going to get a little of the tenderloin' – in other words, stipends from proprietors for turning a blind eye to their crimes, warning them of police raids, and protecting them from crooks who were aiming to muscle in; also from the latter, if they were willing to pay more than the proprietors.

A Woman Kissed Thaw.

Just as the policeman started into the elevator with Thaw, a woman described as dark-haired and short of stature reached up to him and kissed him on the cheek. This woman some witnesses declare was Mrs Thaw.

The crowd was then scrambling wildly for the elevators and stairs. The employees of the Garden who knew Thaw, and nearly all of them did, as he visited the place often, did not seem greatly surprised at the tragedy. When Thaw entered the Garden in the early part of the show he seemed greatly agitated. He strolled from one part of the place to another, and finally took a seat in a little niche near the stage.

He was half hidden from the audience, but could see any one who might enter. It is believed that he knew just where White would sit, and had picked out this place in order to get at him without interference.

Henry Rogers of 222 Henry Street was seated at the table next to the one at which White was sitting when he was killed. He says that Thaw fired when the muzzle of his pistol was only a few inches from White's temple.

Another witness said that after firing three shots and looking at White as if to be sure that he was stone dead, Thaw uttered a curse and added:

'You'll never go out with that woman again.'

Here is another story of the killing of Mr White told by a man who sat a few feet from the table where the shooting occurred:

'The show was going along nicely, and my attention was on the stage until I noticed a strange-looking fellow who walked about in a nervous sort of way. His throat was muffled up, and it appeared to me that he was a man who seemed on the verge of delirium tremens. I said to the man friend who was with me that the fellow who was muffled up was either a prizefighter or an athlete in training, but when he came near us I saw that he was wildly excited.

He muttered to himself several times and paced up and down the floor, turning now and then to see who was near him, as if he thought he was being followed. As he passed toward the rear of the place, a woman near the man who was shot later leaned forward and whispered something. It seemed to me that she was afraid of somebody or something.

A waiter came along and I called his attention to the muffled man, remarking that he seemed foolish. The waiter said he had noticed the fellow around all evening and that something was wrong with him.

Just then the fellow walked over to the side of the building where the tables were and craned his neck forward as if he suddenly spied the person he was looking for, and quickened his pace.

"That fellow's going to grab somebody," I said, turning to my companion, and when I again looked in the direction of the fellow, I saw him with pistol in hand and pointing it downward at the man at the table near by. Then he fired.

Immediately after the shots were fired the man who did the shooting leaned forward and said something to the woman. It sounded like "It's all right, don't worry. I'm not sorry I did it."

That settled the show. All about, women were frantically pleading with their escorts to take them out of the place and into the street, but the escorts couldn't find a way out so easily.

As that man who did the shooting had his neck muffled up, it seemed to me that he was trying to disguise himself while preparing to kill the other man.'

A Woman Sat Near White.

At another table adjoining that at which White was killed sat a woman dressed in white. It was believed for a time that she was a companion of White's, and it was reported that she leaned over and kissed the face of the dead man, but this could not be verified, and it is positive that White was alone when he entered the Garden.

Some one in the audience hurried to the fallen man to see if assistance was needed. A great pool of blood had quickly formed on the floor. The tables had been pulled back and in the bright glare of thousands of electric lights it was quickly seen that White was beyond any earthly help.

A number of the actors and actresses left the stage, and away from the calcium and the footlights their painted faces showed strangely in the group of employees and friends of Thaw and the dead man which formed as the last of the audience left.

Thought it a Stage Trick.

Two of them said that the reason the fright of the audience was not worse when the shots rang out was that just before the tragedy a dialogue concerning a burlesque duel had been carried on by two of the characters, and many people thought that the old trick of playing in the audience had been tried again.

As the lights of the Garden were dimmed, the body of White was straightened out, the arms brought to the sides, and the legs placed together. A sheet was obtained in one of the dressing rooms, and this was stretched over it.

While all of this was going on, Policeman Debes and his prisoner had reached the street entrance. Thaw never once lost his composure. His linen and his evening suit showed no signs of ruffling. Only the paleness of his face showed that anything had happened to excite him.

'Here's a bill, officer,' he said to the policeman before he started for the station. 'Get Carnegie[1] on the telephone and tell him that I'm in trouble.'

The policeman and prisoner then walked through the crowd to Fifth Avenue, up the avenue to Thirtieth Street.[2] As they turned the corner at the Holland House [a posh hotel at Fifth Avenue and Thirtieth Street] a number of cabmen who knew Thaw tipped their hats to him and he recognized their salute in return.

The trip up Thirtieth Street, across Broadway and Sixth Avenue, was without any excitement, and the prisoner reached the station without the usual crowd of curious people following.

Thaw did not seem to be intoxicated, but walked in a sort of daze. He made few comments on the way to the Tenderloin Station. Sergt. McCarthy asked him what his name was, and he answered:

1 One of Thaw's brothers-in-law, George Lauder Carnegie, was a nephew of the Scottish-born millionaire industrialist (and philanthropist), Andrew Carnegie.
2 Madison Square Garden was at the intersection of Fifth Avenue and Broadway. (The present Garden, opened in 1968, is part of the Pennsylvania Station complex, at Eighth Avenue, between Thirty-First and Thirty-Second Streets.)

'John Smith, 18 Lafayette Square, Philadelphia.'

'What's your business?' he was asked.

'I am a student.'

No charge was made on the books against this 'John Smith.' The detectives were sent out to investigate fully before a charge was made. Sergt. McCarthy asked him:

'Why did you do this?'

'I can't say,' he replied apathetically.

Cards found on the prisoner read 'Harry Kendall Thaw, Pittsburg.' He made no comment when they were pulled out of his pocketbook.

Thaw Sent for Two Friends.

Young Thaw walked dazedly to the back room. The reporters asked him to make a statement. He refused to do it.

Young Thaw had lighted a cigarette while he stood in front of the Sergeant's desk. In the back room he sat on a long bench between two big policemen. He pushed his hat back on his head, stretched out his feet, and lit another cigarette. His eyes had a far-away look.

A number of his friends hurried over to the station to talk with the prisoner, but they were not allowed to see him.

When the detectives put on the case had brought in the witnesses and they had been examined in Capt. Hodgins's room, Thaw was charged with homicide and was locked in a cell.

Thaw Not Ready to Talk.

Coroner Dooley reached the Tenderloin Station at 1.30 this morning and asked to see the prisoner. Thaw had sent the doorman out to buy him some cigars. He was smoking and seemed calm when the Coroner entered.

'Have you any statement to make to me?' the Coroner asked after he had made himself known.

'I don't care to make any statement now,' Thaw replied. 'I would appreciate it if you would tell Burr McIntosh or ex-Judge Hornblower or Joseph H. Choate of what has happened.'[1]

'Mr McIntosh is upstairs,' he was told. 'Do you want to see him?'

'No,' he replied, 'just tell him to call up Mr Hornblower or Mr Choate. Tell him not to call up Mr Choate until morning. I would not like to get him out of bed.'

Mr Choate is at Stockbridge, Massachusetts.

Coroner Dooley said that he found Thaw in good mental condition. He added that he believed the murder was done through jealousy.

When Thaw was searched in the station, $125 in paper money, $2.36 in coin, two silk handkerchiefs, two gold pencils, a gold watch, and a little pocket combination mirror case were found. These were taken by the Sergeant.

**Mrs White at St James,
Long Island.**

Mrs Lizzie Hanlon, housekeeper for Mr White at his residence, 121 East Twenty-First Street, had not heard of the shooting when a reporter

---

1 Burr McIntosh, a fashionable photographer and an acquaintance of Thaw's, had also attended the first night of *Mamzelle Champagne*. Joseph H. Choate was the doyen of trial lawyers.

from THE TIMES called shortly before midnight. She expressed the utmost horror, and could suggest no explanation.

The house is one of the most magnificently decorated in the city. Standing amid elaborate Italian decorations with carved marble and graceful fountains on every hand, Mrs Hanlon gave what information she could. She said:

'Mr White has been alone in the house for some time. Mrs White has been away in the West for about three weeks or a month, but is now at her country residence at St James, Long Island.

Lawrence White, Mr White's son, came down from Harvard the other day. Both he and his father came in and dressed for dinner to-night, but they did not go out together, Mr White leaving alone a few minutes before his son. I do not know where either of them went.'

'Has Mr Thaw been to the house to see Mr White recently?' Mrs Hanlon was asked.

'Mr Thaw? I never heard of him. As far as I know, Mr White did not have any visitors here to-day.'

Young White, with a friend, Leroy King, dined with his father last night at the Café Martin.[1] Mr White, his son says, was in the best of spirits and said nothing about any trouble.

After the dinner the party entered an electric automobile and went up to the New Amsterdam roof garden.[2] There the two boys asked the elder White to stay and see the performance.

He said: 'No, I thank you,' adding that he was going elsewhere.

That was the last they saw of him.

Only One Bullet in Head.

After the body was taken to the undertaker's a hasty examination was made. Three wounds were found. The fatal bullet entered the left eye. The other two bullets grazed the shoulders, leaving a flesh wound on each. The top of the head showed a mark, this having been caused by striking the edge of the table as the body fell to the floor.

1 One of Manhattan's smartest restaurants, between Fifth Avenue and Broadway on Twenty-Sixth Street. Gerald Langford, in his book *The Murder of Stanford White* (Gollancz, London, 1962), says that 'the Broadway side of the establishment had been fitted out as a French-style café with marble-topped tables and cushioned wall seats, where the patrons lingered on after dining to play chess or to scan the file of risqué Parisian illustrated papers. The main restaurant, with its imposing array of white linen beneath the panelled ceiling and elaborate chandeliers, was on the Fifth Avenue side. Upstairs were private dining rooms, awaiting the spur-of-the-moment parties that could be formed in a special foyer open to women without escorts.'

2 The New Amsterdam (on the south side of Forty-Second Street, close to Times Square) housed two theatres, a large one and the Aerial Roof Garden. On the night that *Mamzelle Champagne* opened at Madison Square Garden, the popular farce, *The Governor's Son*, written by George M. Cohan and featuring 'The Favorite Family of Fun-Makers, the Four Cohans,' opened at the Aerial Roof Garden. (Fourteen years later, on the night of Thursday, 10 June 1920, the Aerial Roof Garden was again the penultimate place visited by a murder-victim: Joseph Bowne Elwell, the great bridge-player. See *The Slaying of Joseph Bowne Elwell* by Jonathan Goodman [Harrap, London, 1987; St Martin's Press, New York, 1988].)

Detectives Look for Mrs Thaw.

Mr and Mrs Thaw have been stopping at the Lorraine, Fifth Avenue and Forty-Fifth Street. Detectives were sent there to get her as a witness, but she had not returned at 3 o'clock this morning.

At that hour Policeman Debes, who arrested Thaw, gave this account of what happened:

'I was on post at Twenty-Sixth Street and Madison Avenue last night, and asked the manager of the Garden if there would be any shooting in the show. I did this because the use of firearms at Hammerstein's Theater last week made me hurry and scurry for a while, thinking the shooting was done on the street. He told me there was not.

I heard three pistol shots and started for the Garden. I met the electrician of the place, who was on the run. He said that a man and a woman had been shot in the audience. I hurried upstairs, and the first I saw was a woman who had fainted. Then I found Thaw with the fireman. I asked him if he had shot the man whose body I could see by the table.

"Yes," Thaw replied.

Then he added that the man had ruined his life—or wife—I could not distinctly make out.

"Is he dead?" he asked.

I told him he was.

"Well, I made a good job of it and I'm glad," he added. Then a woman, who Manager Lawrence told me was Mrs Thaw, ran up and embraced him and kissed him.

"I didn't think you would do it in this way," she said. He whispered to her, patted her on the shoulder, and said that it would all come out all right.

When we got to the street, a number of women shook hands with the prisoner and sympathized with him.

Some wanted to know why he had killed White, but he did not answer.'

A dispatch from Pittsburg last night said that Thaw and his wife were to have sailed for Europe tomorrow.

Mrs William Thaw, mother of Mr Thaw, sailed for London on the Atlantic Transport liner *Minneapolis* last Saturday. She is on her way to visit her daughter, the Countess of Yarmouth, who was Miss Alice Thaw.

WHITE AIDED MRS THAW.

George W. Lederer Tells How He Gave Her Financial Assistance.

Special to The New York Times.

CHICAGO, June 25.–George W. Lederer, the theatrical manager, formerly of New York, now of the Colonial Theater here, tonight told about the friendship between Stanford White and the former Miss Florence Evelyn Nesbit, now Mrs Harry Thaw. Mr Lederer introduced Miss Nesbit to the stage. He said:

'Miss Nesbit was the daughter of a Pittsburg lawyer, and when she was 11 or 12 years old her father died, leaving an estate much involved. His widow found it was necessary for her to pitch in and make a living, and she went to Philadelphia, where for a couple of years Evelyn posed as a model. Then she moved to New York, where she continued to pose.

When she was only 15 or 16 years old, she met Mr White, and subsequently he became a close friend of her and of her mother's. I think that, throughout, his friendship for the girl was entirely platonic. He was a persistent first-nighter, and liked pretty girls.

He took a strong personal interest in the Nesbits, assisted them financially, and made them comfortable in every way. Subsequently the girl went on the stage, first appearing in *Florodora* in the Casino.[1] Mr White remained her very good friend and she in turn was grateful to him.

She is of frivolous disposition and no doubt refused to break off her friendship for him after marrying young Thaw, who is a cigarette fiend, and always seemed half crazed to me when I saw him.

Now, Mr White was a great "rounder," but from all I observed and from talking many times with Miss Nesbit's mother, I am firmly convinced that his friendship for Miss Nesbit and the help he gave her grew out of sheer good-heartedness. Of course, he was a man who always liked to talk to pretty girls and to be with them.'

—————

Friends of Mr Thaw said last night that there had long been feeling between the men because of the interest that Stanford White had taken in the former Miss Florence Evelyn Nesbit, now Mrs Thaw.

Mr White was greatly interested in the stage, and was one of a group of men, young and old, who frequently were seen about the theatres where musical comedies were playing and at restaurants and other places with actresses. Mr White cultivated the friendship of various theatrical managers, and for years had enjoyed the privilege of going behind the stage at various productions. He had befriended many young actresses, helping them to better themselves in their profession. In fact, it was known that a word from him would often get a girl a chance to come out from the back row of the chorus and play a part.

It was through this influence that Mr White gave Miss Nesbit her first opportunity. She had been brought to New York by her mother, a Pittsburg widow, and had attracted the attention of several artists and photographers, who employed her as a model. It was through this employment, it is understood, that Mr White became acquainted with her. He found that she had a leaning towards the stage, and helped to persuade her mother that she should have a chance to make a career.

When the consent of the mother had been gained, Mr White aided her to get into *Florodora*. Afterward he asked George W. Lederer to engage her for *The Wild Rose*, which was then about to be put on at the Knickerbocker.[2] It was largely because of his friendship toward Mr

—————

1 *Florodora* opened at the Casino on 10 November 1900, and ran there for five hundred and fifty-two performances.

2 *The Wild Rose* opened at the Knickerbocker on 5 May 1902, and ran there for one hundred and eighteen performances.

Newspaper readers would soon be reminded that, a few hours before the first night of this musical comedy, with Evelyn as the eponymous gypsy rose, she had been named corespondent in a divorce suit brought by Mrs George W. Lederer; her name had been withdrawn before the suit went to court.

During the run of *The Wild Rose* – and perhaps before, and perhaps afterwards – she had had a torrid affair with the actor, John Barrymore (who, so she said, had once made love to her after wrapping her in the cloak his father, Maurice, had worn as Romeo – and more than once informed her that she was 'a quivering pink poppy in a golden whirlwind of space'). Only because of his footnoting here, it is worth mentioning that Barrymore detested footnotes, grumbling that having to read one was akin to having to go downstairs to answer the door just when he was coming.

White that Mr Lederer took up the young woman and boomed her as a new beauty. Her success was such that she soon had her pictures in the newspapers, and became popular with the young men who frequent stage doors.

Miss Nesbit, however, was grateful to Mr White, and generally preferred to take any late suppers she might have in company with him and such friends as he might choose. Mr White often went behind the stage at the Knickerbocker to see her. He helped her in learning the arts of the stage. They were seen together, with friends, driving and dining often.

It is understood that it was through the influence of Mr White that Miss Nesbit was afterward taken up by Mrs Robert Osborn, when she started Mrs Osborn's Playhouse. Miss Nesbit was one of the beauties there, and it was said that Mr White was one of the financial backers of the enterprise. At any rate, he was frequently seen at the playhouse, and again had the privilege of going behind the stage.

When Mr Thaw entered the field as an admirer of Miss Nesbit, the influence of Mr White was eclipsed. After their marriage, however, the architect still let his friends understand that he felt the same friendship for the young woman and that he would be glad to aid her in any way possible in case the Thaw family should continue to frown upon her husband because of his marriage to her.

STANFORD WHITE'S CAREER.

He Designed Many of the Finest Buildings in This Country.

Stanford White was born in this city on Nov 9 1853. He was the son of

Richard Grant White and Alexina B. Mease. His father was well known as a critic, journalist, and essayist, and for more than twenty years served as Chief of the United States Revenue Marine Bureau for the District of New York. His mother was a daughter of Charles Bruton Mease of this city.

The American head of the family was John White, who came to this country in 1632 from England, a passenger on the ship *Lion*, and settled at Cambridge, Mass. He became a freeman the second year after his arrival, and was then a salesman of the town. He removed to Connecticut with Pastor Hooker's company in 1636, becoming one of the founders and proprietors of Hartford. He later settled at Hadley, Mass., which place he represented in the General Court in 1664. He died in Hadley in 1683.

Stanford White's great-grandfather was Calvin White, for many years rector of the St James Protestant Episcopal Church at Derby, Conn., but in his later years he became a Roman Catholic layman. His grandfather was Richard Mansfield White, a shipping merchant of New York City. Stanford White was educated in the private schools of New York and by tutors, and received the degree of M.A. from New York College in 1883.

He began the study of architecture in the office of Charles T. Gabrill and Henry H. Richardson. From 1878 to 1881 he traveled and studied in Europe, and on his return formed a partnership with Charles F. McKim and William R. Mead, under the firm name of McKim, Mead & White.

The name of this firm is associated with some of the most notable architecture of the country, many examples of which were designed by Mr White himself. He was the architect of the Villard house, on Madison Avenue, now the property of Whitelaw Reid; of the Madison Square Garden, the Century and the Metropolitan clubhouses, the Washington Arch, on Washington Square; the New York University, the University of Virginia, and many private residences throughout the country.

Among his most conspicuous special works are the architectural features for the sculptures of Augustus Saint-Gaudens, notably the pedestal of the Farragut Statue, Madison Square; the pedestal for the Chapin Statue, Springfield, Mass., and the pedestals for the Lincoln and Logan Statues and the Adams Tomb, Washington, DC.

He was the creator of interior designs which won great praise for him. Specimens of his work in this direction are shown in the Players and Metropolitan Club houses, the Villard residence, the Church of St Paul the Apostle, and the Church of the Ascension, all of this city.

A work by which he will always be remembered, and which is considered by many of his friends as the best specimen of his genius, is the Marble House, which he built at Newport for Mrs William K.

Vanderbilt. Its construction marked the zenith of his fame. He received carte blanche as to material and decoration. His bust now stands on a pedestal in the hall as a recognition of the success he achieved.

He had charge of the interior decorations for the Metropolitan Club. When the time came for building the University Club, the committee in charge called him in and told him that, while the Metropolitan was superb, they did not want him to copy it in the new structure.

Although only a few years had elapsed since the Metropolitan was completed, he had discovered certain things which he thought he could improve, and these he embodied in what is said by many to be the handsomest and most complete clubhouse in the world.

Mr and Mrs White have not been living together recently, and while the husband nominally retained his home at their house at Gramercy Park and Lexington Avenue, he spent but little of his time there.

Madison Square Garden, designed by him, and where he met his death, was known as his 'pleasure house.' When the Garden was nearing completion, he stipulated that he should have a suite of apartments in the tall tower. He had had it ever since.

From the *New York Times*, Saturday, 13 April 1907 (starting at the top of the front page):

THAW MISTRIAL; JURY WAS 7 TO 5

Majority for Conviction After Forty-seven Hours of Deliberation.

NEW TRIAL IN OCTOBER

Jerome Says It Can't Be Before That
—Will Oppose Release on Bail.

CROWDS AWAITED VERDICT

Cheered Thaw's Wife and Family When They
Left After Hearing of Disagreement.

Failing to agree on a verdict after more than forty-seven hours of deliberation, the Thaw jury was dismissed at 4.30 o'clock yesterday afternoon, and all the work done since the first juryman was examined on Jan 23 had gone for naught.

But Harry K. Thaw will be tried again for the murder of Stanford White. District Attorney Jerome[1] says it will be October before the new trial can be moved. When court reconvenes on April 20 an application may be made for admitting the prisoner to bail. Mr Jerome will oppose it.

IN THE JURY ROOM BY JUROR NO. 6

Story of the Long and Fruitless Session
Told by One Who Took Part In It.

THEY BEGAN WITH PRAYER

And Strove Earnestly and Conscientiously
to Reach a Verdict.

ONE WAS FOR ACQUITTAL

But that Was the Only Change
After the First Real Line-up.

---

1 William Travers Jerome. One of his first-cousins, *neé* Jennie Jerome, was the wife of Lord Randolph Churchill; one of the Churchills' sons was named Winston.

EVIDENCE THAT COUNTED

Wife's Story and 'Dementia Americana' plea Figured Very Little in the Result.

BY HARRY C. BREARLEY
Juror No. 6

The members of the jury were greatly surprised when at the close of Mr Jerome's summing up on the Wednesday afternoon the Judge announced his intention of immediately charging the jury upon the law points. It had been generally supposed that if the case closed by the middle of the afternoon a recess would be taken until the following morning, for the jurors were all wearied by the close attention given to the long and detailed summing up; most of them had lost sleep through consideration given to the facts of the case, and a sense of the solemn responsibility soon to devolve upon them, and they had hoped to be able to begin their real labors in the refreshed condition of a morning session. However, they straightened up in their chairs and fixed their gaze upon the dignified Justice as he read with great impressiveness his luminous charge.

At 5.20 o'clock the jurors were excused to go into the jury room, and marched through the immense crowd to the rear door. The prisoner and his wife, both of whom showed evidence of the strain under which they had been long laboring, fixed anxious glances upon them as they passed.

The events of the next forty-seven hours must be considered as in some sense sacred, and the writer has no wish to violate any of the proprieties. It is manifest that every juror has a proprietorship in his own perso-

nality, hence the writer considers it necessary to omit all names, as well as any indications of the identity of the different members.

If any further warrant were needed, the fact that this case is in every way a public matter, and that the public has a distinct right to a knowledge of how certain general classes of evidence are regarded by jury, makes it to some degree a public duty to throw a degree of light upon the proceedings.

Deliberations Began With Prayer.

It can be distinctly stated that the jury walked to their room with a deeply solemn sense of responsibility to render a careful, deliberate, fairminded and thoroughly conscientious verdict. By unanimous impulse, the first action was to gather about the long table in the centre of the room and stand with bowed heads while an opening prayer was made. Then, with the Foreman in his chair at the head of the table and the other jurors in the places to which they were accustomed at meal times, parliamentary rules were adopted, and the formal discussion was under way.

Upon motion, an initial ballot was taken preceding all argument. This ballot occurred at 5.30 o'clock, ten minutes after the jury entered the room, and revealed six votes for conviction of murder in the first degree, two votes for manslaughter in the first degree, and four for acquittal upon the ground of insanity. The two manslaughter ballots were immediately changed to murder in the first degree, the respective jurors explaining that they had so voted, not from any doubt of the completeness of the People's case as charged in the indictment, but to suggest a possible basis for an ultimate compromise ballot should such ultimately prove to be necessary.

The line-up then stood eight for murder in the first degree to four for acquittal upon the ground of insanity. Argument then began with the seriousness and almost the formality of a Congressional debate. The jurors very generally respected the rights of the speaker to an uninterrupted privilege of address after recognition by Mr Smith. Thus was secured early freedom from any long wrangling.

'Unwritten Law' Ignored.

One of the first things developed was the completeness with which the covert but perfectly obvious defense of the 'unwritten law' [the notion that a person has the right to kill, given sufficient justification] – so conspicious in Mr Delmas's[1] address and in his case in chief – was ignored. The defense of legal insanity was the only thing considered to be properly competent for discussion. The addresses made were earnest, forceful, and in many cases rising to a degree of impassioned oratory. They were also long, and continually referred to supporting points of evidence as recollected by the speakers.

Attention was almost immediately fixed upon the events of the fateful June evening from which all the subsequent events have grown, and throughout the succeeding two days probably no words were quite so frequently spoken as these:

'Did he know the nature and quality of the act he was doing, and did he know that it was wrong?'[2]

Opinions differed. Nay, more: opinions earnestly differed, and each man was so conscientiously sure of the correctness of his deductions that to each it seemed only a question of fully stating his viewpoint to secure unanimous agreement. Unhappily this hope was destined to recede as the long hours wore themselves away, and to be finally extinguished to an accompanying disappointment almost too deep for words. It is hard to see how any jury under any circumstances could have striven more earnestly to avoid such an unfortunate termination.

In the midst of an animated debate which was being conducted with such keen interest that no note had been had of the flight of time, a knock on the outer door hushed all voices. The opening disclosed Capt. Lynch, who asked the jurors to assemble for a trip up town to dinner at the Broadway Central.

---

1 Delphin Delmas of San Francisco, known as 'The Napoleon of the Western Bar,' who, prior to his becoming Thaw's leading counsel (at a fee reported to be $100,000), had secured nineteen acquittals in nineteen murder cases.

2 A paraphrase of the M'Naghten Rules regarding the legal meaning of insanity. The Rules were formulated by English judges in 1843, following a furore over the acquittal on the ground of insanity of John Bellingham, who had shot and killed Edward Drummond, the private secretary of the prime minister, Sir Robert Peel, in mistake for that politician.

Jury's Idea of Thaw.

Despite the lateness of the hour – after 7 o'clock – and the continuous effort of the day, the men were not a little disappointed at the enforced interruption. Soon after 9 o'clock they were back again in their places, and a third ballot taken before 10 o'clock evidenced no change in the alignment. In due course the formal debate broke up naturally into individual arguments between pairs or among small groups, scattered about the room as they strove earnestly with each other. The hope in the minds of all was for some early agreement, and efforts of the most zealous nature were put forth.

Those contending for conviction acted upon absolutely impersonal grounds. There was not the slightest suggestion of a spirit of bloodthirstiness in anything that was said. Rather the feeling was one of all proper sympathy for the defendant and the members of his family.

It was freely admitted by some of this number that Thaw was hardly to be considered an absolutely normal man by their own standards. He impressed some as of a marked degenerate type, and some thought that he had justified himself in the shooting. But, as was repeatedly stated, the verdict must not be reached upon any question of Harry K. Thaw's own moral standards, but upon his knowledge of the law as it related to the taking of human life.

First All-Night Debate.

Almost every speaker for conviction stated with solemn earnestness that he had mentally struggled against his formed convictions as the evidence had piled up, and even now would thank any one who could point out to him conscientious reasons for a change of opinion.

By a process of elimination it was endeavored, in some instances, to discover all possible elements of agreement in order to localize the points of dispute. It was found that not a few of these rested upon difference in recollection of certain points of evidence. As the night wore away, it became increasingly apparent that little progress was being made and that little could be made until the opening of court made it possible to secure enlightenment. The vigor of discussion finally lapsed into a lull, broken now and again by sporadic outbreaks, and various exhausted jurors curled up from time to time in the cramped confines of their chairs, or upon the hard table, in the attempt to get a little sleep. Some succeeded measurably, but some had had no sleep whatever when the early morning light began to show in the Walker Street windows.

The coming of morning awakened anew the spirit of argument, but by 7 o'clock, the time of starting out for breakfast, it was pretty generally agreed that the next step must be the securing of additional information from the court.

Anxious Faces of the Defense.

The streets were astir with the early morning workers when the party went again to the hotel. Upon return, there were so many different exhibits and points of testimony desired that a rather formidable list was sent in to Justice Fitzgerald, and shortly thereafter the whole party were ushered into their accustomed jury box seats, where they faced an expectant roomful. The defendant and his wife were obviously cheerful, although they gazed very earnestly at the faces of the jurymen. These in turn attempted to betray no expres-

Architect of a Murder

Evelyn Nesbit Thaw and Stanford White

The Madison Square Roof Garden

Above: A New York *Recorder* caricature of William F. Howe and his little partner, Abe Hummel

Below:
A picture postcard postmarked 'BIRMINGHAM/ MAR 13   07, addressed to Miss Willmott, Diglis Locks, Worcester; the message was 'Dear Flo, I hope you like this P.C. I will send you [George] Robey's. When are you coming over to Brum again, I shall have a trip to see you one of these next fine days so don't be surprised, love and best wishes, Alice'.

sion which should indicate their position as to a verdict. As the various parts of testimony were read, the writer thought that he detected a somewhat more anxious air at the table of the defense, which might have been due to the fact that the points in question very largely concerned the events of the night of the shooting, and of that alone.

Thus were consumed several hours. Luncheon followed in the jury room, and then the key of Capt. Lynch turned again in the lock and attention became at once occupied with the many exhibits which had previously been in dispute.

Value of Clinch Smith's Testimony.

For one thing, the testimony of James Clinch Smith [a brother-in-law of Stanford White] came in for a great deal of discussion. Whether or not from his seat it would have been physically possible for him to follow with his eye the figure of Thaw as he walked down the Madison Avenue aisle of the roof garden, and thence to the entrance, was considered to have an important bearing. Recourse was had to the diagram of the roof garden for light upon this point.

James Clinch Smith's story was rehearsed in full. The fact that the defense had accepted it in full, as was apparent from Mr Delmas's summing up, made it unnecessary to question its veracity. A very large part of the argument of those who advocated conviction was based upon what he testified to. Mr Smith testified, it will be remembered, with great explicitness to the details of a conversation in which Thaw did most of the talking and discussed a wide range of current topics, including a criticism of the performance then taking place upon the stage, the condition of the stockmarket, various aspects of ocean travel, companionship with young women, mutual acquaintances, and various other casual matters, in a way which it was contended indicated a state of mind far removed from uncontrollable insanity. He also testified as to Thaw's getting up and looking over the heads of the audience in the general direction of White's table, and then walking about the Madison Avenue and Twenty-Eighth Street aisles, but always turning his head in such a way as to direct his gaze towards that immediate section.

The significance of his passing out of sight through the door by the elevator has already been indicated. The return, with eyes still directed as before, the ascent into the gallery where presumably he might get a better view of the exact situation on the floor below and his return to his seat, seemed all points of much significance.

It was argued that Mr Delmas's ingenious supposition that this showed him only to be looking for a vacant seat was nullified by the fact that he had had a very good seat with Smith and was evidence in its turn of the importance attached by the defense to this point.

Where Thaw Kept His Pistol.

The testimony in regard to Thaw's pulling a revolver from his pocket was regarded as very important. Mr Jerome in his summing up had referred to the fact that when Thaw stepped out into the hall beside the elevators he had time in which to slip his revolver from the holster in his pocket and place it in the more convenient pocket of the light overcoat he wore. It had been warmly debated during the evening before whether the testimony actually bore out this contention.

If Thaw had had the revolver in his overcoat pocket it was argued that it would have shown distinct premeditation for the following reasons: The overcoat must have been of a very light nature, consequently it is not to be thought that Thaw had previously had his revolver in that pocket. It was recalled that he and his wife had just been dining at the Café Martin [as had Stanford White], and that Thaw's overcoat must have been handed to a check boy or waiter. Anything so conspicuous as a heavy revolver in the pocket would have been exposed to the possibility of investigation by any of the employees of the restaurant. Clearly, therefore, the revolver must have reposed in the holster later taken from it, and must have been in its accustomed place in his hip pocket when he left the restaurant and reached the Garden.

There was no evidence to show that he expected to find White there that evening, although a 'first night' performance at the Garden roof pavilion might have suggested such a possibility. It seemed distinctly more likely that Thaw caught sight of his enemy, quite by accident, later in the evening. If it could be shown that the revolver was in his overcoat pocket instead of his holster at the time he approached his victim, it would be a strong indication of the fact that the impulse to kill antedated the moment when he stood near him.

This was the controlling motive in asking for the testimony of [four eye-witnesses of the shooting,] Blaese, Cohen, Paxton, and Brudi; but unfortunately none of them seemed to make an explicit statement upon this point. Whether or not the confirmation of Mr Jerome's assumption could be found in other portions of the extremely voluminous records, both direct and cross, might have been determined in course of time. So much time was consumed in going through the installment of the morning's request, and so much material for consideration was thereby produced, that no further search for the overcoat pocket evidence was then attempted.

Thaw's Great Self-Possession.

The events succeeding the shooting were of equal interest, and about this there was much more difference of opinion.

Some felt that Thaw's various actions, such as raising the pistol butt upward, making no attempt to escape, telling Mrs Thaw that he had probably saved her life, and so on, could not have occurred had he been in an approximately sane condition; and others drew a directly opposite deduction from the same incidents.

Argument was made to as whether, if Thaw had been approximately rational immediately before the shooting, and rational enough to be cognizant of many points including the disposition of his wife, telephoning to George Lauder Carnegie, referring to the danger of remarks in the street being overheard by reporters, desire to consult counsel, invention of a false name and address, refusal to speak before he had consulted with counsel, and even his ability to comment upon the character of the cigars furnished him, his insanity must be localized in the very short period of the shooting itself, and evidenced by that incident alone. If that were the case and the killing of a man was, in itself, incontrovertible evidence of a man's legal insanity upon the point of killing, it was argued that such a thing as a murder trial for anybody at any time under any conditions became necessarily a farce, and that the same logical process would include every other form of criminal action, and criminal law become simply a matter for expert alienists. This whole subject gave rise to more thousands of earnest arguments than is restful to recall.

The story of Evelyn Nesbit Thaw was rather surprisingly forced into the background by the line of discussion developed. There was some difference of opinion as to its credibility, and yet, so far as it developed, the balance of opinion seemed to be rather in her favor.

It must be remembered that the harrowing details which occupied so much time in the conduct of the case bore largely upon the unavowed defense of 'unwritten law.' There-fore the jury's virtual ignoring of the unwritten law made comparatively little place for discussion of her story. It was virtually admitted that, while staying with Thaw in Paris in 1903, she had told him that she had been Stanford White's mistress; some members of the jury convinced themselves of this fact by a re-examination of the letters written by Thaw to the then Miss Nesbit.

It was generally agreed that she had been a remarkable witness. There was some division of opinion as to her character, but no great amount of discussion. Whether or not she was correctly defined by Mr Delmas as an 'angel child,' it was felt that there was an element of distinct heroism in her going through the ordeal of the witness stand. What-ever doubt was cast upon her story came more from the circumstances of its telling and from collateral referen-ces in other testimony than from the famous Hummel affadavit.

[Evelyn had testified that, in the autumn of 1903, soon after her return from Europe, she had spoken about Thaw to Stanford White: 'He said he would fix things so that I wouldn't have to see him [Thaw] . . . Mr White told me that he was going to take me to see a great lawyer; that his name was Abraham Hummel[1] . . . When I saw Mr Hummel, I must not be frightened. He said Mr Hummel was a bore, with a tiny little body and a very large head, and that he had warts on his face and was very ugly, and he said that Mr Hummel looked like an abortion. And then we rode to Mr Hummel's office, and there were pictures of actresses all over the walls, and then he told me about them; that he got divorces for them . . . Then he asked me where I had met Harry Thaw and how I had happened to go abroad . . . He asked me why we had quarrelled, and I

1 Instances of illegal work done by Hummel and his partner William Howe are given by Richard H. Rovere in his book, adapted from a series of *New Yorker* articles, and entitled *Howe & Hummel* (Farrar, Straus & Co, New York, 1947).

said we had quarrelled all the time, that we couldn't get along together at all . . . Then he shook his head and said it was very terrible, that I was a minor, that I was not of age, and it was a very mean thing for Mr Thaw to do. Then he said Thaw was a very bad man; he had a case in his office against Thaw . . . He said above all things I must be protected against Harry Thaw, that it was very necessary to get Harry Thaw out of New York and keep him out of New York. Then he sent for a stenographer . . . I was very nervous and excited, and I think I cried. Then Mr Hummel dictated to this man, but before he came in he told me I must not interrupt what he had to say. Then he put in a lot of stuff that I had been carried off by Harry Thaw against my will, and I started to interrupt and he put up his hand for me to stop . . .'

The 'Hummel affidavit', which Evelyn had said that she had signed without knowing what she was signing, read as follows:

SUPREME COURT, COUNTY OF NEW YORK
EVELYN NESBIT, PLAINTIFF

Against

HARRY KENDALL THAW, DEFENDANT
City and County of New York, ss.:

Evelyn Nesbit, being duly sworn, says: I reside at the Savoy Hotel, Fifth Avenue and Fifty-Ninth Street, in the city of New York. I am eighteen years of age, having been born on Christmas Day, in the year 1884.

For several months prior to June, 1903, I had been at Dr Bull's Hospital, at No 33 West Thirty-Third Street, in this city, where I had had an operation performed on me for appendicitis, and during the month of June went to Europe with my mother, at the request of Harry Kendall Thaw, the defendant above named. My mother and I had apartments on the Avenue Mantignon, in Paris, France, and from there traveled to Boulogne, during which time we were accompanied by Mr Thaw. Mr Thaw left at once for London, England, while my mother and I remained at the Imperial Hotel about three weeks.

While the said Thaw was in London he wrote me a number of letters. He then returned to Boulogne and took my mother and myself back to Paris, where we stayed at the Langham Hotel. We lived there about two weeks, after which the said Thaw, my mother and I returned to London, where we located at the Claridge Hotel – that is, my mother and I lived at that place, while Mr Thaw stayed at the Carlton Hotel, in the city of London.

My mother remained at Claridge's Hotel for some little time and then moved to the Russell Square Hotel, in Russell Square, London. I went with Mr Thaw to Amsterdam, Holland, by way of Folkestone.

I was ill during this entire period. Mr Thaw and I then traveled throughout Holland, stopping at various places to catch connecting trains, and then we went to Munich, Germany. We then traveled through the Bavarian Highlands, finally going to the Austrian Tyrol. During all this time the said Thaw and myself were known as husband and wife, and were represented by the said Thaw and known under the name of Mr and Mrs Dellis.

After traveling together about five or six weeks, the said Thaw rented a castle in the Austrian Tyrol, known as the Schloss Katzenstein, which is situated about half way up a very isolated mountain. This castle must have been built centuries ago, as the rooms and windows are all old-fashioned. When we reached there, there were a number of servants in the castle, but the only servants I saw were a butler, the cook and the maid. We occupied one entire end of the castle, consisting of two bedrooms, a parlor and a drawing room, which were used by us. The balance of the house was rented by the said Thaw, but was not occupied by us. I was assigned a bedroom for my personal use.

The first night we reached the 'schloss' I was very tired and went to bed right after dinner. In the morning I was awakened by Mr Thaw pounding on the door and asking me to come to breakfast, saying the coffee was getting cold. I immediately jumped out of bed and hastily put on a bathrobe and slippers. I walked out of my room and sat down to breakfast with the said Thaw.

After breakfast the said Thaw said he wished to tell me something, and asked me to step into my bedroom. I entered the room, when the said Thaw, without any provocation, grasped me by the throat and tore the bathrobe from my body, leaving me entirely nude except for my slippers. I saw by his face that the said Thaw was in a terrific, excited condition, and I was terrorized. His eyes were glaring, and he had in his right hand a cowhide whip. He seized hold of me and threw me on the bed. I was powerless and attempted to scream, but the said Thaw placed his fingers in my mouth and tried to choke me. He then, without any provocation and without the slightest reason, began to inflict on me several severe and violent blows with the cowhide whip. So brutally did he assault me that my skin was cut and bruised. I besought him to desist, but he refused. I was so exhausted that I shouted and cried. He stopped every minute or so to rest, and then renewed his attack upon me, which he continued for about seven minutes.

He acted like a demented man. I was absolutely in fear of my life; the servants could not hear my outcries . . . The said Thaw threatened to kill me, and by reason of his brutal attack, as I have described, I was unable to move . . . The following morning Thaw again came into my bedroom and administered a castigation similar to the day before . . .

It was nearly three weeks before I sufficiently recovered to be able to get out of my bed and walk. When I did so, the said Thaw took me to a place called the Ortier Mountain, where Italy, Switzerland and Germany conjoin. Then we went into Switzerland. In Switzerland we remained at the Hotel Schweitzerhof that night, at Santa Maria. The next morning I made some remark, and the said Thaw took a rattan whip, and while I was in my nightgown, beat me over the leg below the knee so violently that I screamed for help. When I began to scream, the said Thaw again stuffed his fingers in my mouth. During all the time I traveled with the said Thaw, he would make the slightest pretext an excuse for a terrific assault on me . . .

One day my maid was in my room taking things out of the drawers and packing them away. I found a little silver box, oblong in shape, and about two and a half inches long, containing a hypodermic syringe and some other small utensils. I went to the said Thaw and asked him what it was and what it meant, and he then stated to me that he had been ill, and tried to make some excuse, saying he had been compelled to use cocaine.

I realized then, for the first time, that the said Thaw was addicted to the cocaine habit. I also frequently saw the said Thaw administer cocaine to himself internally by means of small pills. On one occasion he attempted to force me to take one of these pills, but I refused to do so . . . During this entire period, while I was in this condition of non-resistance, Thaw entered my bed and without my consent repeatedly wronged me. I reproved the said Thaw for his conduct, but he compelled me to submit thereto, threatening to beat and kill me if I did not do so . . .

I have not seen my mother since I left her in London, and am informed within the past two weeks that she returned to the city of New York from London on the steamship *Campania* . . .

I have been repeatedly told by the said Thaw that he is very inimical to a married man, whom, he said, he wanted me to injure, and that he, Thaw, would get him into the penitentiary; and the said Thaw has begged me time and again to swear to written documents which he had prepared, involving this married man and charging him with drugging me and having betrayed me when I was fifteen years of age. This was not so; and so I told him, but because I refused to sign these papers, the said Thaw not alone threatened me with bodily injury, but inflicted on me the great bodily injury I have herein described.

(Signed) EVELYN NESBIT

Howe & Hummel, attorneys for the plaintiff.

Hummel, speaking on the phone to Thaw's lawyer, had told him about the affidavit, and suggested that he should warn his client that Miss Nesbit was a minor (which, if her birth-date in the affidavit was correct, she was not: she had reached the age of eighteen on Christmas Day, 1902).

Evelyn had married Harry Thaw on 5 April 1905; since then – so she had testified – she had been 'pursued' by Stanford White against her will . . . and had told her husband of the unwelcome pursuing.]

Several of the jury gave some little weight to this affidavit; but to most of those who discussed it, the reputation of Hummel so affected consideration on any production of his that it was even a trifle amusing to think that Mr Delmas had wasted so much breath and oratory in neutralizing it.

Juror Switches to Insanity.

The advocates of acquittal based their judgment upon a variety of points: testimony that from child-hood Thaw had been subject to strabismus [squinting], St Vitus's Dance, and other nervous ailments, indicating that he was of a strongly neurotic character, the probable effect upon such a constitution of the life of dissipation that he had led since growing up, the probable effect of the receipt of the story in Paris, the strongly melancholy strain running through the letters – although the letters themselves seemed distinctly lucid – his actions when in Pittsburg as related by his mother, his manner with Drs Evans and Wagner when they examined him [for the defense] in the Tombs,[1] and his manner and appearance in court.

The most interesting argument upon this side was made well in the afternoon of Thursday, when one juror, originally an advocate for conviction, after an hour or two of careful inspection of the documents secured from the court, got up at last to speak in his turn and surprised every other member of the jury by announcing that his mind had been changed, not by any arguments he had listened to but by his own deductions.

Talks as Well as Delmas.

The speech in which he stated his conclusions was in the matter of genuinely fervid oratory of a character quite worthy to rank with the handling of the subject by Mr Delmas himself, and the fact that it was a strictly extemporaneous effort made it, in the opinion of all the body, distinctly a remarkable performance. He was warmly complimented by both sides at its conclusion, and his unquestioned genuineness of conviction introduced a new feeling into the atmosphere of the jury room, where something of a deadlock had previously prevailed.

The Sole Change – Request for Cots.

However, his was the only accession to the ranks of the minority – indeed, the only definite change in the original grouping of the body effected during the entire forty-seven hours. Answering arguments were immediately made by several who held that an analysis of the events

based upon a strictly intellectual judgment made it impossible for them to reach this conclusion, and the remaining seven continued unshaken throughout the balance of the forty-seven hours.

The advocates of acquittal made a strong point of the fact that when Dr Allan McLane Hamilton was called to the stand by the defense, Mr Jerome very strenuously objected to his giving his opinion and succeeded in keeping out the testimony while the jurors were in the room. As Dr Hamilton was the only expert alienist said to have examined Thaw in the Tombs with the exception of Drs Evans and Wagner, they held that this action, by inference, justified their position. The testimony of Drs Evans and Wagner was made much of, and the jury returned twice to the courtroom in order to have read to them that section of the Judge's charge which dealt with the weight properly to be given to such testimony.

On Thursday afternoon a communication was drawn up addressed to the Judge, and making request for cots in case a verdict could not be reached before a reasonable time. It was pointed out that the health of the jurors was directly involved, and that in a public service of such importance this health should be safeguarded.

This letter was signed by all of the jurors, and delivered by kindly Capt. Lynch, who returned word that Justice Fitzgerald made a special search for authority which would permit him to comply, but could find none. Hence chairs and tables became again the order for the night for the very slight rest secured. The writer, for example, had an aggregate

---

1 The New York City Prison – next door to the Criminal Court Building, and linked to it by the 'Bridge of Sighs'.

of two hours' sleep out of the entire forty-seven.

Eight Ballots Taken in All.

Eight ballots in all were taken, and in some of them a strong effort was made to get together upon the compromise verdict originally suggested. Almost numberless private arguments were had between different individual jurors, and strong appeals were made before the parliamentary body of the whole, developing the fact that, while every one of the advocates of conviction agreed to the modified form, provisionally upon its being unanimous, none of the other side save one, and he the speaker before referred to, cast such a ballot in any of the votes, his reason being given as the belief that Thaw was now insane and should be restrained in the public interest in the only way open to the jury – that is, by a term in prison.

Upon the final ballot, taken just before sending word to the Justice, all of those who modified their votes went back to their original position, leaving the ballot seven for conviction of murder in the first degree and five for acquittal upon the ground of insanity.

———————

Thaw's Disappointment Bitter.

Thaw, while bitterly disappointed at the result, bore up bravely. His family seemed more downcast.

The young Pittsburger had earlier in the afternoon again bundled up the mass of letters and documents which he meant to take with him from his cell. He was even at the eleventh hour hopeful of acquittal. He thought that the appeal of Mr

Delmas, who pictured him as a Sir Galahad rescuing forlorn damsels, would influence the jury so greatly that he would be liberated before the setting of yesterday's sun.

When he was told by Mr [Russell] Peabody and Mr [Daniel] O'Reilly of his counsel that there would be a mistrial, he dropped his bundle of documents to the floor. The bitterness of his disappointment was beyond words. He faced months more of confinement and then the strain of another trial.

After some words of encouragement from his lawyers, Thaw braced himself and followed his prison guard into the courtroom. He slipped into his chair at the head of the table reserved for the lawyers for the defense so quietly that few of those in court noticed him.

Evelyn Nesbit Thaw slipped into the room from the door which leads to the Justice's chamber. Instead of taking her accustomed seat, she swung a chair beside that in which her husband sat. She knew the result; she had been told by the lawyers who had made the fight for her husband's life and liberty.

As she sat close to him, Thaw dropped his right hand toward her, caught her gloved hand, and held it fast.

Jury is Dismissed.

Some court attendant pressed a button and the drab of a cloudy April afternoon was relieved by the glare of many electric lights. Clerk Penney arose from his seat and called to Thaw to stand and face the jury. He then turned to Foreman Deming B. Smith and called to him and his eleven associates to face the defendant.

Thaw stood up. In the glare of the electric light, his face showed plainly the pallor that comes from long imprisonment. The lines from the curve of his nostrils down to the chin seemed to have deepened, as if the keenly sharpened plow of adversity had suddenly furrowed them. A few moments before, he had sat with his pitiful little treasures in his lap, all neatly parcelled, and ready to carry them to the great outer life of which he had been deprived for nearly a year. He had even arranged for a tour abroad with his wife.

As Thaw rose, he threw back his heavy shoulders and put his chin in the air. He looked squarely at Foreman Smith, and Mr Smith looked at Justice Fitzgerald.

The end of the case was brought quickly. Clerk Penney asked if the jury had reached a verdict. Mr Smith said, simply, that it had not. He then plumped himself suddenly into his chair, and Thaw sank into his.

Then Justice Fitzgerald said:

'Gentlemen of the jury, I have kept you deliberating so long because I regarded it as my duty to do so, as long as there was any possibility of reaching a verdict. I have reached the conclusion that this is now impossible. I have advised the People's representative and the defendant's counsel that I do not intend to longer insist that you continue your deliberations. I therefore discharge you from further consideration of the case. Do I have the consent of the public prosecutor and the counsel for the defense?'

Mr Jerome and Mr Hartridge both said: 'We consent.' Mr Jerome added: 'For reasons known to your Honor, this case should be kept open, and I therefore request that you do not, when you adjourn,

adjourn *sine die*, but to a date which your Honor may choose.' Court was then formally adjourned until April 29, when application for bail may be made.

The jurors jumped from their seats in the box, entered the jury room, grabbed their hats and overcoats, and hurried from the building.

Sad Parting for Thaw Family.

Harry Thaw, realizing that for the time being his hopes of freedom were dead, looked about him in a dazed fashion. His mother and his sisters, Lady Yarmouth and Mrs Carnegie, and his brothers had slipped into the room and were sitting behind his chair. The mother dropped her veil, and if she wept none saw it.

Evelyn spoke to her husband, pushed back her chair, and hurried through the throng of newspaper reporters and court attendants.

Thaw pulled his overcoat over his arm and once more stood up and turned to follow his prison guard. At the door leading to the path towards the Tombs, Thaw turned and looked over his shoulder in the direction of the place where his mother sat. He seemed to desire a moment with her or with some one of his own kith and kin. Evelyn Thaw had already left the room. Her face was placid; her husband's was terribly drawn.

Lady Yarmouth stared towards the bench, which Justice Fitzgerald had already abandoned. Mrs Carnegie, whose face has shown almost as haggard as the face of her brother on trial, stretched out her hands, and to Mrs William Thaw signified that it was time for them to depart. The police cleared a way to the waiting automobiles. Josiah and Edward Thaw walked together from the building.

The Final Day of Strain.

The day was one of anxiety not only to Thaw and his family, but to his counsel and to Mr Jerome. In the early morning, after rumor had it that a verdict would be reached within an hour or two, Evelyn Nesbit Thaw, still attired as a schoolgirl,[1] sat in the room adjoining the chamber of Justice Fitzgerald with others waiting for the final word of the jury.

All of them felt that the end was near, as the hour for dinner recess approached. There was still the slight hope that the jury would agree and bring in a verdict at 1 o'clock. When that hour came, the hope was not met.

Out of the building straggled the waiting groups, and they had to fight their way through the crowds that swarmed about the Criminal Court Building. The one among them who was most calm and pleasant of countenance, who was not worried by the crowds, nor dismayed by the multitudes of trampling and curious people, was Evelyn Nesbit Thaw.

She went with one of the counsel for her husband, not to the French Café on Franklin Street, where a great crowd of people had congregated to look at her, but to a restaurant on Park Row, where she enjoyed a meal undisturbed.

On her return, there was such a swarm of curious humanity about the Criminal Court Building that Sergt Kellerer, in charge of the court squad of police, was compelled to ask for assistance. Again, from Mulberry Street and from the Tenderloin, came the crowds, anxious to see the woman who was depicted by Mr Jerome as the 'angel child.' In this mob were many women; some of them carried children in their arms. The police were compelled to use force to clear a way for the prisoner's wife.

Meanwhile, over in the Tombs, Thaw had written a communication to all of the newspapers, explaining his action in going armed while in New York.

During this noon hour, Thaw was told that the child of one of his

---

1 From *Evelyn Nesbit and Stanford White: Love and Death in the Gilded Age* by Michael MacDonald Mooney (William Morrow, New York, 1976): 'For the part she was to play Evelyn had chosen her costume carefully. Before the trial began Mr Delmas had interviewed her for hours on end so that, he said, he would not be met with any surprises. Among the knowing members of the press, reports circulated that the price of Evelyn's testimony would be one million dollars, but of course such reports were surely exaggerations because any payment of a witness for his or her testimony would be illegal under the laws of the State of New York and of the United States of America. When Mr Delmas finally seemed satisfied with his rehearsal of Evelyn's testimony he asked how she would dress when the day came for her appearance in the courtroom. Evelyn told him she would wear what she always wore in the daytime – a plain, dark blue, tailored suit; a shirtwaist and a boyish collar. It would be almost the costume of a schoolgirl, and she thought its simplicity would put her best foot forward – her youth and her innocence. "Quite right," Mr Delmas had said. "And what hat?" For Mr Delmas she tried on nearly every hat she owned before he would settle on a black velvet trimmed with violets. She appeared in the approved costume every day, with the result that even before the selection of the jury could be completed, her costume had become the new fashion on the streets of New York. Copies by the thousands suddenly appeared, taken from the newspaper drawings made by the artists engaged to sketch the trial. Every store sold all the violet-trimmed black velvet hats it could stock.'

keepers was dying. Thaw said to him, 'Old man, you are in a sadder plight than I.'

After his luncheon, Thaw was again brought back to the guards' room outside the court room for another long wait. This ended with the summons at 4.20 o'clock that he was to appear to hear the jury report, and then came the final scene of the trial, the jury's dismissal.

Thaw's Comment on the Jury.

Following his return to the Tombs, Thaw issued a second statement. It read:

'First statement since the disagreement and second and last statement to-day.

I believe that every man of the jury, possessing over average intelligence, excepting possibly Mr Bolton,[1] comprehended the weight of the evidence and balloted for acquittal.

All my family bid me good-bye with courage.

I trust, D.V., we may all keep well.'

This statement was signed with Thaw's name. The reference in it to the balloting of the jury aroused considerable comment and discussion as to just what Thaw meant by it. It became generally accepted, however, that it had been thought advisable by the Thaw counsel to keep the real ballot of the jury from him, and that the prisoner may, in consequence, have issued his statement in the belief that the jury had stood at ten or eleven for acquittal.

Jerome Tells His Plans.

District Attorney Jerome was unwilling to comment at length upon the outcome of the case.

'There is little that I can say with propriety,' he declared. 'I may say, however, that, in view of the evidence which has been presented and the attitude of the jury, I feel it my duty to again present to a jury the evidence for the acquittal or conviction of this defendant.

There are, however, many homicide cases now under indictment: fifteen of them are murder case of the first degree. These demand attention, and it would be improper to try them in any other than their regular order. In the meantime, the retrial of Thaw must wait.'

In regard to the admission of Thaw to bail, Mr Jerome said:

'Application for admission to bail is a motion which any defendant has a right to make, and which the court must entertain. In view of the evidence adduced at this trial, however, and in view of the discussion which has gone on in the jury-room and the attitude of the jury on the question of whether Thaw is guilty or not guilty, I should consider it my duty to oppose such an application, and when the facts in this case become known to the court, I am of the opinion that no judge under any circumstances would grant admission to bail.'

Change of Venue Not Necessary.

Mr Jerome was asked concerning

---

1 In the middle of February, the trial had been interrupted for a couple of days because of the death of Juror Joseph Bolton's wife from pneumonia. Thaw had been vexed: 'I'm sorry for Mr Bolton,' he had told his jailors without convincing them, '– but why, oh why, did this have to happen? It's just my luck – I always get the worst of it.'

the generally accepted belief that a retrial of the Thaw case will be held elsewhere than in this city. He replied: 'I see nothing at present which leads me to believe that twelve men cannot be selected from the lists of those liable to jury duty in this great county, twelve men who will be able to serve acceptably to this great County of New York, and who can give a fair trial to this defendant.'

Think Jerome Is Elated.

Despite Mr Jerome's refusal to divulge his own opinion of the outcome of the case, persons who have had an intimate knowledge of the trial from its beginning declare that the District Attorney cannot feel other than elated at the result – more pleased perhaps at the disagreement than he would have been at a conviction.

It is pointed out by these persons that almost from the beginning of the trial Mr Jerome has felt that Thaw, if not insane in the legal sense, was certainly mentally deranged from a medical viewpoint. A conviction would, therefore, these persons point out, have placed the District Attorney in the unenviable position of having successfully prosecuted for murder in the first degree, a man whom he himself believed beyond the pale of the law.

As the case now stands, Thaw will be kept in the Tombs Prison for several months. The mental suspense as well as the physical strain of these months of imprisonment and enforced idleness cannot, it is believed, fail to bring to a crux any mental ailment Thaw may now be suffering from. Jerome's course in such an event would be easy. He would no longer be compelled to bring Thaw again to trial for his life. Instead, he might, this time with some hope of success, apply for a Lunacy Commission which would send the young Pittsburger to Matteawan Insane Asylum.

Should Thaw, on the other hand, successfully withstand the ordeal to which he will be submitted for the next few months, those who think they know Jerome's own feelings say that his last doubt of Thaw's sanity will have been removed, and he will be enabled to bring him to the Bar the second time with the full accord of his own conscience.

Thaw's Lawyers Undecided.

Clifford W. Hartridge, counsel of record for the defense, said late last night that he could not discuss the matter of an application for bail for his client at that time.

'It will be necessary for counsel to get together and consider this matter,' he said.

Thaw's Family Surprised.

When the members of Thaw's family reached their hotel, the Lorraine, reporters were waiting for them, but they would say nothing. In the hall was an acquaintance of the Countess of Yarmouth, and to her she spoke as she waited for the elevator.

'Isn't it terrible? I can't understand it,' she said.

It was said that the Countess sent a cable message to her husband, saying:

'Great disappointment.'

Evelyn Nesbit Thaw arrived a few minutes after the others. She was alone. The same dull incomprehension of what had happened and why it had happened was the note of her cry. As she was asked what she thought of the end of it all, she said:

'I can't understand it. I don't see why they couldn't have come to an agreement.'

'They say the jury stood seven to five for conviction,' some one said.

'I don't believe it,' she cried. 'On the evidence they ought to have acquitted him.'

Neither callers nor messages were received by the Thaws last night. For a long time no word could be had from their apartments, but at length a telegram was delivered to Mrs William Thaw. It asked her if there was anything she wished to give out and whether there was anything in the rumor that Thaw intended to drop all his counsel excepted Daniel O'Reilly. To this she sent the reply:

'Mrs Thaw has nothing to say. She has made no statement since she has been in New York; neither will she make any.'

HOW THE DAY PASSED.

Thousands in the Streets Awaited News from the Thaw Jury.

The disagreeing jurors in the Thaw case were awake all of Thursday night. The court attendants were in almost as hard a fix as the jurors. They had to act as attendants in court all day and as special officers at night. One of them said yesterday that in fifty-six hours he had been asleep for exactly three.

The jurors left the Criminal Court Building soon after 7 o'clock. As they straggled up Broadway to the Broadway Central Hotel, they were guarded closely by Capt Lynch and his men, but there was no attempt to interfere with them. They looked a thoroughly washed-out lot, hardly able to drag their feet along.

Breakfast made a vast difference in them. It revived their spirits, and almost as soon as the meal was over they began to argue together again. They seemed careless of appearance in their anxiety to reach a verdict, and men who passed the hotel to their work could see part of the deliberations which would decide the fate of Thaw carried on in full view in the window. Malcolm B. Fraser was to be seen gesticulating with energy as he tried to convice Oscar A. Pink that the insanity plea was utterly out of the question, and Joseph B. Bolton, the juror the death of whose wife delayed the trial for so long, could be made out reclining wearily in the chair while Charles D. Newton talked to him.

Bernard Gerstman and Harry C. Brearley were together in a corner, apparently running over the arguments which already for many hours they had been enforcing upon the attention of their colleagues.

In the procession back to the Criminl Courts, which began soon after 8 o'clock, the same preoccupation seemed to possess all of them, and only Bernard Gerstman and Oscar A. Pink seemed to have found any subject on which they could chat without serious disagreement.

Thaw's Troubled Night.

Thaw himself had passed nearly as troubled a night as his jurors. He tossed from side to side on his prison bed and caught only naps the whole night through. He had been warned by his counsel that the jury had already almost endured more than the human frame could stand, and he was haunted by the idea that their disagreement would condemn him to at least another six months' weary confinement, or that those who favored his acquittal might submit to a compromise which would send him to Sing Sing for the best days of his life.

Still he kept up the marvelous pluck which has astonished all who have come near him. When he was called, he declared he felt 'fine,' and ran to the shower bath for a toning up for all the day might bring forth.

He was over in the Criminal Court Building by 10.30 o'clock, the hour set for the convening of the court, and settled himself in the Sheriff's guardroom to await a summons to appear before the jury. He appeared somewhat worn and pale as he passed across the Bridge of Sighs, but to inquiries called to him as he went by he replied with his stereotyped:

'I'm fine; thank you.'

For a time he was left alone with Mr Hartridge. His wife and family had come down to the Criminal Court Building and were ready to stand by his side when the last ordeal came, but for some reason or other they did not hasten up to the Sheriff's room. They remained in the little room which has been placed at the service of witnesses for the defense since the trial began, and allowed the defendant to pass the first part of the morning without their comfort.

This seems to have been because Thaw had made up his mind that he should issue another statement. Mr Hartridge did all he could to dissuade him. He assured him that it would be absolutely useless so far as his own case was concerned, and that it might be misconstrued. He pointed out that the jury were absolutely beyond

the reach of outside influences, and the utmost that it could accomplish would be to satisfy morbid curiosity. The defendant, however, insisted, and about 11 o'clock Thaw's latest thoughts were revealed to the world.

Thaw Tells of Being Armed.

At the very moment when his fate hung in the balance, when hundreds of men and women were gathered in the building to hear at the first possible moment the verdict of the men who had tried him, he seemed to worry most about the opinion than the outside public might have of his personal courage. He wrote:

'I wish the jury and every one else to understand that no one despises a person who carries concealed weapons more than I.

That only after my life was in jeopardy, as I was informed by persons and as was communicated to me by professional detectives, did I protect myself. Then I employed the Pinkertons, and they could neither prove these attempts so I could invoke the protection of the law or disprove them so I could safely continue defenseless.

Then, doubting my judgment, I consulted an ex-Chief of Police and respected in his community, and he advised that my duty was to protect myself.

In this trial I wished my case solely and simply based on the law of the State and upon the evidence which had convinced not only me, as I reviewed all this evidence in quiet, but also the District Attorney, that I am innocent under the written law of the State.'

Efforts to Get Into Court.

To get past the police lines which

The Art of Murder

barred the way to the courtroom, all sorts of subterfuges were used. But by Justice Fitzgerald's order none but reporters were to be admitted, and women particularly were barred. One tackled the big Sergeant who has been so conspicuous a feature of the scenes of the trial.

'I represent a London paper,' she said.

'Don't you know the Lee Avenue Station at Brooklyn?' replied the Sergeant.

'Why, yes.'

'I used to be stationed there.'

'And?' she asked innocently.

'There's no "and" about it. I was stationed there and that's all there is about it.'

'What a wonderful memory for faces you do have,' said the woman. 'I used to think I could get around any man, especially the handsome ones.'

Even that did not touch the Sergeant's heart, but somehow or other later in the day persistency won. The woman actually got seated in the courtroom, and was turned out immediately by the hard-hearted court officers. She spent the rest of the day in the corridor, watching for the lawyers as they passed to and fro.

The Crowd Outside.

Just after noon it was made known that the jurors saw no chance of early agreement, and that they thought it would be well to get something to eat. This was taken as a sign that nothing would happen until the middle of the afternoon. Justice Fitzgerald announced that the court was adjourned until 2 o'clock, and went off himself to lunch.

Twelve o'clock is the dinner hour in all the workshops in the neigh-

borhood of the Criminal Court Building. Thousands pour out on the streets at that hour, and a goodly proportion of them thought that they would like to get a glimpse of the woman of whom they had heard so much in connection with the trial. They came down to the Courthouse, and would have gone in if the police, had not been ready for them.

Then they stood outside on the White Street side and looked at the automobiles standing at the side entrance, waiting for Mrs William Thaw. Others preferred Franklin Street and hoped against hope that before they had to go back to work they might catch a glimpse of two shadows passing over the Bridge of Sighs which they might interpret as the signs that Thaw and his guards were passing that way.

Inspector McCluskey was on hand to keep them in check. He had fifty men under his orders, and the crowd was pushed back up the side streets nearly as far as Broadway.

Rush to See Thaw Family.

The first amusement the spectators got was the departure of Mrs William Thaw, Mrs Carnegie, and Lady Yarmouth from the building. As usual they got into their automobiles and started rapidly uptown for the Hotel Lorraine. At once the crowd broke through the police lines. The women scrambled upon trucks, the men surged across the street, and children came running up from all directions. Two or three thousand people were rushing wildly along to see three heavily veiled ladies drive away in automobiles. They were wildly excited and cheered the relatives of the defendant heartily. However, the automobiles

138

soon escaped them, and they turned to see who else was worth notice.

Evelyn Nesbit Thaw was the next to come out. She was too anxious to go as far from the Court House as the hotel and she wished to be back again as soon as her husband had returned from his lunch in the Tombs. At the same time, she had no wish to go through the unpleasant experience of Thursday, when she was mobbed on her way back from Pontin's. So, with Daniel O'Reilly, she decided to go to a restaurant on Park Row, where her identity would not be so likely to be discovered. She started in an automobile and was greeted with the same cheers and the same rush as Mrs William Thaw and the others.

Small Fire in the Building.

After the family of the defendant had departed, the crowd had an unexpected excitement. From the windows of the Criminal Court Building, directly below the Bridge of Sighs, smoke was seen issuing. A rush was made along Franklin Street. However, the police managed to restore order, and hearing that the fire was slight and already under control of the court attendants, prevented an alarm being turned in.

As a matter of fact, it was Harry K. Thaw himself who discovered the fire. As he was going across the bridge to his lunch he smelled smoke. He called the attention of his guard to it and Superintendent Coppers of the building was also warned. He instituted a search immediately and found that the smoke was coming from a small examination room attached to the Tombs Police Court.

An old umbrella thrust behind a radiator was the cause. Some one had

thrown a cigarette end upon it and the fabric was smoldering. It was quickly extinguished, but in order to do so a part of the partition had to be chopped away.

Although no one expected that the jury would have anything to report before 3 or 4 o'clock, every one was on hand again promptly at 2 o'clock. Once more Thaw was led across the Bridge of Sighs to the Sheriff's guard room, and once more his family took up their weary watch in the little room set apart for them. Every now and then one or other of them would go upstairs for a few minutes and keep him company, but most of the time he was alone with his guards or his lawyers.

Counsel, court officials, and reporters had been under a great strain for hours and were expecting a still greater one. They sought relief in the best way they could, but kept an anxious eye the whole time upon Capt. Lynch of the court squad.

From him only could authentic news of the jury's proceedings come. The guard sitting outside the door of the conference chamber had to report to him, and he took such action as the occasion demanded. He was willing enough to give out any information that was legitimate, but sternly refused to give a hint of the way they were getting along with their deliberation.

About 3 o'clock a rumor spread that there was almost a fight behind their closed doors. Angry voices, it was said, could be heard even at the distance that the jury room is separate from the court. But Capt. Lynch professed himself ignorant of anything.

'Nothing to say,' he replied to all enquiries.

Soon after 4 o'clock, however, he

had news of the utmost moment to communicate, and at his intimation that at last the jury were coming in, counsel and the reporters flocked in from the hall, and everybody was on the alert for the end of the great trial.

While the jury was in court, the doors were closed and locked. By the courtesy of Capt. Lynch, arrangements were made by which bulletins could be passed out by the side door leading past the Judge's chambers to the mainhall, but no one was allowed to disturb the proceedings by leaving his seat.

Within the police lines outside the court, a number of reporters stood waiting the first intimation of what had taken place. Others were at the telephone booths, holding the wires to their offices. As the bulletins were passed out they tried to intercept them, but they were handed quickly to boys and rushed out of the building. For five minutes no one could tell what was in progress.

Crowd Hear the Result.

Suddenly the door leading to the passage-way from the side door of the court was burst open. Three or four men rushed out. 'Disagreement!' they shouted. They plunged wildly for the stairs leading to the telephone booths, and it was lucky no one was in the way of their rush.

'Disagreement,' took up the crowd in the corridor and a great shout went up. Down the stairs pelted the reporters, and in a minute the news was being flashed over the wires to the newspaper offices and called along the street.

Inspector McCluskey had been just outside of the side door of the court while the jury was in. He rushed out at the clamor and gave hurried orders to the police. He bade them clear every one off the main floor of the building, whether they had legitimate business there or not. Happily the men who have been guarding the courtroom for the last three months have got on good terms with the reporters. They knew that there was no one there but had work to do, and they interpreted the Inspector's orders with judgment. They made the crowd move, but they cared not where they went. The reporters stepped quietly behind them and were able to attend to their business without molestation.

The jury were sent back to their room as soon as they were discharged. There is an unobtrusive little door leading to it which has been provided for just such occasions as this. From it the twelve men issued and vanished as quickly as they could down the elevator.

THAW NEWS IN TIMES SQUARE.
A Bulletin of the Disagreement Was In Place in Four Minutes.

Immediately the disagreement of the Thaw jury was announced, a huge sign reading 'Thaw Jury Disagrees' was posted on the TIMES's bulletin board on Broadway, an eager crowd quickly gathered, and the man who was placing the bulletin, anticipating how great was their curiosity to learn the latest news from the Criminal Courts Building, posted the single word 'disagreement' first.

It was the first bulletin posted in upper Broadway, and the news that the Thaw trial, that had lasted so many weeks, was at an end, for the time at any rate, spread with great rapidity. Soon a crowd that blocked the street had assembled to read the bulletin and make sure the reports were true. Street cars stopped in front of the building to let the passengers read the news, automobiles paused, and even the traffic policemen craned their necks to ascertain the latest news without leaving their posts.

Comments on the result were few, and at no time was there anything approaching a demonstration. Everybody had expected exactly what happened, the result being that there was a chorus of 'I told you so's.' The disagreement was announced at the Criminal Courts Building at 4.25 pm. Four minutes later THE TIMES bulletin was in position.

GREAT INTEREST IN LONDON.

Extras Giving the Result of the Trial Eagerly Bought.

LONDON, April 12. – Interest in the trial of Harry K. Thaw for the murder of Stanford White, which at first was intense here, lagged towards the end of the proceedings, but the unexpectedly prolonged deliberations of the jury and the novelty for the British public of the circumstances surrounding the final scenes, raised curiosity here to a fever point to learn what the outcome of the strange case would be. Within a few minutes of the receipt of the cable dispatch announcing that the jury had disagreed, the streets of London, in spite of the lateness of the hour, echoed with the shouts of the newsboys, the newspapers were bought up eagerly, and the people everywhere discussed with unusual avidity the likelihood of another trial.

All the papers publish long editorial articles on the Thaw case, and most of them review the various stages of the trial. It is declared that American prestige has suffered severely, and the case is called a 'a signal proof of the utter inefficacy of American statesmanship to evolve a practical legal system.'

One paper says: 'Law, dignity, common sense and order, all have been wanting.' Another says: 'A strong English judge would have made short work of the trial, reducing to a minimum its degrading sensationalism.'

From the *New York Times*, Saturday, 2 February 1908 (starting at the top of the front page):

THAW INSANE; IN MATTEAWAN

He is Found Not Guilty of Murdering White Because He Was Crazy.

SENT AT ONCE TO ASYLUM

Jury Deliberated 25 Hours and at First Stood 8 to 4 for Acquittal.

NO WRIT FOR RELEASE YET

Prisoner Loudly Protests, However, That He Is Sane Now – Littleton Says Verdict Was Fair.

After deliberating twenty-five hours, the jury which tried Harry Kendall Thaw for the second time for the murder of Stanford White on Madison Square Roof Garden on the night of June 25, 1906, returned to the courtroom at 12.40 o'clock yesterday with a verdict acquitting the prisoner of the crime on the ground that he was insane when he shot White.

Supreme Court Justice Dowling at once ordered the prisoner to the State Asylum for the Criminal Insane at Matteawan, and Thaw was taken there, leaving the Tombs a few minutes before 4 o'clock in charge of Deputy Sheriff Bell.

Just before he boarded the train, Thaw dictated this statement:

'I am perfectly sane now, but I am going to Matteawan on the advice of my counsel, who thought it unwise to sue for a writ of habeas corpus at this time. Counsel will proceed in the matter of my release as soon as they can get together the proofs they will present that I am at present sane. I am confident that my stay in Matteawan will be for a short period of time only.'

Justice Dowling had allowed counsel for the defense until 3 o'clock yesterday afternoon to confer with Thaw pending the beginning of the journey to Matteawan. In that time it was decided that no fight would be made for the present to keep Thaw out of the asylum.

Thaw staggered to his feet when he heard the verdict. There was in his mind the conviction that Littleton[1], whose eloquence and constructive power in the defense had brought about this verdict, would save him from Matteawan. The prisoner stood, with shoulders braced squarely, before the jury as the verdict was announced, and he seemed possessed with a strong desire to extend to the twelve men his thanks. He bowed to the foreman, bending his body in the middle, and he bowed to Naething, the second juror. He bowed to the third and the fourth jurors, and the fifth and the sixth, but none of them looked at him. Instead they extended their hands to Martin W. Littleton, congratulating him on his work, and passed on out of the jury box to shake the hand of the prisoner's wife.

All the while the prisoner stood bowing his thanks to the jurors. Not a juror lifted his eyes to the sallow-faced man over whose fate he had wrestled for twenty-five hours. The last man of the twelve contented himself with a word of appreciation to the chief counsel of the defense and a word of congratulation to Evelyn Nesbit Thaw.

The jurors had been ordered to the jury room at 11.40 am Friday. From that hour until 12.40 yesterday afternoon they were away from the court and the public, weighing in the balance the claim of Thaw to the life of White. These twelve men cast fourteen ballots. The first ballot cast showed eight for acquittal on the ground of insanity and four for a verdict of murder in the first degree. Two jurors changed to a verdict of acquittal during Friday night, and the vote then stood ten to two.

The jurors were taken up to the Hotel Knickerbocker yesterday morning for breakfast, and afterwards another juror changed his vote to not guilty. This left only one of the twelve sticking for a verdict of guilty of murder in some degree. Five

1 Martin W. Littleton, who had replaced Delphin Delmas as Thaw's leading counsel.

minutes before word was sent to Justice Dowling that a verdict had been agreed upon, this twelfth juror switched over, and the verdict on the ground of insanity was agreed upon.

Veteran Got the Table.

During the night of physical torture pending the reaching of a verdict, the jurors, with one accord, agreed to give the use of the table in the room to Juror Cary, the senior member of the body. He is a grizzled veteran of the civil war – on the Confederate side. He stretched out on the hard boards and slept from 2 until 4 o'clock in the morning and then got up and resumed the discussion of the case.

All morning Thaw fidgeted about in the prisoner's pen of the courtroom. His wife did her best to calm him. He had packed up his pictures, clippings of newspapers, and letters preparatory to walking out a free man. The thought of being held a prisoner any longer was far from his mind. When he was told that the jury had reached a verdict, he seemed dazed and hardly able to comprehend what it meant to him. He walked into the courtroom with a Deputy Sheriff behind him. He seemed to walk as by effort. He smiled at his wife with a twitching of the corners of his lips and sat down beside his counsel.

Clerk Penney arose and asked whether the jury had found a verdict. Foreman Gremmels replied that the jury had, and announced in clear tones that the verdict was not guilty on the ground of insanity at the time of the killing of White.

Evelyn Nesbit Thaw was the only woman of the family in the courtroom at the time. She leaned far over in her chair, and for the first time since the trial of her husband she showed genuine anxiety in her face. Her usually smooth, babyish face was seamed from the curve of the nostrils to the chin. She looked a woman suddenly aged.

Thaw, who had been standing facing the foreman of the jury, sat down and shelled his left ear to catch what the Judge would say. He seemed to anticipate the order sending him to Matteawan. He and his wife listened keenly to every word that came from the bench.

Despite the fact that Justice Dowling had given a foreword to those in the courtroom that there should be no demonstration when the verdict was announced, it had hardly been given when one spectator began to clap his hands vigorously. Nobody else applauded, and it was an easy matter to find the offender.

Cost Pell $25 to Applaud.

'Who is that person?' demanded Justice Dowling of Capt. Lynch, in charge of the court squad.

'Here is the man,' was the reply, and the offender was taken up to the bench. The captive said he was Theodore Roosevelt Pell, named after the President but not a relative. He said he had just dropped in to hear the verdict. Justice Dowling fined him $25, and the Sheriff declined to take his check. He was compelled to remain in the Sheriff's office until a friend arrived with the cash to pay his fine.

This incident disposed of, Justice Dowling said:

'The only testimony in this case upon which a verdict of insanity could be based was to the effect that the defendant was suffering from a manic-depressive form of mental derangement. This testimony and the diagnosis of the form of insanity were based upon prior outbreaks of the defendant as testified to by witnesses from London, Monte Carlo, Rome, Paris, and Albany.

It also appears from the testimony, and the court was careful to inquire into this, that recurrences of the periods of mania are reasonably certain. In the depressive stage there is danger of a recurrence of suicidal tendency.

There has been no testimony adduced here to show that a person suffering from this form of insanity ever can be cured. It appears, however, that the person suffering from this form of insanity, during the maniacal form of the disease, is likely to commit dangerous assaults or murder.

Therefore, upon all the evidence in the case, the court deems that to allow the defendant to go at large would be dangerous to the community and to the public safety. The decision of the court is that the defendant shall not now be discharged, but, being in custody, shall be so held and committed with all dispatch to the State Hospital for the Criminal Insane at Matteawan. The Sheriff of the county is directed to take custody of the defendant and deliver him to the State authorities at Matteawan.'

Thaw Demanded a Writ.

As Justice Dowling was thus committing Thaw to Matteawan, Thaw leaned over Lawyer O'Reilly's shoulder and whispered to Mr Littleton, his chief counsel. Mr Littleton asked that the court grant a stay of his order until he could confer with his client. District Attorney Jerome, who seemed well satisfied with the verdict, made no objection, and Justice Dowling granted the counsel for the defense a stay of two hours.

Mrs William Thaw, the prisoner's mother, had been notified of the verdict by telephone. She and Mr Littleton then had a long conference. Thaw was for an immediate application for a writ of habeas corpus. The form of the writ had been drawn up the day before by Lawyer Peabody. Everything was in readiness for a fight against Matteawan – all, except Mr Littleton. The chief counsel for the defense believes that Matteawan is better for him than Broadway, and the carefully prepared application for a writ of habeas corpus was not used.

The final disposition of the Thaw case is to come when application is made under a writ of habeas corpus for his release from Matteawan. When this is made, a court of the State will appoint a commission which will pass on his sanity. His form of mental disease – paranoia – is said to be of such nature that cunning in deceit as to the state of his mind is highly developed. His own witnesses have described his mental condition as such that an outbreak may be expected, and it is believed that, for the sake of the community, Mr Jerome will fight any effort that may be made to get him out of Matteawan. Mr Littleton's failure to resort at once to habeas corpus proceedings is taken as an indication of his desire to end his own connections with the case and accept the verdict.

Mrs William Thaw, the mother, and the other members of the Thaw family hope eventually to see the prisoner put in some private asylum and held there for the rest of his life.

Verdict Pleased His Wife.
Evelyn Nesbit Thaw seemed pleased with the result. In her home, which she occupies by herself and without the companionship of any of the Thaw family, 446 Park Avenue, she said yesterday afternoon:

'Considering everything, the verdict was very satisfactory. It was all that we could expect under the circumstances. Further than that I must not say anything, for my lawyers have forbidden me to talk.'

Her husband was not so calm. As he crossed the Bridge of Sighs to get his belongings and start on his journey to Matteawan, he turned to his guard, Deputy Sheriff Bell, and asked who would go with him to the asylum.

'Another deputy and myself,' replied Bell.

'No,' exclaimed Thaw angrily. 'I only want you to go.'

'It doesn't make any difference whom you want to go, young man,' replied Bell, 'for there will be another.'

Thaw's hope for absolute freedom seemed based on the application for a writ of habeas corpus. He expected that an application for it would be made during the afternoon and that it would keep him out of Matteawan. When he found that Mr Littleton would not make the application, he became very angry.

'I will not go to Matteawan; I don't want to go there,' he exclaimed.

'You've got to go,' responded Mr Littleton. 'There's such a thing as public sentiment in this town, and you can't have cold water one day and warm the next.'

'Where did you expect to be sent?' asked Lawyer O'Reilly. 'Rector's or Martin's?'[1]

Thaw was subdued, and left with his wife in the Sheriff's office.

By 4 o'clock he had packed his belongings, and in a few minutes he was in his wife's electric brougham, speeding for the Grand Central Station. There the prisoner, in charge of two deputies, took the 4.54 train for Matteawan. Lawyers O'Reilly and Peabody accompanied him to the asylum. Evelyn Thaw said goodbye with no show of regret. The parting between mother and son occurred Friday afternoon.

Martin W. Littleton said last night that he thought the verdict a righteous one. He would not discuss the matter of probable future effort to get Thaw out of Matteawan.

---

1 Gerald Langford (op cit): 'While Sherry's and Delmonico's catered particularly to the Four Hundred [elite] and their imitators, Martin's and Rector's were more bohemian in their clientele. Located on Long Acre Square (renamed Times Square in 1904), Rector's was a special favourite for after-the-theatre parties, and its green and gold, mirrored main dining room was the regular gathering place for such glamorous stars as Lillian Russell, laced into the hour-glass silhouette that fluttered men's hearts, and Frankie Bailey, whose appearance [on stage] in tights . . . had shown off such stunning legs that "a pair of Frankie Baileys" became Broadway parlance for any good-looking legs. Between the theatre and a stop at Rector's, however, women who were careful of their reputation made a quick trip home to change from low neck to high. To appear décolleté would have given them a label which on some later occasion it might have been embarrassing to disclaim.'

HE'S NO. 719 AT THE ASYLUM.

Thaw Bunks in a Dormitory with 50 Other Male Inmates

Special to The New York Times.

MATTEAWAN, N.Y., Feb.1.—
Harry Thaw, or 'No. 719,' as he will
be known during his stay at the State
Hospital for the Criminal Insane,
arrived at Fishkill Landing on the
6.44 express to-night, and, after
spending nearly three hours over a
good dinner in the village with his
lawyers and the Deputy Sheriffs, was
driven out here. He arrived at the
hospital at a little before 10 o'clock in
a closed carriage in a driving storm of
sleet and rain. An hour later he was
shown into the big dormitory where
he will sleep with fifty other men.
Under the eyes of an unsympathetic
attendant, he undressed and turned
into an iron cot.

When Thaw stepped from his
carriage at the gates of the asylum, he
looked for all the world like a small
boy who had been caught playing
'hookey.' There was a peculiar smile
on his face which seemed to signify
satisfaction at his surroundings and
discomfiture at being in them. He
was dressed in a long, heavy, mixed
gray ulster over a dark sack suit. He
wore a derby, small black bow tie,
and heavy calf shoes.

His party brought no baggage with
them, except a small bundle, which
Thaw carried under his arm, as if he
was momentarily afraid of dropping
it. This bundle was unobtrusive and
small, but it excited the suspicions of
the Third Assistant Deputy Superintendent, who was detailed to take
Thaw's pedigree while the head of
the asylum talked to the reporters,
and he asked Thaw what was in it.

With a sheepish grin, he replied in a
scarcely audible voice, 'Nothing but
an extra shirt.'

When Thaw left the Tombs with
Deputy Sheriffs Bell and McFadden,
County Detective Moore, Lawyers
O'Reilly and Peabody, and his wife
just before 4 o'clock, he was trailed
by a small army of photographers
and reporters. The party managed,
however, to escape the battery both
of questions and flashlights and got
to the Grand Central Station without
being intercepted. There Thaw bade
his wife farewell and she returned to
her home.

When the party entered the
Poughkeepsie Express, they found
the car that had been practically
reserved for them filled with newspaper men and photographers. Thaw
immediately lighted up a big black
cigar and proceeded to issue another
of his 'statements.' All the way up in
the train he sat in the midst of a circle
of reporters, lawyers, and Deputy
Sheriffs, and, between grins,
discussed the weather and kindred
subjects.

Arriving at Fishkill, the photographers got their batteries into
action, but O'Reilly succeeded in
getting in front of Thaw and gave
him the benefit of an eclipse. The
party literally ran across the street to
the Riverview Hotel, where all hands
had a drink. Then they called
carriages and were driven to the
Hotel Holland, where an elaborate
spread had been previously ordered.

A Farewell Feast.

It was without doubt the greatest
feast that any one ever saw in
Fishkill, and surely the best that an
insane prisoner of the State of New
York ever sat down to before enter-

ing the Matteawan Asylum. There
was everything that a Broadway restaurant could produce, from
cocktails to nuts, followed by many
cold bottles and black cigars.
Through it all, the Fishkill folk who
gaped in through the partially drawn
curtains saw Thaw sitting with his
meaningless grin and whispering
into the ears of Mr Peabody in the
same manner that he did through the
trial.

The drive through the rain to the
hospital was without incident. There
again the photographers had
gathered at the gates of the grounds.
They were taken unawares, however, having used up all their flash-
light powder on a carriage load of
reporters which had driven up ten
minutes before.

All they were able to get into
action was very much dampened by
the rain, and the pictures were taken
with sputtering and dim-light
powder.

Thaw walked up the gravel path
beside Lawyer Peabody, tightly
clutching the little bundle under his
arm and paying little attention to his
surroundings. He hardly looked to
right or left. He was met at the door
by an attendant who showed the
party into the reception room. There
seemed to be no excitement about the
hospital over the arrival of the prisoner, and Dr Robert B. Lamb, the
Superintendent, paid no attention to
him at all, but devoted himself to
explaining to the newspaper men just
what Thaw's daily routine would be.

Mr Graber, the Third Assistant
Deputy Superintendent, who was
detailed to look out for Thaw,
received the party and took the
prisoner's pedigree. Thaw answered
the usual questions as to where he
lived and what his name was with a

pleased sort of grin, and then shifted
his little bundle to his lap. Mr Graber
spied it, and the presence of the shirt
and the absence of other baggage
came out.

Then Thaw arose and said good-
bye to the lawyers and deputies,
shaking hands all around, and was
led away to his little iron bed in the
big dormitory. Here he will sleep in
the same room with many other
insane prisoners until his case has
been diagnosed by the doctors and
his assignment to a particular ward
made. Then it is probable that more
comfortable and secluded quarters
will be arranged for him, possibly to
the extent of a room by himself.

The Simple Life for Him.

Thaw's daily life will be very
simple. Until his diagnosis is made,
he will be placed in the Observation
Ward, probably for a week or ten
days. This is a large, airy room, fitted
with chairs and other furniture that
the inmates cannot throw at each
other. About fifty men sit there all
day long. The rising bell in the dormitory rings promptly at 6 o'clock,
and the men then get up and dress
and stand in line for the toilets,
which are too few for the number of
prisoners.

At 7.20 o'clock the inmates of each
ward breakfast in the big dining
room together. Then they file to the
ward, where they sit until luncheon.
Then they have two hours for exercise in the indoor court during bad
weather and out of doors under the
constant eye of an attendant during
good weather. This is the time when
the inmates are allowed the greatest
amount of freedom.

The dining hour is 7, and every
one is sent to his room at 9. Lights are

147

out as soon as they have time to undress.

Thaw will not fare so badly for food if his people do not forget him. Prisoners are allowed to run an account with the asylum cook by which they can order anything they want that is approved by the doctors.

Liquor is forbidden entirely, as is also tobacco, but, as Dr Lamb explained last night, the physicians do not believe in a man who has been used to tobacco being cut off from it immediately. If Thaw happened to have a couple of packs of cigarettes done up in that shirt and he lights one while 'on exercise,' the attendant will probably look the other way for the first week or so. Thaw will not be obliged to wear any regulation uniform, as there is no such thing at Matteawan.

He can see his friends any time they care to visit him. There are no regular visiting days or restrictions on the number of guests an inmate may have.

Postscript (by Jonathan Goodman)

From May 1908, three months after Thaw's arrival in the asylum at Matteawan, his lawyers – an entirely new pack of them – tried to get him out. His first writ of habeas corpus – contested by Jerome, and unsupported by Evelyn (who, it was said, had been bought off by his lawyers from testifying against him) – was dismissed. Evelyn then instituted proceedings to have herself named as custodian of his estate; nothing came of that. In June, Thaw demanded the right to a jury trial to determine whether or not he was sane; having been turned down several times, he took his case to the United States Supreme Court, which ruled against him in December 1909. Meanwhile, he had obtained a second writ of habeas corpus; Evelyn had testified against him, saying that she believed that he was congenitally mad, and so had a retired madam of a Manhattan whorehouse, who recalled that she had rented him rooms, for the ostensible purpose of training girls for the stage, but actually because he wanted sound-proofed quarters in which to pleasure himself by whipping the girls (who, loud at that time, had been paid to be silent during the murder trials); Thaw had rebutted the madam's evidence, saying – in a voice described by a reporter as being 'weak, effeminate, with the hint of an English accent' – that he had visited the brothel solely in the hope that members of the staff might provide him with proof that Stanford White was an immoral person.

By the time of a third habeas corpus hearing, in the summer of 1912, Evelyn was back on the stage, as a vaudeville performer both in America and abroad. While in Europe in 1910, accompanied by a reporter whom she had engaged as her manager, she had given birth to a son – who, she insisted, was Thaw's too, the outcome of a happening during a visit she had paid him in his suite at the asylum. Thaw said that – never mind that Evelyn had named the boy Russell William Thaw – someone other than himself was the founding father. Tit for tat, Evelyn had volunteered to speak against his third habeas corpus application – had stated, under oath, that he had threatened to kill her the minute he was free to do so.

A small conspiracy was revealed in the following spring: then, Thaw gave evidence before a grand jury that a lawyer, not one of his regulars, had asked him for $120,000, twenty thousand of which would go to the superintendent of the asylum, who would, in return, certify that he was sane. The lawyer was convicted of attempted bribery, and (meaning, surely, that the attempt had been successful) the superintendent was sacked.

While all that was going on, Thaw and some of his employees planned his escape. The employees recruited half a dozen small-time crooks, and Thaw bribed the gate-keeper of the asylum – who, early on the morning of Sunday, 17 August 1913, turned a blind eye as Thaw walked through the gate, which had been opened to let a milk-float through, and scampered into a parked car, which headed north a few miles to where another car was parked; Thaw changed cars, and was driven farther north – at 70 mph, according to a man who was nearly knocked over by the car – to a railway station, where he and some of his crook chaperones boarded a train going still farther north; alighting near the Canadian border, Thaw hired a car to take him across it – to the village of St Hermingilde de Garford. Some hours earlier, his escape had been reported by the gate-keeper to the new superintendent; a reward of $500 had been offered for his capture; constables had been posted at every entrance to the hotel in Manhattan where Evelyn was staying – not to stop reporters getting to her, though. She told them:

Harry has threatened to kill me, and I believe my presence in New York prompted him to escape. Four years ago, he told me, 'I suppose I'll have to kill you next.' The State of New York has a great deal to answer for in this case. What Harry Thaw has been allowed to do at Matteawan is an outrage to think of – bribery connived at and keepers bullied by the power of his money. And now he is allowed to escape. I suppose twenty or thirty thousand dollars looks pretty good to some people . . . Harry won't stay in hiding long. A few drinks make him a raving madman, and when that happens he'll head straight for New York . . . He's terribly revengeful. He was that way before he killed Stanford White. In fact, Harry's trouble with Stanford White started over another girl long before he met me.

During the train-journey part of his trip north, Thaw had chatted with another passenger; had told him who he was. The passenger, who happened to be a deputy sheriff, trailed him to St Hermingilde de Garford.

Thaw was arrested there on Tuesday morning. Later in the day, he was taken to Sherbrooke. The eighteen thousand residents of that town having been told of his coming, nearly all of them turned out to welcome him, many chanting, respectively in French and in English, 'Let him go!' and 'Hurrah, hurrah, for British fair play!' Clearly touched, though not surprised, by the reception, Thaw behaved as he believed conquering heroes were supposed to behave in the circumstances.

William Travers Jerome travelled to Sherbrooke to 'talk extradition' with the Quebecian authorities. In his opinion, they were obstructive; after a day or so of hearings, he complained that 'the fine points of Canadian law were such that he would not feel justified in even guessing at the outcome'; he himself was arrested for playing a penny-ante game of chance, stood trial, and was acquitted.

On 10 September, Mounties smuggled Thaw back across the border – into New Hampshire, the authorities of which were quite as obstructive as those of Quebec. It took a year, till December 1914, for Jerome to get Thaw back to New York. In the following year, Thaw tried yet again to prove that he was sane, and on 16 July, at the end of an elongated trial in which much of the evidence presented at his trials for the murder of Stanford White was recapitulated, twelve good men and true found in his favour. The *New York Sun* – suspicious, like many other papers, of how the verdict had been obtained – published an editorial entitled 'How to Be a Hero':

> He guzzles and drabs. The riotous folly of his feast makes Europe sneer at the country that produced such a specimen of the new rich. One night, primed with highball courage, he murders a man of genius. Then for years the courts are full of his fame, and the lawyers of his money. Insane in the act of murder, he escapes its consequences, if murder has any consequences save financial ones for assassins with the price.
>
> At length the long, ignominious drama is ended. The paranoic walks forth free, declared sane by a jury of his intelligent fellow-citizens; and he becomes, as he had previously become even in sober New Hampshire, a conquering hero, the idol of 'the populace'. Cheering crowds crush around him. Women weep over him. Men esteem it an honor to shake the hand crimson with the blood of Stanford White. Washington or Lincoln could not be more deified than this murderer 'with the price'.
>
> In all this nauseous business we don't know which makes the gorge rise more, the pervert buying his way out, or the perverted idiots that hail him with wild huzzas.

As soon as he was officially sane, Thaw sued Evelyn for divorce, citing as corespondent a newspaperman (Evelyn said that she was too busy rehearsing with her new dancing-partner, Jack Clifford, to comment on her husband's sanity or suit), and then went home to Pittsburgh (without the h in the *Times* reports I have quoted; that was the usual spelling then), where thousands of the natives cheered him through the streets to his mother's mansion.

Eighteen months later, Thaw, who was then forty-six, was indicted in New York for the kidnapping and whipping of a Kansas City youth, Frederick Gump, Junior. He went into hiding and meanwhile tried to commit suicide by slashing his throat and wrists with a razor. One of his bodyguards was arrested, and was found to be carrying letters from a number of youths replying to Thaw's offers of jobs at the Highland Iron Works of Pittsburgh, of which Thaw was a non-executive director. So as to save him from being extradited to New York, his mother, saying that she was 'unable to resist the facts that demonstrate his insanity,' arranged for a commission on lunacy to declare him insane and commit him to the mental ward of the Pennsylvania State Hospital, Philadelphia. The Gump family brought suit for $650,000 in damages, and six years later, at the start of 1924, settled out of court for $25,000.

By then, Thaw was trying to get himself declared sane – and Evelyn was insisting that he was as mad as a March hare, always had been, always would be, and that 'their' son had 'an expectant interest in the estate of Harry Thaw . . . and that if he should be freed from restraint and his estate restored to him, he would dissipate and probably wholly destroy the interests which the said Russell William Thaw has as aforesaid'; she received support from staff at the Pennsylvania State Hospital, who gave instances of Thaw's irrational acts, among them his habit of throwing pet rabbits as high as he was able and then pinching and biting them. Twelve good men and true decided that Thaw was as sane as each of them was. Evelyn was 'not surprised at the verdict; there was dirty work at the crossroads, that's all.' She, by the way, had meanwhile married and divorced Jack Clifford.

For a year or so, there were only snippety news items about Thaw and Evelyn: rumours that they were getting together again, that he had bought a house in trust for William Russell Thaw, that he hadn't, that he, as a backer of the next edition of Earl Carroll's *Vanities*, had been a guest at a party during which a chorus girl had taken a bath in a tub filled with champagne till emptied by the thirsty party-goers, who had thereby contravened the Prohibition law. More newsworthily, Evelyn, who was appearing solo in night-clubs, singing songs such as 'I Could Love a Million *Men*' and 'I'm a Broad-minded Broad from Broadway,' broke her contract with a club in Chicago by missing several performances, owing to the fact that she had drunk half a pint of Lysol.

Recovered by the end of 1927, she opened a speakeasy, Chez Evelyn, on West Fifty-Second Street in Manhattan. Thaw turned up there one night, in the company of bodyguards and showgirls, nodded to her while looking puzzled, as if he vaguely recognized her but couldn't think from where, and, at the end of the evening, when presented with a bill for two hundred dollars, emphasized his refusal to pay by overturning a table laden with bottles and glasses. 'It was one of Harry's mild tantrums,' she afterwards remarked. 'You know what he's like.'

Next year, he travelled to Europe; he was refused permission to land in England, so went to Paris instead, and then on to Vienna. Cabled that his mother was seriously ill, he returned home – as did her other surviving children: Margaret, formerly Mrs George Carnegie, now the Countess of Perigny; Alice, formerly the Countess of Yarmouth, now a Mrs Whitney of the Boston Whitneys, and Josiah. Starting before and ending long after his mother's death, Thaw was involved in a series of legal actions brought by a night-club hostess, who claimed that he had beaten her up. In 1937, he was again sued for damages, this time by a waiter whose eye he had blackened during an argument over a bill for champagne. He was not often in the news thereafter. He died on 22 February 1947 in a rented house in Miami; he was seventy-six.

Towards the end of 1928, Chez Evelyn had to be closed because Evelyn and whoever her backers were could not afford the increased pay-offs demanded by Prohibition agents. During the next few years, she ran clubs, or simply sang in clubs, in Atlantic City, Manhattan, Chicago, and Panama City (where the club, called the Kelly Ritz, was actually a brothel). Then little was heard of her till after the Second World War, by which time she was living in a lodging house in Hollywood, apparently supported by her son. She visited Manhattan in 1955 for the première of a movie called *The Girl in the Red Velvet Swing* (that object said to have been installed by Stanford White in his apartment, specially for Evelyn to swing in), starring Ray Milland as White, Farley Granger as Thaw, and Joan Collins as Evelyn. Returning to Hollywood, to the lodging house, she seems to have become obsessed with theosophy; between religion-studying times, she painted and potted. In the early 1960s, then being looked after in a nursing home, she told a visiting reporter: 'Stanny was lucky – he died. I lived.' Supposing that her birth-date in the Hummel affidavit was accurate, she was eighty-one when she died in 1966.

★　　　★　　　★

Of course, Evelyn and Thaw respectively gave their names to books of Revelations advertised as being STARTLING. Nowadays, the one of those books most easily acquired secondhand is that which appeared, ostensibly the work of Evelyn, in 1934: the American edition, published by Julian Messner Inc, New York, is called *Prodigal Days: The Untold Story*, while the English edition – from John Long Ltd, London – uses the sub-title solitarily. There are clear signs that the so-called autobiography was borne by an anonymous literary surrogate.

One of the most perplexing biblio-mysteries is why certain books, having sold gratifyingly to their publishers, become rare, in some instances almost unobtainable, when out of print. Nearly all dealers in and collectors of criminous literature believe that there is only one book, *The Untold Story*, said to be the work of Evelyn. They are wrong. John Hogan, who by 1982 had the most complete collection of the writings of Edgar Wallace, then, as he now explains, added to it:

Edgar Wallace did not employ ghost-writers, but he did ghost-write for another.

While sorting through copies of the many agreements made between Wallace and various publishers, I came upon one which immediately attracted my attention. There was a letter on Grand Hotel, Paris, notepaper, dated 24 May 1913, in Wallace's handwriting but addressed to himself:

Dear Mr Wallace,

On condition that you write and prepare for publication a book provisionally entitled 'The Story of My Life' by Evelyn Thaw I agree to share the proceeds of all sales and royalties equally (fifty per cent and fifty per cent). It is understood that you bear all preliminary expenses and that you will dispose of all right, serial, book, etc, on terms mutually agreeable to ourselves.

Yours faithfully
EVELYN THAW (her signature).

With this letter there was a statement also written on Grand Hotel, Paris, notepaper, and again written by Edgar Wallace, reading:

Drawing by Birch Burdette Long of Madison Square Garden, 1891

A Literate Killer

Pierre-François Lacenaire

I authorise Edgar Wallace to act as my literary agent for the disposal of 'The Story of My Life': a book of 60,000 to 80,000 words. I agree to allow him to dispose of all rights on my behalf on such terms as shall be mutually agreed between us.

EVELYN THAW (her signature).

The letter and statement were attached to a copy of a Memorandum of Agreement made on 23 July 1913 between Edgar Wallace and John Long for the latter to publish *The Story of My Life* by Evelyn Thaw:

BETWEEN EDGAR WALLACE of Shoe Lane in the County of London, hereinafter termed the 'proprietor', of the one part and JOHN LONG of 12, 13, 14 Morris Street, Haymarket, in the same county, hereinafter termed 'The Publishers', of the other part. Whereby it is mutually agreed . . . as follows:

1. The Proprietor shall deliver to the Publishers in complete form ready for the printers within three weeks from the date hereof a work to be written by Evelyn Thaw under the title of 'THE STORY OF MY LIFE' together with Portraits of the leading characters and herself, such Portraits to be delivered to the publishers free of charge and copyright . . . Upon such delivery as aforesaid the Publishers shall at their own expense produce the Work as a Demy 8vo volume (that is eight and three quarter inches by six) incorporating therein reproductions of the aforesaid Portraits, publish at the price of seven shillings and sixpence per copy, and advertise . . .

(The agreement runs to eleven numbered paragraphs and is signed by 'John Long, Managing Director', and initialled by Edgar Wallace.)

Reference to Jonathan Goodman brought the loan of, among other books, *The Untold Story*. Within a few more days, Gerald Austin of John Long Ltd (then part of the Hutchinson Publishing Group) confirmed that they had published *The Story of My Life* in April 1914, an 8vo book with eight illustrations and 254 pages. This is the only known instance of Edgar Wallace ghosting a book. While I learned that there were copies in the British Library, the Bodleian, and the National Library reserve in the Lawnmarket, Edinburgh, I searched for several years to find a copy for my collection.

On the day in 1982 when I was asked to speak at the Edgar Wallace dinner in Greenwich, celebrating the 50th anniversary of his death, I heard from an old bookdealer-friend that he had found a copy of the book for me. I believe it to be the only copy held by a collector.

Harry Thaw called his book *The Traitor* – but, feeling that those couple of words were inadequate, added, *Being the Untampered With, Unrevised Account of the Trial and All That Led to It*. The verso of the title page carries the copyright date, 1926. On the title page itself, the publishers are said to be Dorrance and Company, Philadelphia; however, at the foot of the spine of the crimson-and-black dustjacket are the words 'ARGUS Publisher' – and confusion is worse confounded by the back of the jacket, which carries an advertisement for books published by Ben Abramson, of 3 West Forty-Sixth Street, New York 19.

What seems to have happened is that Thaw arranged for Dorrance and Company to publish the book at his expense; but, having fallen out with them after the book had been printed and bound, paid them off and made a deal with Abramson-cum-Argus to wrap jackets round the copies and to act as distributors. That doesn't explain the schizophrenia of Argus and Abramson on the jacket. Going by the advertisement, Abramson seems to have specialized in short runs of literary curiosities (one of the books he offers is *The Circus of Dr Lao* by Charles Finney, 'a wonderful, mad, magnificent work . . . Gay and fantastic illustrations! Limited edition, $5.00'): therefore, it may be that, treating the large number of copies of Thaw's book as a sideline, he coined the name Argus for that book alone, differentiating it from his own productions.

Unlike Evelyn's books, Thaw's was all his own work. There is no doubt about that. His madness clouds every page. The title-tagging claim, *Unrevised*, is horrifyingly true – but *Untampered With* is inaccurate. There are several signs of tampering, the most obvious relating to a reference in Chapter XII to a letter said to have been written by Stanford White: 'It is in Chapter XXVII,' Thaw writes – and adds, 'but do not read that yet.' Ignoring that order, one turns to Chapter XXVII – only to find, beneath the words, 'See the letter, a classic, seemingly so harmless yet nakedly so appalling:', a space, blank apart from the explanation: 'Censor Cuts This Out'. Although the eponymous Traitor is not named, there is a littering of clues to the fact that Thaw's paranoia was aimed at Judge William Olcott, a family friend who, soon after the murder, offered to defend Thaw but was dismissed because of his insistence on commissioning 'bug-doctors' to testify that Thaw was crazy.

Reverting to Evelyn's *Untold Story*, a number of things said in the book contradict things she said at the trials of Thaw for the murder of Stanford White. For instance, most of the incidents referred to in the Hummel affidavit appear also in the book. Though she testified that she had hated White, the *Untold Story* has her loving him and wanting to keep him all to herself: '. . . when I came across a little book in which he had recorded the birthday of every pretty girl he knew, I became violently jealous . . . Like a silly child, I wanted to make him jealous of me.'

If it was with that intention that she took up with Thaw, she may also subsequently have wanted to make *Thaw* jealous – by overstating White's devotion to her. Thereby, she would have given a madman a motive for murder.

A Literate Killer

Rayner Heppenstall

26 May 1969: I saw *Les Enfants du Paradis* shortly after the War. I was principally taken, like everyone else, with the miming of Jean-Louis Barrault and an extraordinary comic performance by Pierre Brasseur. I did not then know that most of the characters were based on historical figures or that the book was by Jacques Prévert. I did not know this for some years after meeting both Prévert and the actor, Marcel Herrand, who had played the murderer Lacenaire, of whom at the time I had never heard . . . I have been watching for a repeat showing of the film and noticed only this morning that it was on at the Academy cinema today, Whit Monday. M. [Mrs Margaret Heppenstall] and I went to see it this afternoon. Less good in a number of ways than it seemed when I first saw it, but still very nice.[1]

PIERRE-FRANÇOIS LACENAIRE was born in Lyons, the second son and third child of Jean-Baptiste Lacenaire and Marguerite Gaillard. The date of his birth was 20 December in the year 1803, according to legal and military records, but 1800 by his own insistence. Much of his short working life was spent as a lawyer's clerk or legal copyist, and he was to show natural gifts as a barrister.

Thirty years older than his wife, Jean-Baptiste had retired from business as a dealer in pig-iron but, after marriage, returned to it as a silk-merchant. In politics he was very much a

---

1 An entry in *The Master Eccentric: The Journals of Rayner Heppenstall 1969–81*, edited by Jonathan Goodman, Allison & Busby, London, 1986.

throne-and-altar man and under Jesuit influence, abjectly so according to his son. Pierre-François was put out to wet nurse and long kept away from home, so that, perhaps justly, he believed himself to be detested by his mother, to whom, however, later he was bound by close ties of love. He had a favourite sister, and he disliked, but would remain charitable about, an older brother, who was thought in the family incapable of wrong but in fact stole from his parents and taught his younger brother to do so, himself never found out. A story shows young Pierre-François and his father out walking one evening and seeing the guillotine set up in a public square in Lyons. Father inevitably said that it was to that the boy would come unless he changed his ways. Lacenaire was to make much of this later. In his dreams, he would say, he had lived with the guillotine ever since. It may be so, and fathers ought to be careful, but the observation is one we may imagine millions of French fathers making to their sons over a period of a century and more, perhaps especially in the provinces.

For reasons of personal turbulence, free thought and forbidden reading or unpopularity with masters and with the parents of his schoolfellows, the boy was, it seems, expelled from three schools in Lyons before going to the seminary at Alix near Villefranche. In due course, he was expelled from that, too, though a brilliant pupil and remembered with affection by at least one of his masters, no more than a few years older than himself, Reffay de Lusignan, presumably at the time not yet in full clerical orders but later Rev. Fr. Reffay de Lusignan, S.J. A schoolfellow, Laput, who became a lawyer, was not to remember Lacenaire with affection. Coeur and Sauzet, who were to rise to dizzying heights, were no doubt pre-occupied with their own ambitions, ecclesiastical or political. In his Memoirs, Chief Inspector Louis Canler speaks of Lacenaire as having been the most gifted pupil in his year and as having many friends when he left at the age of seventeen, which would be either in 1821 or in 1818, at any rate under Louis XVIII.

A lawyer's office in Lyons, a first visit to Paris, a first enlistment and desertion, a return to Lyons and some attempt to earn a living as a commercial traveller in wines and spirits, a second visit to Paris, a return to Lyons with forged bills of exchange, possibly visits to Italy and Switzerland, occupied the young man until he was rising either twenty-five or twenty-eight, when he re-enlisted in Montpellier (giving, he says, the wrong age, making himself out to be younger than he was) and may have served in the Morea campaign. That was in 1828. The Memoirs[1] published eight years later in his name were, certainly, written in large part by him (he was to be seen writing them in prison), but nobody knows with certainty who got at them or to just what extent before they appeared on the market, nor does anyone know to what extent Pierre Lacenaire was a compulsive liar, though a totally creditable police chief, Pierre Allard, is on record as considering him a man of honour, his word to be trusted once he had given it. We should, I fancy, totally reject the claim in his Memoirs that Lacenaire ever travelled in England and Scotland, and we may doubt his eight duels and two early murders, one with a pocket pistol in Italy, one by tipping a man late at night over the parapet of a bridge.

It is certain that he was not of powerful physical constitution and that soldiering cannot have suited him, though he was wiry and not without stamina. From engravings we may see that he was thin and that his eyes were widely spaced, somewhat deepset and at times wild in expression, his nose long and prominent, his chin rather weak and cleft, the mouth small and shaded by a drooping moustache, the forehead high, the darkish hair not thick. A physician who also told bumps (phrenology remained in fashion) describes Lacenaire after trial in terms which suggest degeneracy, even premature senility (and gives the colour of his eyes as tawny, his complexion as pale and sometimes livid). He was a heavy drinker, but no great womaniser. He wrote verse with exceptional facility, but set little store by it, and there is every reason to believe that already on his first stay in Paris a vaudeville sketch by him was performed and that later he ghosted for Eugène Scribe.

Army records show that Private Lacenaire, P.-F., deserted from the 16th Infantry of the Line in March 1829. He made his way to Lyons and found nobody at home. His father had gone bankrupt and fled with his family to Brussels. An aunt who had lost money in the business refused to help him. He went to Paris

1 Editor's note: An English translation of them by Philip John Stead was published by Staples Press, London, in 1952.

and was there greeted stonily by another aunt, who also had lost money in the business. He tried various journals for which he had written before, but there was no work for him. His mother sent him five hundred francs from Brussels, but that was soon gone.

> In fact, within a matter of days, I was reduced to the point at which I almost died of hunger. From that moment I became a thief, and at heart a murderer. . . I resolved to become the scourge of society, but could do nothing alone; I needed associates, but where to find them? I had never quite known what it was to be a thief by profession, but latterly I had read *Les Mémoires de Vidocq*;[1] this had given me an idea of that class in a state of constant feud against society. . . It was essential that I should spend some time in the company of those people . . . Thus I crossed my Rubicon. I must next commit some theft which did not bear too heavy a penalty.

And then he must learn thieves' slang, of which indeed *Les Mémoires de Vidocq* had already provided him with a smattering. The date of decision was 10 May 1829, and we may note that at this juncture Lacenaire, posted as a deserter, adopted his mother's maiden name and was known as Gaillard.

What he in fact did to get himself into prison and learn thieves' slang was steal and sell a hired cab. He thereafter made no attempt to evade arrest, but quite the reverse. More interestingly, it appears that between theft and arrest, he fought a duel with the nephew of Benjamin Constant (author of *Adolphe*) and killed him. The occasion of this duel is obscure. Then, tried and sentenced under the name of Gaillard, Lacenaire went to prison in August for a year. This was longer than he had intended. He had expected six months. At Ste Pélagie, he made the acquaintance of the poet Béranger, there for the second time on account of his fourth published collection of songs. From Ste Pélagie, Lacenaire was transferred to Poissy, where he found the company tedious but made satisfactory progress in his study of *argot*.

★ ★ ★

1 Editor's note: An anonymously translated abridgement of them was published by Bell, London, in 1928.

After his release from Poissy in August 1830, he seems to have practised theft successfully for a while but presently to have settled down for two years as a legal copyist, a life with which it appears he was not dissatisfied and which evidently kept him safe from cholera and street riots. Things did not again go seriously wrong for him until the beginning of 1833, when some theft of stamped paper or carelessness in copying an engrossment made his name one no longer to be heard around the Palais de Justice. He called on a number of literary people, among them Jules Janin, with whom he had been at school in Lyons, and Eugène Scribe, for whom he had worked before. These two gave him small sums of money, or, he is reported to have said, he would have killed them.

The next racket was blackmailing homosexuals, employing a boy as *agent provocateur*. Lacenaire and a man he had known at Poissy would appear, pretending to be policemen, and catch the boy and his customer *in flagrante delicto* in the Champs Elysées. There was also, if we may trust the Memoirs here, an attempt on a man closely watched at the gaming tables. This took place on 14 March, and Lacenaire and his friend went to it armed with sharpened bradawls. The attempt failing, they took to stealing silver forks from restaurants, and Lacenaire was caught. By July, he was in La Force, to start a sentence of thirteen months. Among his fellow-prisoners, some were there for political offences, and it seems to have been to amuse these that he, not himself politically minded, wrote what was to become the best-known of his poems.

THIEF'S PETITION TO A KING
HIS NEIGHBOUR

Sire, of your grace, listen to me;
I have just come from the hulks. . .
I am a thief, you are King,
Let's work together, like friends and brothers.
Honest folk give me the creeps,
My heart is hard, my soul vile,
I am pitiless and devoid of honour:
Ah! set me up as a policeman.

Good! here I am a policeman now!
It isn't much of a reward;
Appetite grows with what it feeds on,
Come, Sire, indulge me a little;
I am as peevish as a cur,
And my malice is that of an old ape;
I should do France as much credit as Gisquet:
Make me prefect of police.

I am, I hope, a satisfactory prefect;
No prison is big enough;
This profession is nevertheless not adequate,
I do really feel, to my deserts.
I know how to gobble up funds,
I can cook the books.
I will sign myself: 'Your subject';
Ah! Sire, let me be a minister.

Sire, dare I still lodge a complaint? . . .
But listen to me without anger:
The wish I am about to express
Might indeed cause you some displeasure.
I am two-faced, miserly, spiteful,
Mean, ruthless, greedy.
I drove my kinsman to hang himself;
Sire, give up your position to me.

The last line but one has been taken to refer to the death of the Prince de Condé,[1] which had benefited the house of Orleans even if it were the unaided work of Sophie Dawes.[1] Lacenaire evidently accepted the official view that it was suicide, and so presumably at that moment did his Republican friends.

1 In August 1830, the aged Condé was found hanged or, at any rate, suspended by the neck in his bedroom. In September, a judicial inquiry found that it has been suicide. Nobody believed this for a moment, and there is a good case to be made for the belief that the old man was murdered, because of the threat of a change of will, by a Baronne de Fleuchère who is more properly known to us as Sophie Dawes, a whore from the Isle of Wight, and whom the prince had won at cards in London twenty years before. The will as it stood divided the estate between her and the juvenile Duc d'Aumale, the king's son, so that Carlists, Republicans and Bonapartists alike were ready enough to believe that she had smothered the prince in his bed and suspended him (not that she lacked the strength) with Orleanist help.

In July 1834, Poissy again disgorged him. By that time, he knew *argot* only too well and did not wish ever to spend a third term in prison. He would, he said, even prefer one of the convict stations, for in those at least you caught a glimpse of the sea. He knew well enough, all the same, that his was not the physical constitution to thrive in the naval dockyards at Toulon, Rochefort or Brest. It would be better to be executed. The thing was not to steal except in circumstances which precluded a long prison sentence. To be on the safe side, each theft should be accompanied by murder. If you got away with it, that would be nice. Lacenaire would have consented to become rich by undetected theft with murder, but the crime had to be such that a capital sentence would ensue upon its discovery. At Poissy, Lacenaire had become acquainted with a short, raucous-voiced man, Victor Avril, who, though he had been deprived of the advantages of education, had been brought to a similar conclusion. Avril, however, would not be out till late October.

In the meantime, there was always the literary and theatrical world, where there might be pickings for a man who knew his way around. A newspaper proprietor encouraged Lacenaire to write about his prison experiences, but appears to have cheated him. At the Folies Dramatiques, Frederick Lemaître had not that time revived *L'Auberge des Adrets* in its old form but got the authors to collaborate with him in a play derived from it, called *Robert Macaire*, which did not need imposed codding, for a strong element of farce had been written into it. Lacenaire saw this play and seems rather to have missed the point.

From the Memoirs of Chief Inspector Louis Canler:

On 14 December 1834, a horrid crime spread alarm and terror among the inhabitants of one of the most populous neighbourhoods in the capital. An old woman, Widow Chardon, who lived with her son in Red Horse Passage off the Rue St Martin, was found murdered at home, and the same hand which had struck the mother had also struck the son. Their apartment consisted of two rooms, each with a window, one opening on to the Rue St Martin over the passage entrance, the other on to the passage itself. In the first room, the son Chardon was lying in a pool of blood; a blood-stained axe, abandoned near by, and the manner in which his head was split, showed clearly enough how the crime had been committed. In the second room, the mother's body was found on the bed; sheets, pillows and covers were piled upon it, as though the murderer had wished to spare himself the sight. On every hand, moreover, broken furniture, forced locks and scattered linen abundantly testified that theft had been the prime motive of the murder, and that both the one and the other had been committed.

The son Chardon was nicknamed 'Auntie' and widely known for his *antiphysical* tastes, and so it was on abject creatures known to share these that suspicion first fell. Several of these filthy fellows were arrested and then released for want of proof. Others were simply watched, but without result.

On 31 December, at about half past three in the afternoon, a bank messenger, Genevey, a youth of eighteen, went to a house in the Rue Montorgueil, to collect payment on two drafts from a Sieur Mahossier, on the fourth floor at the rear. The name MAHOSSIER was written in white chalk capitals on a door. He knocked: two men appeared to be expecting him in a room furnished only with two bales of straw and a basket with a board over it. As soon as he entered, the door was shut behind him. One of the two unknown men tried to take off him a portfolio containing 10,000 francs in bank-notes and a satchel containing 1100 francs in coin, at the same time striking at his right shoulder a blow with a sharp, triangular instrument which pierced almost through to his breast, while the second man sought to stifle the victim's cries, hand over his mouth. But Genevey was a robust young man; in spite of his wound he fought back, and shouted so loudly that the two murderers took fright and ran off, shutting the alley gate and themselves crying: 'Help! Thief!' in the street.

They escaped, and at first the Sûreté had no success with this matter either. For the moment, Chief Inspector Canler was unavailable.

A man who had led an attempted prison riot at La Force had nevertheless been released before the end of the year. His name was Desjardins. He was seen around La Courtille, a neighbourhood to the north-east of Paris full of dram-shops, billiard saloons, dance-halls and brothels, much frequented by the criminal fraternity. This meant that he was *en rupture de ban,* the whole Paris area being out of bounds to him. Canler with six of his men and two informers therefore went off to arrest him, a perilous undertaking which they accomplished in the face of a drunk and threatening crowd of two hundred or so assorted villains and screeching tarts. That was on 7 January. No sooner had Canler handed Desjardins in at the Belleville guard post than he was fetched to deal with the murder of a hatter elsewhere. On the 9th, however, the case of the assault on the bank messenger was assigned to him.

His first visit was, naturally, to the greengrocer who owned the house in the Rue Montorgueil. The name MAHOSSIER was still on the door in white chalk. The greengrocer described this Mahossier, but the description meant nothing to Canler. The greengrocer couldn't remember the other man. Canler trudged round hotels and lodging-houses near the Temple, on the Île de la Cité, up the hill to Montmartre. He found the name 'Mahossier' in the books of one in the Rue du Faubourg du Temple, No 107, and underneath it 'Ficellier'. The two had been there only one day. They'd shared a bed. The landlady, a Mme Pageot, described Ficellier, a big, red-haired man. It sounded to Canler uncommonly like one François, who'd been picked up for false pretences at a wineshop only a few days before. He was still at the central police station.

I visited him in his cell, and, taking my notebook out of my pocket, I opened it and pretended to be looking for a name I'd forgotten: 'François,' I said, 'I've been racking my brains all day, wondering what made you book in at Ma Pageot's under the name of Ficellier. You tell me you'd nothing to do with that bit of fraud you're charged with.' 'No,' said he, 'I hadn't. But there was a warrant out for me, wasn't there? and they always say: "If they reckon I've pinched the towers of Notre Dame, I'm off, quick." I wasn't such a muggins as to give my real monicker, when the dicks was after me.'

So it had been François. I made out a report in which I designated him as one of the authors of the crime committed on 31 December. Next day I went back to the hotel in the Rue du Faubourg du Temple. Pageot was out, and his wife was more communicative on this occasion. The Sieur Mahossier had stayed there before, but not under that name. Then he had booked in by the name of Bâton.

Bâton was traced and arrested. He bore no resemblance to the descriptions of Mahossier. Neither the greengrocer in the Rue Montorgueil nor the bank messenger recognized him. Bâton had to be released. But Canler had heard of his intimacy with a man called Gaillard. They'd been 'school friends'. That is to say, they'd been in prison together, at Poissy. Bâton was asked to describe this Gaillard. It sounded as though he were Mahossier. So now Canler went round looking at hotel books again for a Gaillard. He found no fewer than twenty in the past year. One of them had stayed at No 15, Rue Marivaux des Lombards.

I asked the landlady whether this individual had ever had visitors and what sort of people he mixed with.

'Oh, Lord, sir,' she replied, 'I never saw anybody call, except a woman with a handkerchief over her head. She came quite often, but I don't know her name or where she lived.'

'Did he leave anything behind? Any clothing, papers?'

'Yes, I'm forgetting. On a shelf in that room I discovered a bundle of Republican songs. I've got them here in a drawer.'

There was also a draft of a letter addressed to M. Gisquet, the prefect of police. It was not very respectful. But the handwriting, those capitals! I had seen them in white chalk on a door. They had spelt the name MAHOSSIER. I made my report to M. Allard. He told me to fetch François Ficellier, who'd been moved to another prison. I went for him with a cab. He sat beside me, handcuffed.

'Yes, his name's Gaillard,' said François, 'and there's something else I can tell you, Monsieur Canler. This has got nothing to do with the bank messenger at the Rue Montorgueil. I know who did the Widow Chardon and her son on 14 December. I'll tell you how I know. I was crossing the Place Royale on New Year's Day, about one o'clock. I met this Gaillard with a geyser I hadn't seen before. He came along with us to a wine-dealer's, and we had a big spread, but then this fellow went. Me and Gaillard, we had another bottle and then another and then another. I don't know how many bottles we had, but we were still in that wineshop at one o'clock in the morning. Then he begins to talk. He says he done 'Auntie' Chardon and the widow while the geyser who just left kept a look-out in the street. Then he has a look round. All he found was a few twenty and forty franc pieces, not much of a lay when you think of the trouble he took.'

At La Force, the prisoner Avril had intimated that he wanted to talk. Avril was in for a year. He'd just begun the sentence. We don't know what it was for. Avril knew Gaillard, he said. Nobody knew him better. If M. Canler would get him out of La Force, he'd find Gaillard. Avril was released and followed, without result. Gaillard must have left Paris, he said. He gave Canler another lead. In the Rue Bar-du-Bec, Gaillard had an aunt, an old girl, quite rich, Mme Gaillard. Canler and his chief, Allard called together on Mme Gaillard. She peered at them through a judas in the door. They said that they were police officers and that they wanted a word with her nephew, Gaillard. She let them in. That wasn't his name, she said. She was afraid of him, afraid of being murdered. That was why she'd had a judas put in the door. If he'd come, she wouldn't have let him in. His name was Lacenaire. That was the name of the man her poor sister had married in Lyons. He'd had all her money, and now they were in Belgium.

A few days later, the prefecture had a letter from the district attorney in Beaune, where Lacenaire, under the name of Jacob Lévy, had been caught passing a forged bill of exchange. He had in fact left Paris on 9 January, the day on which the bank-messenger case had been assigned to Louis Canler. The date of his arrest in Beaune had been 2 February. He was sent to Paris fettered. Canler and Allard went to see him in his cell at the central police station. The man lying on the camp bed, with fifteen pounds of iron on his feet, answered to the descriptions Canler must have received from the greengrocer, the hotel keeper, François and Avril (thin, pale, didn't look very strong, high forehead, hooded eyes, moustache, long nose, very well-spoken, an educated man, might have been a gentleman down on his luck, so we may imagine those brief acquaintances saying). Both Chief Inspector Canler and Superintendent Pierre Allard were, for a variety of reasons, to take more than the usual interest in their prisoner.

We talked to him about the crime in the Rue Montorgueil; he admitted to being one of the authors of that crime, but without effrontery as without remorse. He spoke of the affair as a business man might speak of a deal which hadn't come off. We then asked him who his accomplices had been, but he answered vehemently:

'Gentlemen, we villains have our code. Our self-esteem requires us not to denounce our accomplices, unless they have first betrayed us. So please do not ask for names.'

'It wasn't really necessary to ask you that question,' I said. 'We know who your accomplice was: it was François.' (Lacenaire denied this with a smile.) 'And I can also tell you that it was you who killed Chardon and his mother.'

Then I told him what François himself had revealed.

'Ah!' he said to us when I had finished, 'ah! François said that! Well, all right, when I'm at La Force, I'll find out a bit more, then we shall see . . .'

'Not only did François split on you, but for a week I walked about the streets of Paris with Avril, from lodging-house to lodging-house, from wineshop to wineshop, looking for you, Avril being engaged, at his own request, for the purpose of pointing you out.'

'Ah! him too,' continued Lacenaire, 'really, him too? Well, gentlemen, I'll go into that also, and no doubt I shall then have the honour of seeing you again.'

And, indeed, some while after this conversation, we were told, my chief and I, that Lacenaire wanted to talk to us.

After having been transferred to La Force, he was removed from there by order of the examining magistrate, and we found him in the mousetrap, a big underground room in which prisoners wait when they are due for interrogation . . .

What Canler does not tell us, but what we may discover not only from the Memoirs but from the trial proceedings and from a contemporary engraving by J. A. Beauce, is that Lacenaire's enquiries at La Force and perhaps threats uttered by him led to him being savagely beaten up by friends of François, so that, prior to his reappearance at the Conciergerie, he had spent some weeks in the infirmary. The *souricière* in the basement of the Palais de Justice seems to have been the place in which prisoners normally saw their lawyers before going up to the *juge d'instruction*'s office. Apart from members of the armed constabulary on duty, it is likely that the police did not ordinarily go there. It would be in order for Allard and Canler to see Lacenaire in the mousetrap, since he had asked for them, but even so Canler speaks of them being introduced to the place by a warder's wife, whom he names.

. . . Lacenaire was alone; he greeted us and said:

'Gentlemen, when you came to see me at the central police station, you informed me what François had said about me and what Avril had done to procure my arrest. I told you that I would make my own inquiries; I have made them and am satisfied. I said to you also that villains like myself denounced only those who had betrayed them: well, then! everything François told you about the Chardon murder was true, except that in first discussing it with him I incriminated a third party, who is entirely innocent. I shall now give you full particulars of that double crime and who my accomplices were, both in that and in the Rue Montorgueil affair. In the latter, M. Canler was not mistaken, it was indeed François who was with me at the time. I know very well that, for the Rue Montorgueil, I shall be sentenced to hard labour for life, while for the earlier matters I shall take my head to the scaffold, but there we are, it's the only means I have of avenging myself on Avril and François, who betrayed me in so cowardly a manner.'

Thereupon, with indignation fed by his rancour, Lacenaire recounted to us the details of the two crimes, details which I shall not report here, since the trial made them sufficiently familiar, but which incontestably established the guilt of François and Avril.

In his Memoirs, Lacenaire speaks very highly of Pierre Allard (he does not mention Canler). He also puts in a good word for all the prison staff and the magistrates in Paris (by contrast, apparently, with those in the provinces and especially Beaune). In the first place, the examining magistrate on the bank-messenger case seems to have been a M. Jourdain, but we read only of Lacenaire having to do with a M. Michelin, to whom we may suppose that the Chardon murders had been allocated before connection had been established between the two crimes. When the composite case came up for public hearing, the presiding judge would be M. Dupuy, counsel for the prosecution M. Partarrieu-Lafosse. To defend Lacenaire, M. Dupuy appointed a young advocate, Maître Brochant, François's defending counsel was to be Maître Laput, who had been a fellow-pupil of Lacenaire's at the seminary near Villefranche in Reffay de Lusignan's time. Hearing of the case, M. Reffay wrote to Lacenaire asking whether there was anything he could do. Later, he came to Paris.

To be in Paris suited Lacenaire. He felt that he would be appearing before his natural judges. It had depressed him to be caught in Beaune.

> It was in Paris that I wanted to die. I shan't hide the fact, it would have been most disagreeable for me to have to do with a provincial executioner. Dear Paris! Dear Barrière St Jacques! . . .

No doubt there is some dandyism in that, but the prospect of death at the hands of Executioner Sanson and his men really does seem to have appealed to Lacenaire. In the Memoirs, he speaks of sitting, one late evening, on the parapet of the Pont des Arts, near where they had buried 'those stupid heroes of July' (it was at the time of his first release from Poissy in 1830), and of having a vision. From that moment, his life was a revengeful suicide. He no longer belonged to himself, but to cold steel, not the knife or the razor or, presumably, the sharpened bradawl, but the great, consoling blade of the guillotine. The guillotine was his bride, his lovely betrothed.

Lacenaire was formally moved to the Conciergerie in the last week of October. The journey from La Force to the Conciergerie was a short one. The prison of La Force, a formal ducal mansion, stood at the corner of the Rue Pavée, which still exists, and the Rue des Ballets, which doesn't. The *panier à salade* (no longer constructed of wicker, the term still reserved facetiously to police vans) turned into the Rue St Antoine (which is a continuation of the Rue de Rivoli, and in 1835 still ran through the narrow Arcade St Jean to be pulled down a year or two later to make room for extensions to the City Hall) into what had once been the Place de Grève and then along the embankment. Lacenaire would have made the journey quite frequently before, in a small rear compartment separated by a grating from an usher and a town policeman, while a mounted constable rode alongside.

The trial of Lacenaire, François and Avril was due to open on 12 November, a Thursday. The rule now is that the judge appointed to preside over a case before the Court of Assize must visit the accused in his place of confinement not less than five days before the trial opens. It was perhaps thus immediately after M. Dupuy's visit to Lacenaire that the latter held a kind of press conference in what is said to have been the infirmary at La Force. There were doctors and barristers present as well as journalists. Their conversation was reported partly in *Le Constitutionnel* and partly in *Le Charivari*.

Lacenaire sat by the stove, in the middle of us, talked literature, morality, politics, religion, with a pertinence, clarity of thought, a reflective depth and a precision of memory which left the greater number of us speechless.

A Doctor:	How is it that your intelligence did not protect you against yourself?
Lacenaire:	Ah! there came a day in my life when I had no other alternatives than suicide or crime.
Doctor:	Why, then, did you not choose suicide?
Lacenaire:	I asked myself whether I was my own victim or society's.
Doctor:	Those you struck had done you no harm.
Lacenaire:	I was sorry for them, but they were part of the whole against which I had taken up my stand.
Doctor:	So you were murdering systematically.
Lacenaire:	Yes, I had adopted murder as a means of livelihood.
Doctor:	Were you never in one of those states of frenzy which make crime seem pleasurable?
Lacenaire:	No.
Doctor:	In that case, you did what you did coldly, as it might have been a commercial transaction?
Lacenaire:	Yes.
Doctor:	How did you manage to stifle any feeling of pity in yourself?
Lacenaire:	A man does whatever he chooses to do. I am not cruel by nature; but the means had to be in harmony with the end.
Doctor:	And so you never experienced remorse?
Lacenaire:	Never.
Doctor:	Nor fear?

Lacenaire: No. My head was at stake. I wasn't counting on impunity; for, if there is one thing we are forced to believe in, it is justice, for society is founded on order.

Doctor: The idea of death doesn't frighten you?

Lacenaire: Not at all. We must all die, mustn't we? When I see old men dragging themselves along and fading away in a long and painful death, I say to myself that it is better to die at one *stroke*, in the possession of all one's faculties.

Doctor: If you were able to, would you commit suicide now to escape the ignominy of the scaffold?

Lacenaire: No, I could have done that before shedding blood. A murderer, I saw that I had established a bond, a contract between the scaffold and myself, that my life was no longer my own, but belonged to the law and the headsman.

Doctor: For you, then, it will be an expiation?

Lacenaire: No, a simple consequence, the payment of a gaming debt.

Doctor: Do you believe that everything ends with life?

Lacenaire: It is a subject I have never thought about.

Later, however, Lacenaire admits that he believes in the migration of intelligence into all natural bodies. From the calm way in which this man, fortunately exceptional, discourses on the dogmas of Pythagorean philosophy, it might be Plato talking with his disciples on Cape Sunium.

Lacenaire: It seems to me that the principle which animates organic and living beings may, when it leaves them, enter into crude matter, remain there, cause it to live for a while in its own way, then later pass into other bodies. Everything lives, everything feels. This stone has its life and its intelligence.

Doctor: Crude bodies haven't; sensation is found only in organic, living bodies, those in which impressions are transmitted to a common centre, the brain, which perceives them and converts them into sensations; interrupt this communication, and impressions are no longer conveyed to the brain, there is no more perception, no more sensation. This happens

173

with apoplexy and with the paralysis which ensues.
You may cut or burn the paralysed limb, vainly;
impressions are no longer transmitted to the brain;
the individual feels nothing. It is the same with a
man whose head has just been cut off . . .

At these thoughtless words we looked at Lacenaire with some
emotion; none showed on his physiognomy. He left the room a few
moments later.

There can, I suppose, be no doubt that the possibility of a
capital sentence greatly improves the dramatic quality of a
murder trial. As things are in Britain at the moment, so little is
at stake that there seems no reason why television should not at
intervals go over to the Old Bailey as it does to Old Trafford.
The worst that can happen is that, as a result of the judge
carelessly infringing some rule of the game, yet another murderer resumes his place in society, another strange rule having
decreed that he can never be charged again with the same
offence. Two more rules of ours would markedly have altered
the shape of the trial of Lacenaire, François and Avril. We now
firmly demand that the evidence of accomplices, as of juveniles,
shall be corroborated. And the fact that Lacenaire pleaded
guilty to all charges would have put an end to the proceedings.

The charges included stealing a clock, in which also the big,
red-haired Martin François or François Martin, thirty, floor-
layer, of Issy, was implicated. Victor Avril, twenty-five,
carpenter, was indicted as a principal in the Chardon murders.
Pierre-François Lacenaire, thirty-two, commercial traveller,
born at Lyons, was charged with the lot, as well as with forgery
and with passing bills of exchange knowing them to be forged.
He cheerfully admitted everything, questioning only one or two
small points of detail. His sole concern was to see that neither of
his accomplices got off. In effect, he was thus leading for the
prosecution against Avril and François, while with great verve
he incriminated himself. This could have been mortifying to M.
Dupuy, the president of the court, but Lacenaire behaved with
scrupulous politeness and good humour and soon had everyone
on his side, except, of course, François and Avril and François's counsel, with whom he had been at school. He was

eloquent at the right moments, and his timing was extraordinary. It was he, for instance, not the *advocat-général*, M. Partarrieu-Lafosse, who arranged that the crucial witness against François should be produced unexpectedly at the last moment, because otherwise he might have been intimidated. None of the magistracy had known of this witness's availability, although his name was to crop up frequently.

After the opening formalities, Avril and François were removed, and Lacenaire stood alone in the dock in a blue frock-coat, with a display of good linen. In reply to M. Dupuy's questions, he described the Chardon murders in close detail, explaining that afterwards he and Avril went to the Turkish baths, then dined and spent the rest of the evening at the Variétés theatre, separating at eleven o'clock, Lacenaire to go to his lodgings, Avril to a *maison de filles*. The bank-messenger attempt had been the third planned, and François had not in the first place been the intended accomplice. When the bank messenger began to shout, François fled first and at the bottom of the stairs shut the door on Lacenaire, doubtless hoping that his own escape would be likelier if the other were caught.

Avril and François were brought back in turn, and both denied everything. It was during the *interrogatoire* of François that the name of Bâton came up, the court being aware that there existed a real Alphonse Bâton, under whose name Lacenaire had booked in at the Pageot hotel. During this questioning, Lacenaire became hilarious and held his sides with laughter. The afternoon session ended with some consideration of the forgery counts on which Lacenaire alone was indicted. They were exact, and the court rose at five o'clock.

Medical evidence on the Chardon murders was both mystifying and harrowing. There were, it appeared, signs indicative of an unadmitted weapon and a third hand. It further appeared that the mother had still been alive some ten hours after she had been set about with a chopper and had the bedclothes piled on top of her (we may perhaps hope that she remained unconscious most of that time). The two doctors were followed by Pierre Allard, and other witnesses heard that Friday were a blind convict of noble mien, Fréchard, the bank messenger, Louis Genevey, the hotel keeper, Pageot, a laundry-woman, Mlle

Robinet, and a man at whose house Lacenaire and François had shared a bed. Avril butted in repeatedly and desperately. His counsel, Me. Laput, was ticked off by the presiding judge. Lacenaire laughed. The public laughed with him. The court rose at half past six.

The blind convict had cooked Avril's goose the previous day. What had not yet been established was that François had ever met Lacenaire before New Year's Day. The man to do this was Bâton, intended in the first place to serve as Lacenaire's accomplice, who had introduced François to Lacenaire as a substitute (Genevey, the previous day, had failed to recognize either François or Lacenaire). Alphonse-Jules Bâton appears to have been a chorus boy and general *figurant* at the Théâtre de l'Ambigu. His own alibi for 31 December was watertight. A juryman obligingly supplied the principal actor with his cue.

A Juryman: We should have liked to hear this Bâton.
President of the Court, M. Dupuy: He would have been called; but how was he to be found? He is a person of no fixed abode.
Lacenaire: It shouldn't be difficult. At this very moment, he must be in custody somewhere.
President: That can easily be checked.
Lacenaire: A fortnight ago, Bâton was being held at the central police station. The charges against him won't have been cleared up.

The central police station, the *dépôt de la Préfecture*, was not far away. An usher was sent. While the court waited, three minor witnesses were heard.

In a surprisingly short time, the usher returned, followed by members of the armed constabulary with Bâton. Lacenaire smiled benevolently at Bâton. François reddened. Bâton was circumspect, but the presiding judge, with help from the principal accused, pressed him. If he had in fact recommended François to Lacenaire as accomplice in a proposed murder, he would himself be, in our terms, at least accessory before the fact. He was allowed to be evasive about that. The important point was when Lacenaire and François had first met. It was several days before the end of the year. This was made clear. François butted in, but was silenced. Again, a member of the jury obliged.

A Juryman: After the crime, on 31 December, Lacenaire and François apparently met again at Bâton's. Did he see them?

Bâton: I saw Lacenaire and François on 31 December, but they weren't together. They came one after the other in the course of the evening.

President: Which of them arrived first?

Bâton, with much hesitation: It was François.

President: What did they say when they saw each other?

Bâton: Words passed between them.

President: What words?

Bâton, very embarrassed, glancing in turn at Lacenaire and the judge: I don't remember exactly. They were reproachful.

President: Surely you can remember. Tell us the truth now.

Bâton, after a long pause: Lacenaire said: 'You left me.'

President: That is stated in Lacenaire's deposition, members of the jury.

Bâton: I understood him to mean left me on the spot.

President: That wasn't all, was it?

Bâton: I don't remember. Ask Lacenaire, he'll tell you.

Lacenaire: François was surprised to see me come in. He had every reason to be. He said: 'What, you here? I thought you'd been arrested.'

Bâton: Yes, that's it. Lacenaire came in, and François said: 'I thought you'd been arrested.'

President: What did Lacenaire say to that?

Bâton: He said: 'If I wasn't arrested, that's no fault of yours.'

Lacenaire's exclamation at this point is described as one of pure satisfaction. He looked at François, it is said, with cruel joy.

The last witness was a newspaper editor, Vigoureux or Vigouroux, of *Le Bon Sens* and its workers' supplement, *La Tribune des Prolétaires*. In the latter, he had printed an article on prisons by Lacenaire. Lacenaire had also sent him poems from Poissy, and one of these had appeared elsewhere under somebody else's name. It is difficult to imagine who had called this witness or to what purpose: Lacenaire himself probably, in the hope of eliciting, in court, a straight tale about all those editors and publishers who had cheated him and were on the point of cheating him again, a matter about which he felt very strongly indeed, though it had nothing to do with the case.

M. Partarrieu-Lafosse then delivered his *réquisitoire*. The name seems prototypically red-robed. Possibly for quite subjective reasons, M. Partarrieu-Lafosse's lithographed face displeases the present writer. At the Lacenaire trial, there was not much left for him to be nasty about. As we imagine the long jowls wobbling, the small eyes jabbing, we may indeed find his quotations from *Macbeth* a little absurd, but they would seem otherwise to a French audience. There may have been highly educated English visitors with reserved seats, but I have not seen the names of any recorded. The crime rate that year was very high in Paris, and there was nothing foolish in the *advocat-général*'s suggestion that Lacenaire represented a new type of man, who killed not from passion but in the way of business, calculating risks and advantages and convenient dates. Nor was it silly to characterize him as one of those who thought Rome could be built in a day or to think it a dangerous enigma when a poet laid aside his pen and took up a poniard, without afterwards showing a trace of remorse. We may even regard the comparison between Lacenaire and Avril and the Macbeths as witty.

'What hands are here!' says the genius of England, Shagspere.

> *Will all great Neptune's ocean wash this blood*
> *Clean from my hand? No, this my hand will rather*
> *The multitudinous seas incarnadine,*
> *Making the green one red. . .*

But Milady Macbeth knows better. 'A little water clears us of this deed,' says Milady Macbeth. And the cold-blooded killers of our time, murderers in the common way of business, what do they do? They pay a visit to the Turkish baths.

M. Partarrieu-Lafosse spoke little about Avril and François, common assassins. He complimented Lacenaire on his candour. It was truly a merit, he said. He made the further point against him that the man who started life with advantages, the man who wore for a while the cassock of a seminarist, was more, not less, guilty than another. The criminals had not hesitated to strike hard. It was now the duty of the jury to strike hard in their turn. It was a painful duty, but they must not flinch.

Young Maître Brochant was clearly faced with an impossible task. He faced it and did very well. His *plaidoirie* began by tracing the course of Lacenaire's life, so like a novel. Then he twisted logic brilliantly.

FOR THE DEFENDANT LACENAIRE, ME. BROCHANT: A man who starts life with advantages may, indeed, be more guilty than one who started it with none, but he will also feel his later misfortunes more keenly. The boy in the seminarist's cassock was already a stranger in his own home, to which only the false accusations of others returned him. At every turn, this man has met with rejection, commonly accompanied by false accusations. A power beyond his own control seemed therefore to be driving him towards crime. He did not feel hatred towards his victims. It all appeared to him to be a simple fatality. As he waited for the bank messenger in the Rue Montorgueil, he smoked a pipe and read *The Social Contract* by Rousseau. Did he feel remorse, were his nights sleepless? Ask him, ask him, and he will tell you that they were not, as indeed you may see by the smile on his face. Then ask yourselves whether this man is not the victim of a disease. To him, his dreadful life was logical. He thinks himself more reasonable than any one of us. Why, members of the jury? Because this man is mad. That is the answer. He dreamed, as I have told you, gentlemen, of an awful suicide at the executioner's hand. Are you to help him bring that dream about? This man is in the hand of Fate. His will is not his own. Is he then guilty, as you yourselves would be if you had done what he has done? And dare you kill him? No. Imprison him, load him with fetters, see that he does no more harm. But do not help him to commit suicide. Let him work and repent. Condemn him . . . to live! . . .

That, deservedly, made a great impression, and the young barrister sat down to a round of applause. He sat on the bench below the dock. Lacenaire leaned over appreciatively and congratulated him, expressing only the wish that it had been in a better cause.

Me. Vidallot spoke briefly on Avril's behalf. Humanly, there was no doubt much that could have been said. Legally, there was nothing. Me. Laput began his long *plaidoirie* on behalf of François. After an hour, he showed signs of fatigue and asked for a brief adjournment, which was granted. Lacenaire reminded the presiding judge that the prisoners had had nothing to eat since morning. M. Dupuy extended the adjournment. An evening session began at seven o'clock. Maître Laput's continued defence consisted largely of an attack on his former schoolfellow. Lacenaire was then asked, according to rule, whether he had anything further to say. He spoke at some length, easily and without false rhetoric, exactitude his main preoccupation. He ended:

> For myself, I do not cling to existence. I live in memory. For eight months now, Death has sat as my bedside. I shall not ask for clemency. I do not expect it, I do not want it. I have no use for it.

It was eleven o'clock when the jury retired. They returned at two o'clock on what was by then Sunday morning. Lacenaire and Avril were sentenced to death, François to hard labour for life.

I go on with Canler.

> After his trial and sentence, contrary to what is usual in the case of men condemned to death, Lacenaire remained in the Conciergerie, where he wrote his Memoirs. He had been put by himself in a cell at the end of the long gallery to the left; and it had also been thought necessary to take precautions against him hanging himself or opening his veins in a moment of despair or to avoid the shame of the scaffold, so that a guard stayed with him day and night. Whenever I had occasion to go to the Conciergerie, I never failed to

visit him, and as soon as I entered his cell, he'd get up and greet me with a smile, offer me a seat and ask me in the most natural way how I was; we talked about almost anything but his situation. But one day when I found him very busy with his Memoirs, I took it upon myself to address him as follows:

'Ah! ah! so we're working for posterity? they'll find that unusual.'

'They will, won't they? a murderer's reminiscences! that'll be something out of the ordinary. Yes, I fancy they'll be read with great interest because of the novelty.'

'And because of the man who wrote them,' I added.

He inclined his head with a smile, and a flush of satisfaction came to his cheeks . . . He was a man dominated by pride and envy . . . On another occasion, I taxed him with carelessness in the matter at the appropriately named Rue Montorgueil.

'How do you mean?'

'If you'd succeeded in killing Genevey, you'd have cleared out with the money and the bank-notes; but the body would have been found in your room . . . We should still have found out that Mahossier was no other than Bâton, then Gaillard, then finally Lacenaire. You'd have been here just the same, with three murders on your hands instead of two.'

'Don't deceive yourself, sir: when I undertook that kind of thing, I was always careful to foresee and avoid consequences like that. They found, you may remember, straw in the room. Well, if Genevey had succumbed, I should have carved him up and with the help of that straw (which I'd brought along for the purpose) and a sheet, I should have bundled him into a trunk. That task completed, I should have rented a small house with a garden outside Paris. After boiling the remains in water for twenty-four hours, I should have reduced what remained to ashes by fire and dug them into the soil. Not a trace would have been found by all the police in the world, not even yourself. In any case, you'd only have heard that a bank messenger had vanished, everybody'd have thought he'd just made off with the money he was carrying. But, of course, where I did go wrong both there and in Red Horse Passage was in not working alone. I shouldn't have missed Genevey, he owes his life to the cowardice of François who ran for it as soon as the young man started shouting. I should have had twelve thousand francs, I could have lain low three or four years on that, and both these little matters would have been quite forgotten.

'Besides, if I hadn't had François as an accomplice, he wouldn't have talked, he couldn't. And if Avril hadn't been there to give me a hand with the Widow Chardon and her son, I shouldn't have needed, in order to avenge myself on him for squealing, to confess to the double murder in Red Horse Passage and bear my own head to the scaffold so that I could take with me the man who'd given me away. I must admit that, in those two circumstances, I behaved like a raw recruit! Yes, that was foolish. I'd always managed perfectly well on my own. That's something I ought not to have forgotten.'

'What are you thinking of?'

'Oh, little things in the past, long since forgotten.'

'Are you sure?'

'Perfectly, yes. I don't mind telling you about them, since nobody else was involved . . .'

And there follow the stories of the old boy tipped over the parapet of the Morand bridge in Lyons and of a gambler saved by a patrol in the Rue Blanche, which we may also read in the Memoirs Lacenaire was writing at the time.

'You know, Lacenaire,' said I, 'it's a good thing for humanity that there aren't many people like you in the world.'

'You mean,' he replied, 'that this society on which I declared war, and which I have long pursued with implacable hatred, will now be very happy to see my head roll. I know it! Society won, and the *lex talionis* must pursue its course, it is only right that it should.'

Another day, I was trying, as a policeman always must, to extract further information out of him about crimes he'd committed with an accomplice or any others he might know about. I was foolish enough to say that this would be a service to society and that society would be grateful to him.

'But why should you think I want society's gratitude? I would do anything to harm society. No, no, if I gave anything away, it would be to help the police, who've treated me with every consideration, I'm infinitely obliged to them, especially M. Allard. But why should I give anything away? Would it alter my situation? No, and besides I prefer to take with me into the grave the esteem of those unfortunates whom poverty, suffering and society's ingratitude have set upon the way I myself followed.'

That kind of talk about society was to be heard in Paris and elsewhere all through the century, and we may even hear echoes of it today. Lacenaire was not especially prone to it. Of his intellectual capacity and education, we shall not expect to form much impression from the reminiscences of Louis Canler, admirable policeman though he was. But Lacenaire in prison was also being visited regularly by a gifted writer, Jacques Arago, and by his former teacher, Reffay de Lusignan, as well as, less frequently, by more than one phrenologist, by a man to make a life-mask and by other miscellaneous notables, several of whom wrote about their visits. There are letters extant to Fr. Reffay and to Arago, and the two of them were to publish in 1836 a volume, *Lacenaire après sa Condamnation*, in which numerous fragments of conversation are reproduced. There seems to be evidence that, of Lacenaire's class-mates at Alix, the Abbé Coeur did call on him. Jean-Louis Coeur had progressed far in the Church, a year or two later would be preaching the Lenten sermons at St Roch, was to become bishop of Troyes. Maître Laput, as we have seen, was hostile to his former co-seminarist, but was (and this is the point) a clever barrister at the Paris bar, who, though at one juncture rebuked by the presiding judge, had got his man off in the sense of avoiding a capital sentence. A third Alix contemporary, Paul-Jean-Pierre Sauzet, was already a deputy, presently to attain ministerial rank under Thiers, and would for long be *président*, chairman or, in our terms, speaker of the Lower House. At Alix, all three had seemed less bright than Pierre-François Lacenaire, who still bandied Latin quotations with the Jesuit, his former teacher.

It seems to have been almost a first-class mind. The fact would be difficult to establish by quotation from either the Memoirs or the recorded conversations. Both dredged up a fair amount of temperamental mud. The opinions expressed were rational and, in the conversations at least, unemphatic. Lacenaire was, and had been from his schooldays, an atheist, but admitted the benefits and consolations he might have found in Christian belief, especially in the face of death. He even admitted to being superstitious, and one of his more amusing remarks was that he would not like to be executed on a Friday, because he feared that it would then be just his luck to discover that there was a God after all. He spared his intellectual equals the revolutionary small talk about avenging himself on society.

He did talk vengeance. His course of action before and at his trial had been governed by the determination to avenge himself on Avril and François, once he discovered that they had betrayed him. He admitted to Fr. Reffay that at school he had been tormented by a desire to kill anyone who beat him at lessons or in a scuffle and any master who punished or reprimanded him. He had, he said, conquered all his other passions, but not the thirst for revenge. In general, he despised men, hating them because he despised them and not the other way round. Like most of us, he would have accepted society had he found a better place in it. He could have enjoyed the good things of life. He was enjoying them at the moment. Since his conviction, the State denied him nothing. He was drinking ten or twelve bottles of wine a day, including champagne, of which he was especially fond.

In the conversations, we find him saying first that he had never loved anyone and that this was the fault of his mother, but later admitting that he loved children and also warmly recalling his wet-nurse, a simple peasant girl who would do anything for him. He had preferred his mistresses to be ugly. This we find both in the conversations and in the Memoirs. Both mention a Javotte, who was not merely ugly but also constantly drunk and whom Lacenaire had tried to kill (but the first blow struck a locket, and Javotte was too strong to let him get in a second). In the Memoirs, however, we read of a Mme Dormeuil, a married woman with whom there had been five years of happiness. After the unavoidable break with Mme Dormeuil, the guillotine as immortal betrothed was preceded by an ideal and imaginary figure, very much of the Romantic age.

LA SYLPHIDE

Divine being, beauty touching and pure,
Of whom I dreamed from my earliest years,
Whoever you are, spirit or created,
Lend an ear to my concluding accents!
Among the reefs of a turbulent sea,

A Literate Killer

You guided me, mysterious beacon:
I see harbour, and my enchanted soul
Will presently go and seek you in heaven.

I sought you beneath the shining porticos
Where cringe the devoted followers of kings;
I sought you in the humble rustic cot;
Only your shadow appeared at my call.
Alas, my vision may yet be too weak
To bear the refulgence of your reality;
Watch over me, Sylph whom I adore,
Immortal virgin, wait for me in heaven.

In sleep, this tender shade
Blushingly enfolds herself in my arms.
How oft has my ardent bosom
Thrilled to the contact of thy blameless charms!
You responded to this wild intoxication,
But at morn when I re-ope my eyes
The dream has fled, the veil is torn;
Immortal virgin, wait for me in the skies.

I dreamed of you in many a desert grot,
While the hot wind from the south blew furiously;
I dreamed of you beneath the bosky shade,
To the sweet concord of a melodious lute.
Yet suppose that you were but a vain chimaera,
Product of a wayward child's sick heart!
My soul at last will pierce the mystery,
Immortal virgin, wait for me in heaven.

I dreamed of you in the springtime of my life,
Your brow smiling and radiant with colour;
Poor and in protracted suffering,
I dreamed of you, fairer still, in tears.
But now of death I hear the voice severe,
The prism breaks, the rainbow disappears,
Nothing more attaches me to earth;
Immortal virgin, wait for me in heaven.

The poem is dated Poissy, 1829. It appeared in *Le Charivari* five days after Lacenaire's condemnation. When he wrote it, he stood in no immediate danger of death. When it was printed, he did.

It is not, I suppose, a good poem, though it is better than a line-by-line prose or free-verse translation can make it seem. The versification is fluent and exemplary. There are some thousand lines extant of twenty-five poems credibly attributed to Pierre-François Lacenaire, a high proportion of them written in prison after his trial (while he was also writing his Memoirs). These commonly refer more or less directly to his situation. The stanza form varies, and one little poem is in thieves' slang, with a translation into standard French. Some of the poems are serious, others satirical. If one day I were to write a whole book on Lacenaire, I should make some attempt to translate them all. Here, the reader will perhaps take my word for it that worse poems were written and published at the time and that reputations have been based on as little.

Pierre-François Lacenaire was not the only or the first literate killer. At that very moment, among the suspect aliens in France was Thomas Griffiths Wainewright, who in London had flourished in the most respectable literary circles and was also admired as a painter, by Blake for instance. Ninety years earlier, having killed a man out of marital jealousy, Eugene Aram had lived the life of a fine scholar for thirteen years before the skeleton of his wife's lover was discovered. That had been an isolated, violent crime. Wainewright was a calculating poisoner and forger, who did quite well out of his misdeeds and who, after conviction for the lesser ones, lived on to a reasonably ripe age. Their crimes apart, both he and Eugene Aram merit footnotes in literary history. It is difficult to know how confidently the same claim may be made for Lacenaire. It is probable that we should not have known his name but for his crimes, had he nevertheless died at thirty-five. His conviction brought earlier poems to light and started him writing again, as well as causing his *obiter dicta* to be recorded and published.

His performance before the Court of Assize had itself constituted something of an artistic triumph. The play was a bad one, but the leading actor might have been thought to stand on the threshold of a marvellous career. His writings for the theatre

Artist With a Razor

Left Richard Dadd:
a self-portrait, circa
1841

Right Richard Dadd
at work in Bethlem
Hospital, circa 1856

Cobham Hall, with sketching party in foreground, October 1843

'The Fairy Feller's Master Stroke' (*detail*) by Richard Dadd, 1855–64   *Tate Gallery*

have not survived. He himself thought more highly of them than of his poems. He had also thought of himself as an actor. 'You can have no idea,' he said, 'how often I dreamed of success on the stage. If only some producer had opened his door to me . . .' Later, he added: 'Perhaps you think, from the way my life has gone, that, if I had taken up the theatre seriously, I should have excelled in heavy drama? Not at all. I should have preferred comedy, at its lightest indeed and with songs; for even in the face of my victims my thoughts were always amusing.' He had nevertheless failed to enter into the spirit of Lemaître's *Robert Macaire*, upon which he made the curiously humourless observation that, of course, one didn't kill with a laugh like that. He had thought of himself as a barrister, too. At school, he said, in the silence of his dormitory, he would invent difficult crimes in order to imagine how their defence could be most effectively conducted. His own trial and conviction brought him, we may say, to the height of his powers. Acclaimed and stimulated, he lived for a little under two months thereafter, not perhaps in a state of happiness but at least in a state of satisfied vanity, with something resembling clearly defined purpose as to his life's work, which he had missed till then.

It seemed a pity to chop his head off at that point. And yet I do not think that Lacenaire provides us with much of a case against capital punishment, at any rate as a form of punishment. Against it as a deterrent he provides the argument of his own personality. It had not deterred him. Its absence might have deterred him, given the alternatives which then existed. He preferred it, certainly, to the idea of joining François for a life at the seaside. He had appealed, but solely, he said, so that he could be sure of seeing Avril off first. If, unimaginably, he had been acquitted and released, he would, I feel certain, have killed again, unless, even more unimaginably, the public and his new friends had remained faithful to him. He would have done it in order to re-create the situation in which he had once shone, for, bad as it might seem, the play was all of a piece.

Moreover, without its last act, the first act would have seemed very poor stuff. Those were brutal, commonplace murders, carried out messily. With his intelligence and imagination, Lacenaire could have master-minded quite *splendid* criminal operations. That he didn't was a matter of temperament, not of mind. I fancy that he would have been satisfied with his first act. He was, he admitted, lazy. He would have done something of the same kind again, perhaps making a rather neater job of some bank messenger. In the terms of those days, what people did not forgive him was that he would not admit to remorse. It is not a favourite term now, but it means something. Not to feel remorse was as essential a part of Lacenaire's great theatrical performance as not to flinch before the guillotine. But he seems really not to have felt it or anything of the kind. There was a sort of deadness. We may not, with Maître Brochant, think Lacenaire precisely mad, but we must, I would say, in the terms used by psychiatrists today, at least think him afflicted with some ineradicable personality disorder. A dangerous enigma, certainly.

His appeal was rejected on Boxing Day, and so was Victor Avril's. Canler recounts that, in those last days of their lives, the two men, whose hatred for each other had brought them to this pass, became sincere friends. To celebrate their reconciliation, M. Allard and the governor of the Conciergerie gave them a dinner. They joked about the blood of undercooked meat, comparing it with that which they had spilt and their own which must presently spurt. On 9 January 1836, they were transferred to Bicêtre. They knew why. That very evening, Allard and Canler took a cab and went down there with a clerk. It was their job to inform the condemned men that the executions had been fixed for tomorrow, holding out to them the possibility of a reprieve if they made further disclosures, a dirty trick about which Canler himself entertained no illusions.

> Avril was brought to the record office. The chief told him what we were there for, and Avril, in his usual tone of indifference, simply answered: 'I have nothing to say.' Lacenaire was fetched in his turn: he entered, as always, with a smile on his lips and said:
> 'Ah! good evening, gentlemen, how are you both?'
> 'Lacenaire,' said M. Allard, 'I am directed by the Attorney-General and the Prefect of Police to ask you whether there are no disclosures you wish to make.'

But, as he said these words, the chief had turned very pale, and the words were stammered rather than pronounced, for this was in effect the final sentence.

'That's all, is it?' Lacenaire broke in kindly, 'why, set your mind at rest, sir! So, it's tomorrow, eh? Well, tomorrow will be as good a day as any, since it must come. I shall be rid of it sooner.'

Then, after some conversation of no particular interest, he said to us as we were about to leave: 'Well, gentlemen, I hope I shall have the honour of seeing you both in the morning at the Barrière St Jacques?' We both nodded, and he was taken back to his cell. A few minutes later, as we were crossing the yard to pick up our carriage, a well-known voice struck our ears: it was that of Lacenaire who, lodged over the yard and next door to Avril, was talking with his accomplice from one cell to the other.

'I say, Avril,' we heard from Lacenaire, 'I forgot something I wanted to tell M. Allard, do you think I could ask for him?'

We stopped, to listen to the conversation.

'Have him called for,' said the other voice, 'he can't have gone far.'

'Oh, it doesn't matter, it's not worth the trouble, it'll all be the same once it's over.'

Then a moment later, still addressing his accomplice, he called out in a loud voice:

'Avril! the ground will be nice and cold tomorrow!'

'That's true!' replied the latter.

There was a brief pause.

'Papa Thomas!' Avril went on, addressing the warder who was supposed to watch him during the night, 'I'm giving you a lot of trouble, aren't I, old chap?'

'Oh, I have to expect that, my lad, it's what I'm paid for!'

There was no more of that, for Lacenaire, once more addressing his accomplice, called out: 'Good night, Avril, sleep well!'

'Good night, Lacenaire!' replied the other.

Then everything was silent again, and we withdrew, deeply moved at hearing such a dialogue between two men who, ten hours later, would be dying at the hand of the executioner.

The occasion is thus reported in *La Gazette des Tribunaux*:

Because of the state of the roads, it was a quarter to nine before the procession reached the foot of the scaffold. This had been erected during the night by the light of torches. Lacenaire descended abruptly from the closed carriage, his face frighteningly pale, his gaze vague and uncertain; he stammered and seemed to be seeking for words which his tongue would not utter. Then Avril got out with a nimble, resolute step, and cast a calm look at the public. He approached Lacenaire with resignation and embraced him: 'Good bye, old chap,' he said, 'I'll take first turn!' He mounted the steps of the scaffold with a firm tread, was fastened to the fatal plank, he turned again and said: 'Come along, Lacenaire, old chap, do like me, be brave!' Those were his last words, and the knife sent his head rolling on the boards of the scaffold. At that horrible moment, Lacenaire stood at the foot of the steps; the chaplain, Father Montès, tried to turn his attention away from the terrible spectacle before his eyes . . . 'Ah, bah!' replied Lacenaire in a stricken voice, striving in vain to pretend assurance. 'Is M. Allard there?' he said, even more weakly. 'Yes,' replied M. Canler, assistant head of the detective force . . . 'Ah! I am . . . glad . . .' He had said he was going to speak to the people; but had not the strength; his knees gave way, his face was distorted with terror, he mounted the steps supported by the executioner's men, and the fatal fall soon put an end to his distress and his life.

Canler quotes the whole passage in order to refute it. The *Gazette* account was, he says, true as regards Avril, but wholly and deliberately false about Lacenaire.

The celebrity which Lacenaire had gained by his deportment at his trial, the publication of his poems, the announcement of his forthcoming Memoirs, seemed to the authorities to set a dangerous example to others who might feel unappreciated by society and who might be driven to seek fame by no matter what means. In the interests of morality, it was thought desirable that Lacenaire should seem to have weakened in his last moments and to have died like a coward. *La Gazette des Tribunaux* engaged a man of letters to depict the final scene. He could not bring himself to approach the scaffold, and one of the paper's staff went to the Prefecture and was given an account which could be written up from the angle they had chosen.

I saw and heard all that was said and done at the moment of execution. I was standing near by and spoke to those concerned, and every detail is graven ineffaceably on my memory.

Lacenaire descended briskly from the carriage, embraced Avril and, having seen me to his right, nodded graciously, then said: 'Ah, there you are! Good morning, M. Canler, it was nice of you to come! Is M. Allard with you?' 'Yes,' I replied. During this colloquy, Lacenaire's physiognomy bore a smile and denoted no preoccupation of anxiety; Avril boldly climbed the steps of the scaffold; when he was attached to the fatal plank, he threw his head back and called out in a loud voice: 'Good bye, my old Lacenaire, chins up!' To which Lacenaire replied in a firm, energetic voice: 'Good bye, good bye!' Desmarest, the executioner from Beauvais, Sanson's brother-in-law, who had come to help him with this double execution, then went up to Lacenaire, and taking him by the shoulders, forced him to turn round so that he could not see the instrument of torture; Lacenaire had to yield to this, but turning again immediately, raised his head to watch the horrible scene being enacted behind him, he contemplated the knife suspended over his accomplice's head, twice more glanced defiantly at it, saying: 'I'm not afraid! come now! I'm not afraid!' and it was only by force that he was compelled to turn away again. Presently, he himself ascended the scaffold with an assured step, and a second later he no longer existed.

Le Charivari, while less censorious than the *Gazette*, did not quite share Canler's evaluation of Lacenaire's firmness and resolution. In another account, the release mechanism stuck, and the patient had time to turn his head and look up at the blade.

Revenge in Rome

Benvenuto Cellini

(From the translation by John Addington Symonds)

Benvenuto Cellini (1500–1571), the most skilled goldsmith of his age, perhaps of all time, was also a sculptor: his 'Perseus with the head of Medusa' still stands in the Piazza della Signoria, Florence. He wrote his autobiography, some ingredients of which need a pinch of salt, when he was in his sixties. This extract refers to events circa 1525; his brother Cecchino was two years younger than himself.

MY BROTHER, at this period, was also in Rome, serving Duke Alessandro, on whom the Pope had recently conferred the Duchy of Penna. This prince kept in his service a multitude of soldiers, worthy fellows, brought up to valour in the school of that famous general Giovanni de' Medici; and among these was my brother, whom the Duke esteemed as highly as the bravest of them. One day my brother went after dinner to the shop of a man called Baccino della Croce in the Banchi, which all those men-at-arms frequented. He had flung himself upon a settee, and was sleeping. Just then the guard of the Bargello passed by; they were taking to prison a certain Captain Cisti, a Lombard, who had also been a member of Giovanni's troop, but was not in the service of the Duke. The captain, Cattivanza degli Strozzi, chanced to be in the same shop; and when Cisti caught sight of him, he whispered: 'I was bringing you those crowns I owed; if you want them, come for them before they go with me to prison.' Now Cattivanza had a way of putting his neighbours to the push, not caring to hazard his own person. So, finding there around him several young fellows of the highest daring, more eager than apt for so serious an enterprise, he bade them catch up Captain Cisti and get the money from him, and if the guard resisted, overpower the men, provided they had pluck enough to do so.

The young men were but four, and all four of them without a beard. The first was called Bertino Aldobrandi, another Anguillotto of Lucca; I cannot recall the names of the rest. Bertino had been trained like a pupil by my brother; and my brother felt the most unbounded love for him. So then, off dashed the four brave lads, and came up with the guard of the Bargello – upwards of fifty constables, counting pikes, arque-buses, and two-handed swords. After a few words they drew their weapons, and the four boys so harried the guard, that if Captain Cattivanza had but shown his face, without so much as drawing, they would certainly have put the whole pack to flight. But delay spoiled all; for Bertino received some ugly wounds and fell; at the same time, Anguillotto was also hit in the right arm, and being unable to use his sword, got out of the fray as well as he was able. The others did the same. Bertino Aldobrandi was lifted from the ground seriously injured.

While these things were happening, we were all at table; for that morning we had dined more than an hour later than usual. On hearing the commotion, one of the old man's sons, the elder, rose from table to go and look at the scuffle. He was called Giovanni; and I said to him: 'For Heaven's sake, don't go! In such matters one is always certain to lose, while there is nothing to be gained.' His father spoke to like purpose: 'Pray, my son, don't go!' But the lad, without heeding any one, ran down the stairs. Reaching the Banchi, where the great scrimmage was, and seeing Bertino lifted from the ground, he ran towards home, and met my brother Cecchino on the way, who asked what was the matter. Though some of the bystanders signed to Giovanni not to tell Cecchino, he cried out like a madman how it was that Bertino Aldobrandi had been killed by the guard. My poor brother gave vent to a bellow which might have been heard ten miles away. Then he turned to Giovanni: 'Ah me! but could you tell me which of those men killed him for me?' Giovanni said, yes, that it was a man who had a big two-handed sword, with a blue feather in his bonnet.

My poor brother rushed ahead, and having recognized the homicide by those signs, he threw himself with all his dash and spirit into the middle of the band, and before his man could turn on guard, ran him right through the guts, and with the sword's hilt thrust him to the ground. Then he turned upon the rest with such energy and daring, that his one arm was on the point of putting the whole band to flight, had it not been that, while wheeling round to strike an arquebusier, this man fired in self-defence, and hit the brave unfortunate young fellow above the knee of his right leg. While he lay stretched upon the ground, the constables scrambled off in disorder as fast as they were able, lest a pair to my brother should arrive upon the scene.

Noticing that the tumult was not subsiding, I too rose from table, and girding on my sword – for everybody wore one then – I went to the bridge of Sant' Agnolo, where I saw a group of several men assembled. On my coming up and being recognized by some of them, they gave way before me, and showed me what I least of all things wished to see, albeit I made haste to view the sight. On the instant I did not know Cecchino, since he was wearing a different suit of clothes from that in which I had lately seen him. Accordingly, he recognized me first, and said: 'Dearest brother, do not be upset by my grave accident; it is only what might be expected in my profession: get me removed from here at once, for I have but few hours to live.' They had acquainted me with the whole event while he was speaking, in brief words befitting such occasion. So I answered: 'Brother, this is the greatest sorrow and the greatest trial that could happen to me in the whole course of my life. But be of good cheer; for before you lose sight of him who did the mischief, you shall see yourself revenged by my hand.' Our words on both sides were to the purport, but of the shortest.

The guard was now about fifty paces from us; for Maffio, their officer, had made some of them turn back to take up the corporal my brother killed. Accordingly, I quickly traversed that short space, wrapped in my cape, which I had tightened round me, and came up with Maffio, whom I should most certainly have murdered, for there were plenty of people round, and I had wound my way among them. With the rapidity of lightning, I had half drawn my sword from the sheath, when Berlinghier Berlinghieri, a young man of the greatest daring and my good friend, threw himself from behind upon my arms; he had four other fellows of like kidney with him, who cried out to Maffio: 'Away with you, for this man here alone was killing you!' He asked: 'Who is he?' and they answered: 'Own brother to the man you see there.' Without waiting to hear more, he made haste for Torre di Nona; and they said: 'Benvenuto, we prevented you against your will, but did it for your good; now let us go to succour him who must die shortly.' Accordingly, we turned and went back to my brother, whom I had at once conveyed into a house. The doctors who were called in consultation treated him with medicaments, but could not decide to amputate the leg, which might perhaps have saved him.

As soon as his wound had been dressed, Duke Alessandro appeared and most affectionately greeted him. My brother had not as yet lost consciousness; so he said to the Duke: 'My lord, this only grieves me, that your Excellency is losing a servant than whom you may perchance find men more valiant in the profession of arms, but none more lovingly and loyally devoted to your service than I have been.' The Duke bade him do all he could to keep alive; for the rest, he well knew him to be a man of worth and courage. He then turned to his attendants, ordering them to see that the brave young fellow wanted for nothing.

When he was gone, my brother lost blood so copiously, for nothing could be done to stop it, that he went off his head, and kept raving all the following night, with the exception that once, when they wanted to give him the communion, he said: 'You would have done well to confess me before; now it is impossible that I should receive the divine sacrament in this already ruined frame; it will be enough if I partake of it by the divine virtue of the eyesight, whereby it shall be transmitted into my immortal soul, which only prays to Him for mercy and forgiveness.' Having spoken thus, the host was elevated; but he straightaway relapsed into the same delirious ravings as before, pouring forth a torrent of the most terrible frenzies and horrible imprecations that the mind of man could imagine; nor did he cease once all that night until the day broke.

When the sun appeared above our horizon, he turned to me and said: 'Brother, I do not wish to stay here longer, for these fellows will end by making me do something tremendous, which may cause them to repent of the annoyance they have given me.' Then he kicked out both his legs – the injured limb we had enclosed in a very heavy box – and made as though he would fling it across a horse's back. Turning his face round to me, he called out thrice – 'Farewell, farewell!' and with the last word that most valiant spirit passed away.

At the proper hour, towards nightfall, I had him buried with due ceremony in the church of the Florentines; and afterwards I erected to his memory a very handsome monument of marble, upon which I caused trophies and banners to be carved. I must not omit to mention that one of his friends had asked him who the man was that had killed him, and if he could recognize him; to which he answered that he could, and gave his description. My brother, indeed, attempted to prevent this coming to my ears; but I got it very well impressed upon my mind, as will appear in the sequel . . .

I continued working at a jewel for the Pope and dies for the Mint; but I also took to watching the arquebusier who shot my brother, as though he had been a girl I was in love with. The fellow lived in a house near a place called Torre Sanguigua, next door to the lodging of one of the most fashionable courtesans in Rome, named Signora Antea.

It had just struck twenty-four, and he was standing at the house-door, with his sword in hand, having risen from supper. With great address I stole up to him, holding a large Pistojan dagger, and dealt him a back-handed stroke, with which I meant to cut his head clean off; but as he turned round very suddenly, the blow fell upon the point of his left shoulder and broke the bone. He sprang up, dropped his sword, half-stunned with the great pain, and took to flight. I followed after, and in four steps caught him up, when I lifted my dagger above his head, which he was holding very low, and hit him in the back exactly at the juncture of the nape-bone and the neck. The poniard entered this point so deep into the bone, that, though I used all my strength to pull it out, I was not able. For just at that moment four soldiers with drawn swords sprang out from Antea's lodging, and obliged me to set hand to my own sword to defend my life.

Leaving the poniard then, I made off, and fearing I might be recognized, took refuge in the palace of Duke Alessandro, which was between Piazza Navona and the Rotunda. On my arrival, I asked to see the Duke; who told me that, if I was alone, I need only keep quiet and have no further anxiety, but go on working at the jewel which the Pope had set his heart on. Immediately upon this, I opened a very fine shop in the Banchi, and there I finished the jewel after the lapse of a few months.

It had already been said to Pope Clement by one of his most trusted servants, and by others, that is, by Francesco del Nero, Zana de' Biliotti his accountant, the Bishop of Vasona, and several such men: 'Why, most blessed Father, do you confide gems of that value to a young fellow, who is all fire, more passionate for arms than for his art, and not yet thirty years of age?' The Pope asked in answer if any of them knew that I had done aught to justify such suspicions. Whereto Francesco del Nero, his treasurer, replied: 'No, most blessed Father, because he has not as yet had an opportunity.' Whereto the Pope rejoined: 'I regard him as a thoroughly honest man; and if I saw with my own eyes some crime he had committed, I should not believe it.'

I went on working assiduously at the button, and at the same time laboured for the Mint, when certain pieces of false money got abroad in Rome, stamped with my own dies. They were brought at once to the Pope, who, hearing things against me, said to Giacopo Balducci, the Master of the Mint, 'Take every means in your power to find the criminal; for we are sure that Benvenuto is an honest fellow.' That traitor of a master, being in fact my enemy, replied: 'Would to God, most blessed Father, that it may turn out as you say; for we have some proofs against him.' Upon this the Pope turned to the Governor of Rome, and bade him see he found the malefactor. The officials who received these orders were certain clerks of the Camera, who made the proper search, as was their duty, and soon found the rogue. He was a stamper in the service of the Mint, named Cesare Macherone, and a Roman citizen. Together with this man they detected a metal-founder of the Mint. A few days afterwards, Cesare Macherone, the false coiner, was hanged in the Banchi opposite the Mint; his accomplice was sent to the galleys.

In the Name of Love

Kenneth G. Weinberg*

IN THE SUMMER of 1931 the body of a comely twenty-five-year-old woman was found on a shore of Long Island, near New York City. An autopsy revealed that she had died from drowning in salt water (*shallow* salt water, apparently, for there was sand in the lungs); also that she had taken, or had been given, a hypnotic drug shortly before her death.

She was identified as Starr Faithfull, a New York 'party girl'; soon, her lovely name was linked to 'prominent politicians'. One of several presumptions was that she had been thrown, while unconscious, from the yacht of one of those men.

This, of course, was raw meat for the tabloids, and for many weeks titillating front-page stories recounted the victim's affairs with newsworthy persons – some of them yacht-owners.

An assiduous reader of those stories was a young reporter and budding novelist named John O'Hara. Turning Nature into Art, he created a life for Starr Faithfull, calling her Gloria Wandrous, the doomed party girl of his novel, *BUtterfield 8*.

Towards the end of the novel, Gloria Wandrous recalls one particularly wild party.

The party she went to thinking it was being given by a movie actress and it turned out to be a gangster party, where they had all the girls

* Visiting Professor of Law, Cleveland-Marshall College of Law, Cleveland State University.

198

from the show and the gangsters tied sheets to one girl's wrists and hung her stark naked out of the twenty-first floor window, and when they pulled her in they thought she was dead.

There is no other reference to this party in the entire book. It seems to have had little or no influence on Gloria's conduct, and it is difficult to see why the author included the anecdote in a book that otherwise used words with great economy.

Many years later, at least one, and probably two, faithful readers of *BUtterfield 8* found inspiration in that anecdote that readers lacking a perfervid imagination could never glean from the foolish stunt related by Gloria Wandrous.

In the early morning of Saturday, 22 June 1974, the police department of the Cleveland, Ohio, suburb of Cleveland Heights received a report of an accident at 2972 Meadowbrook Road. Responding to the call, the police found the nude and barely alive body of Virginia Lee Love on an outside patio below an open third-floor window.

The woman's husband, David S. Love, a Doctor of Philosophy and an assistant professor of anatomy at Case-Western Reserve University, had initially reported that his wife had slipped and fallen through his third-floor study window while hanging drapes. This story was dutifully reported in the local press the next day, apparently without scepticism, with the additional fact that Mrs Love had died at 8.10 am at University Hospital from internal injuries caused by the fall.

The inherent improbability of an accidental fall of a nude woman hanging drapes by an open third-floor window at six o'clock in the morning ensured that a different version of the death would soon be forthcoming, and even before the newspaper drape story appeared, Dr Love had given a totally different account to the county coroner.

Dr Sam Gerber had been the elected and re-elected coroner of Cuyahoga County for over half a century. His popularity with the voters did not suffer from his unerring instinct for newsworthy unnatural deaths. An attractive, eminently respectable couple fortuitously named Love; a nude body on the patio at six o'clock in the morning; an incredible story of drapes being hung under the most unlikely circumstances – Dr Sam smelled big headlines.

But it soon became clear that Mrs Love had not been the victim of foul play but only of foolish play – or rather, foolish foreplay. The account given by Dr Love to Dr Gerber early on the morning of 22 June, though even more bizarre than the drape story, was, Dr Gerber believed, as close to the truth as the state was likely to get.

Dr Love, aged forty-two, and his wife, Virginia Lee Love, also forty-two, a graduate of the University of Colorado who had worked as a designer and draughtsman, had been married twenty years. They had two daughters, aged six and eleven, and enjoyed a typical middle-class American suburban life-style. They also apparently enjoyed, or at least engaged in, a sex-life that found physical stimulus in physical danger.

Love told the coroner that about 2 am on that fateful morning, the couple had engaged in what the coroner's report labelled 'normal sex', without giving posterity the benefit of a definition of that term. They then decided to try it as they thought it had been done in *BUtterfield 8*, thus reading into that one paragraph much more than Gloria Wandrous of her creator could have intended.

He told how he had tied a rope to his wife's ankles and secured the other end of the rope to the radiator-pipe in his third-floor study.

No missionary position for this daring couple. The idea was for Mrs Love to hang, naked and upside down, out of the window of Dr Love's third-floor study. Dr Love was then to meet her at a second-storey bedroom window, where they were to engage in Eros only knows what kind of acrobatic sexual act.

Dr Love and his wife, it appeared, had frequently engaged in what others might consider unorthodox sexual practices; but the record is unclear whether this was their first attempt at their version of the *BUtterfield 8*. Love told the coroner that after Mrs Love was suspended upside down, the rope slipped from the radiator, Dr Love tried to pull her in, the rope slipped from his grasp, and Mrs Love fell to her death. She was pronounced dead at University Hospital at 8.10 am on 22 June, with death being attributed to lacerations of the liver and various internal injuries consistent with a fall, and with no other signs of violence on the body.

Dr Gerber had heard many strange stories during his fifty

years of investigating accidental or homicidal deaths, but this lurid tale – at first blush, at least – made the drape-hanging story seem almost reasonable. But further investigation – by the Cleveland Heights police, by the coroner's office, and by the county prosecutor's office – disclosed no facts inconsistent with accounts given by family and friends that the Loves were a happy, loving (in their fashion) couple, neither of whom had any reason to do the other harm.

Having no evidence, direct or circumstantial, to contradict Dr Love's account, Dr Gerber was obliged to accept it, and the coroner's verdict was death by accident. No criminality appeared to be involved, and Dr Gerber saw no reason to correct the previous newspaper account of an accidental death while hanging drapes.

Freud believed, or at least said, that there are no accidents. In 1974, the Cuyahoga County prosecutor's office, no nest of Freudians, apparently agreed that there are no accidents – at least when it came to kinky sex – and the office determined to seek a criminal indictment of Dr Love. This presented certain prosecutorial problems, since, before the state could make the punishment fit the crime, it had to find a crime to fit the facts.

The criminal code of the state of Ohio did not appear to include such a crime. The closest the prosecutor could come was involuntary manslaughter, which Ohio Revised Code Section 2903.04 defined in two categories:

A. No person shall cause the death of another as a proximate result of the offender's committing or attempting to commit a felony; and

B. No person shall cause the death of another as a proximate result of the offender's committing or attempting to commit a misdemeanour.

The former was classified as a first-degree felony, and carried a prison sentence of four years minimum and twenty-five years maximum. The latter was a third-degree felony, and called for a minimum sentence of one year and a maximum of ten.

Of course, the weakness in the prosecution case was the absence of any underlying felony or misdemeanour as required by the statute. There was absolutely nothing to suggest that what had occurred was anything more than a voluntary, if slightly demented, act between two consenting adults. The criminality could not be found in the criminal code of Ohio and would have to be found in the imagination of the jurors, just as the Loves' imagination had built upon the offhand anecdote in *BUtterfield 8*.

The grand jury had only to find probable cause that Dr Love had committed a crime, not that he had been guilty – and, as critics of the grand jury system frequently point out, any prosecutor who really wants an indictment can direct and control the secret grand jury proceedings to ensure that an indictment will issue. That was not particularly difficult to do in this case in spite of the lack of any Ohio criminal statute that could be said to have been clearly violated. Nudity, sex and death are all the ingredients a prosecutor needs to cook an indictment. What was more, he had the pictures to prove it. The Loves, who apparently enjoyed being voyeurs as well as participants, had rigged a camera with a delayed shutter, and photographs of the fatal night's activities, as well as other strange and wonderful acts, were among the exhibits displayed to the grand jury.

There have always been those who view sexual revolution as a greater threat to the peace and stability of the world than political revolution. Sex, in 1974 as always, was of great private and public concern. On 24 June of that year, just two days after Mrs Love fell to her death, the Supreme Court of the United States had reversed the conviction of a movie exhibitor in the state of Georgia by holding the obscenity statute under which he had been convicted to be unconstitutional. The movie *Carnal Knowledge* had been ruled obscene at least partly on the basis of a scene suggesting but not really showing an act of fellatio between two fully-clothed actors. If that seemed obscene to movie audiences of those days, the words of a future president of the United States, spoken over and over in a different context, might have been instructive: 'You ain't seen nothin' yet.'

In any event, once the prosecutor had determined not to let the Love case be classified as the tragic, foolish accident that everyone believed it to be, there was no doubt that Dr Love would have to face criminal charges. He had violated a fundamental rule of sexual conduct. At the turn of the century (the last century, not this one which is already starting to turn), Mrs Patrick Campbell, writing to her friend George Bernard Shaw about sex, censorship and private morality, said that one shouldn't care what people do so long as they don't do it in the street and frighten the horses.

Dr Love had done it in the street, so to speak, and the horses were frightened. On 29 August 1974, the grand jury issued a true bill indicting Dr Love for involuntary manslaughter in the first degree, that is, causing death during the commission of a felonious assault. The 'felonious assault' apparently occurred when Dr Love, in the words of the indictment,

> suspended his wife, who was nude, out of the window by a rope around her ankle in order to perform a sex act.

On 30 August, Dr Love was arrested and immediately released on his personal bond in the amount of $1000. On the same date, he entered a plea of not guilty and the case was assigned to Judge Bernard Friedman of the Cuyahoga County Common Pleas Court. Judge Friedman, who was approaching mandatory retirement age and was ineligible to run for re-election, was immune to the seductions of front-page headlines; sensing that Dr Love was perhaps more to be pitied than punished, he refused to make any statements to the press and warned the prosecutors and defence attorneys against trying their case in the news media.

Deprived of all information except what had already appeared in the record, the two Cleveland daily newspapers apparently decided to wait for the trial to have their day in court alongside the defendant, when all the salacious details would be spread before them. Virtually nothing about the case appeared in the papers in the weeks following the arraignment. But there was no doubt that the media were gearing up for a full court press. Judge Friedman reported that he had been deluged with requests from newspapers, radio and TV for seats at the trial, scheduled for November. Also, for the first time in his judicial career, he was getting letters and calls from people volunteering for jury duty.

Meanwhile, Dr Love's attorney had asked for a bill of particulars – seeking, among other things, to pin down the prosecution on the underlying felony or misdemeanour necessary to support the involuntary manslaughter charge. In response, the prosecution could be no more particular than accusing Dr Love of

> hanging her out of a third-storey window upside down, causing death by intending to cause great physical harm.

This was no more particular than the indictment itself. Furthermore, far from 'intending to cause great physical harm', the intention, misguided though it might have been, would seem to have been to cause great physical pleasure. *Degustibus Non Disputantum.*

As the trial date approached, Judge Friedman began to feel more and more strongly that Dr Love had committed no crime and was himself simply another victim, albeit a live one, of a senseless accident. Without directly saying so, he began to suggest to the prosecution that Dr Love presented no threat to society, that failure to prosecute him was certainly not going to lead to any increase in weird sex acts, and that a conviction would most likely be overturned on appeal because the circumstances of the death simply could not be shaped to fit the specifications of the involuntary manslaughter statute.

The prosecutor, whose experience had been with hardened criminal types, had begun to feel considerable sympathy for the respectable, mild-mannered professor who seemed genuinely grieved by the fruits of his folly. Whatever zeal to prosecute might have existed was waning fast, but the political antennae of both the judge and the prosecutor sensed a community demand that this affront to public morality somehow be punished.

The judge, of course, had it in his power to dismiss the case on the ground that the indictment did not spell out a crime punishable under Ohio law, and the prosecutor at any stage could have asked the court to nolle the prosecution on the ground that the case could not be proven. Neither the judge nor the prosecutor, however, was willing to risk the reaction of the horde of reporters who had been waiting for a trial that was certain to become a media event.

Though Dr Love's counsel had not been able to obtain a

dismissal of the charges, he was confident that no crime had been committed under Ohio law and that ultimately there would be an acquittal. But Dr Love feared the embarrassment and humiliation of a trial and despaired at the thought of subjecting his two young daughters to further pain. A plea of guilty, or of no contest, almost certainly would lead to a suspended sentence, but Dr Love would be forever branded a convicted felon.

Then a stroke of fate – or a strike of fate, in the form of a work-stoppage by the Cleveland Newspaper Guild – closed both daily newspapers in October 1974, and gave the judge and the lawyers the chance to reach a compromise solution without fear of second-guessing by the press. A diligent search of the Ohio criminal code turned up a homicide statute classified as a misdemeanour. A guilty plea to this lesser offence would thus not stigmatize Dr Love as a felon.

The offence was designated negligent homicide and provided, in Ohio Revised Code Section 2903.05, that

> No person shall negligently cause the death of another by means of a deadly weapon or dangerous ordnance.

Clearly no deadly weapon or dangerous ordnance had figured in the fun and games at the Love residence on 22 June, and this statute would seem to have been even more inappropriate than the involuntary-manslaughter definition. Indeed, the legislative history of the provision makes it clear that it was directed at gun owners who carelessly left guns lying about, leading to the death of an innocent victim – usually a child. The legislature also hoped to reduce careless hunting accidents. But by this time the judge, the prosecutor and the defendant were all looking for a way out, and a plea-bargain was hastily arranged. Dr Love would plead guilty to the misdemeanour charge, no jail sentence or fine would be sought or imposed (negligent homicide carried a possible sentence of not more than six months' imprisonment and a fine of not more than $1000), and the plea would be entered as soon as possible in the hope that the newspapers would still be on strike.

Accordingly, on 12 November 1974, in open court, with only the judge, his bailiff, the prosecutor, the defendant and his lawyer present, Love entered a plea of 'guilty of negligent homicide'. Judge Friedman continued the personal bond of $1000 pending the mandatory pre-sentencing report. The probation report disclosed nothing negative in Dr Love's background, and the terms of the plea-bargain were carried out.

Following the entry of the guilty plea, Judge Friedman summoned the prosecutor and defence attorney to his chambers and suggested that counsel agree to the destruction of some of the more explicit photographs of the Loves' sex life. These were among many photographs, books, letters and other objects from the Love house that had been confiscated by the police as possible trial-exhibits. Counsel readily agreed to the destruction of the X-rated pictures and they were forthwith burned in the judge's wastebasket.

During the proceedings, Love had said:

I deeply regret the death of my wife and my involvement in it. I feel that the judge and my lawyer said it all. I'm happy to have the opportunity to go back to work, support my family, and try to put our lives back together.'

He lost no time trying to do just that. He resumed his teaching career at Case-Western, where his colleagues were glad to welcome him back. Within a few months after his sentencing, he married a young law school student. Still, though, bad luck dogged his steps.

On a Saturday night in September 1975, less than a month after they married, the couple were accosted near Shaker Square by a pair of armed robbers. When Love told them he had no money, they took two dollars from his wife's purse and shot him in the stomach before fleeing. Love recovered, but the marriage did not. Soon the Loves separated and, after living apart for several years, divorced.

If Love is still trying to put his life together, he no longer is doing it in Cleveland. In 1979, he left his teaching position at Case-Western and moved to Colorado, where things could hardly be worse for him.

Following his trial, Love had filed a motion seeking the return of the balance of his personal property remaining in court custody. Among the items listed was the Loves' copy of *BUtterfield 8*.

It was duly returned, and it is to be hoped that its future readers will make a less expansive interpretation of the story of the dangling showgirl. If Dr Love has read *BUtterfield 8* all the way through, he will know that Gloria Wandrous, grieving over a lost love, dies in a fall from a boat. So both Gloria and Virginia Lee Love fell to their deaths. And both, in a way, died in the name of love.

Artist With a Razor

Molly Tibbs

PARK-LAND. LIMES, CEDARS, AND OAKS, lofty and branchy overhead. At insect-level, mossy banks, fungi, roots, boles and burrows. Cobham Park in leafy Kent, with the rose-red walls and twin Tudor chimneys of the Hall hazy above tree-tops. Early morning, sharp, towards the end of August, with the russets of autumn stippling the green.

Drenched in dew, the body of a man was lying face downwards on the grass, broken, an alien object, imported without congruity into the sylvan setting. It was waiting to be found. Exposed in the open – fully dressed – it lacked all semblance of cover, although an old chalk-pit, named Paddock Hole, was close by and would have served as a kind of grave: even a hyena would have concealed its kill by log or bush. Soon, someone from the estate would surely come that way . . .

Fate, however, chose two outsiders to make the discovery, and, for no other reason than that, to have their names remembered. In the crowded carrier's cart which plied between Rochester and Wrotham Market, on that Tuesday, 29 August 1843, were two country figures: Abraham Lyster, butcher of Eastgate, Rochester, and his nephew, Charles Lyster, who was forced to stand beside him – and so, as they neared the village of Cobham, had a clear view over the park railings. He it was who spotted the still, dark shape some thirty yards from the road. Asleep after the previous day's fair at Strood – or dead? Tentatively, they tried out a call, an almost apologetic salutation in the brisk morning air. No response. Cautiously, then, as the other passengers watched with stolid rustic faces, Charles clambered over a stile and approached the body.

Something paradoxically both limp and stiff in its attitude – with hands raised in awkward angles to the head – told him that the body was untenanted, nothing more in essence than a fallen scarecrow in a field.

After head-scratching consultation, and with the help of a shepherd, George Biggs, who had left his nearby flock when he saw there was something wrong, Charles turned the body over. In its new aspect, there rested no ambiguity: a crime of blood had been committed. The shepherd stayed to watch, while the cart carried the momentous news on to Cobham – to William Dawes, the village constable. He proceeded to the park and solemnly examined the corpse, noting that it was of a gentleman, a person of substance, dressed in a black coat, a green tartan waistcoat, dark trousers, and low shoes. As Dawes unbuttoned the waistcoat, a great clot of blood welled up and moved with a life of its own. The deep gashes in the throat, and the wound in the chest, showed that there was no question of suicide. The man had not died easily – the turf was pocked and rutted with the signs of a desperate struggle. His hat was found ten yards away, squashed into a disc. An open clasp-knife glinted beside the head, and, underneath the body, there was an open razor, very gory.

The body was carried to Cobham and laid temporarily to rest in the wheelwright's shop. As soon as the blood was washed from the face, identification was made by John Adams, a waiter at The Ship Inn. Perhaps he was not altogether surprised. It was little more than twelve hours earlier that a chaise had deposited at The Ship two unexpected visitors. The elder, the father, now identified, was already known to Adams. The other, the son, was a young man of unprepossessing appearance and poor manners. They asked for beds for the night; but there was no room at the inn. Adams offered to find accommodation in the village. 'One bed or two?' he enquired. 'One will do; this is my son, you know,' the older man replied. But the son had other ideas: as the waiter was leaving, he snapped, 'Get two beds if you can.'

Inwardly noting the tone of that command, Adams found

beds at two separate cottages, and returned to serve tea to the visitors. Afterwards, refreshed, they went for a walk. At about seven, they came back for supper: the father ordered cheese and biscuits for his son, whose appetite was clearly delicate, and boiled ham and a pint of porter for himself, after which he turned down his son's suggestion that they should take another walk. 'I am very tired,' he murmured. 'I don't care to go out any more.'

The young man sidled off to the bar, where he asked Emma Gardener, the publican's wife, for a glass of water. His demeanour disconcerted her. His head jerked, and he addressed her abruptly – 'not in the way in which gentlemen usually speak.' He then returned to the parlour and again pestered his father for a walk. Adams left them to it. At nine-thirty, Mrs Gardener saw them departing in the darkness – making for the Park. Time passed – beyond the duration of even the most intrepid walk in the country. Adams, who had not shown them where he had arranged for them to sleep, waited up until after midnight. Still no sign. He ventured out for a short distance. Nothing. Eventually, though still worried, he went to bed.

Now the amiable father lay lifeless and the son had vanished as completely as if one of the great trees had opened up its trunk and engulfed him in an upright coffin. Family circumstances and ominous recent events soon revealed to police investigation the bleak probability that the young man had murdered his father, and fled, bloodstained, from the frightful scene. *Parricide, the taboo crime that goes against nature, the mythological mistake of Oedipus.*

Shocked as they were, some members of the family had feared such a catastrophe, foreseen it even, and, unheeded like Cassandra herself, had warned the father against its coming. The tragedy was all the greater because the son was no ordinary man – or madman – but an artist of glittering promise. Richard Dadd was his horribly punning name. He was born on 1 August 1817 in Chatham, on the river Medway, in Kent. His father, Robert, was an apothecary at the sign of The Golden Mortar in the High Street. It was a good life, quite prosperous, quite cultivated; but the first pointer to what went wrong inside

Richard's mind is the death, in 1824, at the age of thirty-four, of his mother, Mary Ann. She had borne seven children, of whom Richard was the fourth. Within a year or two, a replacement mother had joined the ménage – young Sophia Oakes – but, after bearing two offspring, she herself slipped away, in 1830, aged twenty-eight.

Richard was a scholar at Rochester Cathedral Grammar School, where the education was excellent, but the headmaster, the Reverend D. F. Warner, was a dedicated flogger. The surrounding countryside was a solace for the smartings of boyhood. His favourite haunt was Cobham Park. There he wandered and sketched, his talents already recognized. In 1834, the motherless family moved to London and settled at 15 Suffolk Street, Pall Mall East. Robert had decided to change his avocation and was henceforth a water-gilder and ormolu specialist. Conveniently nearby, the Royal Academy was just moving into the new National Gallery building, and in 1837 Richard entered the Academy schools. Here he won three silver medals, and, together with Augustus Egg, William Powell Frith, John 'Spanish' Phillip and Henry O'Neil, formed the nucleus of a group of young, ambitious painters who called themselves The Clique. At one of their regular meetings, Richard's statement of intent was that he would devote himself 'purely to works of imagination' – another psychic pointer, perhaps.

Dadd works – some, especially diaphanous evocations of fairyland, already showing traces of his characteristic intricacy – began to appear at exhibitions, and he attracted interesting commissions. There was nothing to indicate that he was other than a rising young mid-Victorian artist with a gift for the fanciful, although one authenticated, if retrospective, foreboding is extant: Samuel Carter Hall (the original of Dickens' hypocritical Mr Pecksniff), editor of the *Art Union*, remembered uncomfortable visits to Richard's studio – 'I could never tell why, but, although I liked him much, I had always in his presence a sense of apprehension.'

However, all might yet have been well (although one must doubt it) had Richard stayed safely in London, never roaming further than the reedy marshes of the Medway and the well-remembered woods of Cobham Park. There enters now upon the scene a moustachioed knight, whose intervention unwittingly, through a chain of causation, led to the tragedy. Thomas Phillips, aged forty-one, Mayor of Newport, Monmouthshire, determined upon a Grand Tour to celebrate a series of glories – a knighthood bestowed for reading the Riot Act to an assemblage of seven thousand Chartists and being wounded with bullets, the Freedom of the City of London, and a call to the Bar of the Inner Temple. He needed a travelling companion who, in the Ruskinian mode, could record the romantic and classical sights – and sites – in sketchbooks, and David Roberts, an artist who knew them both, recommended Richard Dadd for his powers as a draughtsman *and his charming, sympathetic character*.

The connection duly made, the expedition set forth on 16 July 1842, copiously equipped, and with confident hopes of an adventure of a lifetime. It was to last for ten months. The variety and exotic richness of the itinerary were overwhelming. From Ostend, they journeyed through Belgium, Germany, Switzerland and Italy to Greece, by rail, coach, steamboat, foot, horse, rowing-boat and mule. Then on and on, to Constantinople, through Asia Minor, the Lebanon and Syria, before, exhausted, in November, they reached their promised land of Egypt. Sir Thomas, eager now for comfort, hired a boat with sixteen crew from the English consul at Cairo, and they glided in a dream, up the Nile to Thebes. Then homewards through Italy, lingering for a month in Rome. Antiquities and museums flowed on in unrelenting procession as Richard struggled to stay the pageant and preserve the moment. The experience was too demanding, too evanescent for him, and he developed feelings of de-realisation – 'A woman at a well, children playing, or a thousand things to arrest the attention . . . all seemed to slip away from me as if unreal,' he wrote in a letter.

Disenchantment of a more personal kind showed in another, guarded letter: 'The officers on board are very civil and attentive, and I perceive the value of my companion's title, as it procures him the smiles of all. I'm very tired of the world, and have seen so much disgusting selfishness since I have left England that I am half a misanthrope.'

Gradually, the hectic journey eroded the young artist's mental equilibrium. The short point is that he left home sane, and returned home quite mad, suffering from what is now termed paranoid schizophrenia. At that time, much was made of a slight attack of sunstroke which afflicted him in Egypt. The Victorians have turned out to be right about the maleficent effects of an overdose of sunshine on the skin, but it takes more than a touch of the sun to cause a violent psychosis. In a way, sunstroke – like, subsequently, shell-shock – was a convenient excuse or euphemism. (The sun even beams its way into the Jack the Ripper annals: 'The Holloway lunatic, who is detained on suspicion in connection with the Whitechapel murders, is a Swiss, named Isenschmid. Some time ago he kept a pork-butcher shop in Elthorne Road, Holloway, and he is known in the trade as a 'cutter-up'. Some years ago it seems, he had a sunstroke, and since then he has been subject to yearly fits of madness. These fits have usually come on in the latter part of the summer, and on several occasions his conduct has been so alarming that he has been carried off to Colney Hatch.'[1])

Michael Bryan, in his *Dictionary of Painters and Engravers* (1903), says that '"symptoms of weakness" had been noted before Richard Dadd went abroad, though this is an isolated assertion, and cannot be traced to source'. No doubt we shall have to wait until Patricia Allderidge, Archivist to the Bethlem Royal Hospital, completes her authoritative biography before we can know if the young artist set sail from England a whole man. What we do already know is that madness also touched three more members of the family – a sister, Maria Elizabeth (who is said to have tried to strangle her youngest child), a brother George William, and yet another brother, Stephen.

In her intense and overwrought novel, *Richard Dadd: His Journals*, Isaure de Saint Pierre, tantalisingly merging accurate research with fictive conjecture, portrays Richard as a homo-sexual, lingeringly seduced *en voyage* by Sir Thomas Phillips, and affected mentally by the experience. There is no hard evidence known to the writer that Dadd was in difficulties over his sexual identity, but one *could* adduce his *Drawing of a Young Boy*, dated about 1837, where the mood and posture are decidedly paederastic. It was Freud, too, who thought that the

1 *East London Advertiser*, 22 September 1888.

distorted thinking of paranoid schizophrenia serves to defend the sufferer against the unwelcome awareness of his own homosexuality!

Because he was a brilliant and imaginative artist with a well-stocked mind, the stuff of Richard's hallucinations and delusions was rich and rare. No commonplace ideas for *him* that the rays of the sun were tuned into his brain – but rather, a complicated and incorrigible belief that he was descended from lion-headed Osiris, god of the Nile, who was slain by Set but rose again to become judge of the dead in the lower regions. Interlocked into this fundamental delusion was a subsidiary theme – a mission, he said, 'To rid the world of those most possessed of the devil'. Authority figures seemed to him to be the most possessed.

When in Rome . . . We come now to an amazing episode in the Dadd story, an event which most commentators trivialize or underplay, bedazzled as they are by the sheer strangeness of the crime of parricide by so ethereal an artist. Richard Dadd is the man who could have killed the Pope. He could have changed papal history, been remembered as another, more successful, Mehmet Ali Agca, who, in 1981, fired a near-lethal bullet at the Pope in a chaotic scene in St Peter's Square. Rarely can a Pope have been in such danger – and never known of it – as Gregory XVI in that spring of 1843, when Richard prowled the piazzas and terrazzas of Rome. Even in those days, however, the pontiff was heavily guarded, and Richard realized that he would come off second best in any attempt to eliminate the 'false' Pope. Thus he 'overcame the desire' and one of J. B. Priestley's 'dangerous corners' was *not* turned.

By the time that they reached Paris, at the end of May, his precarious mental state was apparent to Sir Thomas, who tried to persuade him to see a doctor. Richard fled home, still not a homicide, but a changed man, with a piteous destiny overshadowing him. The Furies of madness hovered about him, but he contrived to carry on painting surprisingly coherent pictures worked up from the sketches which he had made on the tour. He exhibited at the Liverpool Academy exhibition of 1843.

His landlady, Mrs Smith, however, knew the truth about the young artist who shut himself away and worked feverishly in his studio at 71 Newman Street, and – rightly – feared him. Once, he painted all the figures in a picture a startling purple: 'It is my principle,' he explained. Even worse, he had a birthmark on his face, and one terrible day, he became convinced that it was a sign of Lucifer. He seized a palette-knife and hacked out the mark until his face streamed with blood. He stocked the studio with an egg-mountaain, and lived exclusively on them, washed down with bitter ale. One of his close friends from the Clique, it will be remembered, was Augustus Egg, and the pun will not have escaped the wildly whirring ratchets of his deranged mind: Egg was lucky not to have been scrambled! Indeed, portraits of friends propped against the walls were beginning to sprout a new embellishment – a slash of red across the throat.

The authority figure in his home environment was, of course, his own blameless father, and as he brooded and ruminated on the punning significance of 'Dadd', urgings in his head, probably auditory hallucinations, pressed him 'to put a period to the existence of him whom I had always regarded as a parent, but whom the secret admonishings [I had] counselled me was the author of the ruin of my race'. Not knowing, or not facing, the extent of the disease, Robert Dadd procrastinated, while Richard slipped out of his studio and bought from Mosely and Co, Cutlers, of New Street, Covent Garden, a spring-bladed knife and a razor.

Too late, on 26 August, Dr Alexander Sutherland of St Luke's Hospital, one of the most prominent alienists of the day, was consulted. He advised that Richard required constant supervision, since he was no longer responsible for his actions. The sensation of being under observation merely confirmed Richard in his simmering intentions. No strong drugs were available to damp down the delusions; nor, apparently, was restraint an option at that time. Sunday, 27 August, was a blank day of inertia and indecision. Monday, the 28th, the start of a new week, suggested itself to both father and son as a day for a change of scene – but whereas Robert's plans were therapeutic, Richard's were homicidal.

Robert proposed a trip to the Rosherville Gardens at Gravesend, but Richard inveigled him to the more isolated purlieus of Cobham Park. What could be more natural than a desire to return to the green acres which had been his solace and his inspiration in his childhood? There, he told his father, he would 'disburden' his mind to him. Gladly, Robert arranged the outing; they took the one o'clock steam-boat for Gravesend, disembarked at the Town Pier, and walked up the High Street to board the chaise which took them to The Ship Inn . . .

An elder son, Robert Dadd, Junior, made formal identification of his father. The *Maidstone Journal* reported his reaction: 'It will be easily conceived [of] his poignant feelings when he entered the shed, and beheld the lifeless corpse of his parent. He suddenly burst into a paroxysm of grief. "Richard has done this; he has murdered him, and I shall never see him again!"'

The general expectation was, as it would be today, that after such a terrible deed, the killer would turn the knife upon himself, not necessarily out of remorse, but as part of the pattern of his delusions. Richard's mind, however, still feasted on missions and projects which did not include self-destruction. He made for the continent, wrongly thinking, like many a modern fugitive, that there he would achieve anonymity. Colourful tales, mostly apocryphal, are told about his flight. It is known that he had means, but a certain menace in his eye must have protected him from robbery. He managed to replace his blood-stained clothing.

Wearing his new suit, he comes into full view again aboard a train going to Paris. Here, a fellow-traveller had the luckiest escape of his life, and the irony is that he never knew – never thanked God and vowed to lead a better life! In the vivid description of Henry Treffrey Dunn (*Recollections of Dante Gabriel Rossetti*, 1904): 'Dadd, still in doubt, began to fancy his companion was the devil incarnate, whom it was his mission to kill. Through the two windows of the carriage he gazed at the heavens and looked for a sign from it. The sun was setting and the sky was full of rain-clouds. It seemed borne in upon him that if the sun sank in serene and unclouded splendour, his fellow-traveller's life must be spared, but if otherwise, he saw his duty and was resolved to do it. The sun sank below the horizon cloudlessly, and his companion knew little of the fate he had escaped.'

Next, we see this by now very dangerous man, pensive about

his 'duty', seated with only one other passenger, a Monsieur M., in the egg-on-wheels of a stage-coach rumbling through the forest of Valence towards Fontainebleau. Great trees lofty and branchy overhead. Dark. Something mindful of a recent struggle with a stranger who was half his own flesh . . . *This* traveller, indignant, incredulous, terrified, had the closest shave of his life, and knew so! Leaning across, Richard kept on oddly 'lowering' Monsieur M.'s collar and cravat – and then, when asked to desist, whipped out 'an excellent English razor' and carved four quite deep cuts in his throat.

However, this near-second murder was not to be: Richard – weakened, perhaps, by a regimen of eggs and ale – lacked the extra quotient of muscular strength often coiled in the violently insane, and the Frenchman managed – just – to overpower him. Arrived at Montereau, Richard surrendered all his money so that his victim could be cared for, and later, before a justice of the peace, made full confession of his parricide. He was immediately incarcerated, first at Melun and then at Clermont asylum. A hit-list was found in his possession. His father headed the names, presumably with a tick beside him, and one entry was the Emperor of Austria, Ferdinand the First. Again, he could have changed history.

Never again a free man, Richard Dadd, much-admired artist, stood all day gazing at the sun and calling it his father. Osiris reigned in his once fine brain, and he seemed to be a hopeless case. They treated him kindly, and it was months before he was considered well enough to travel. Two Metropolitan policemen escorted him home. On 29 July 1844, he was examined before the magistrates at Rochester, and remanded for one week. He offered two observations: when the charge was being read, he cried out, 'You say I am the murderer, you villain!' and as he was being removed, he told the court, 'It is true, and I have got the money.'

At his second appearance, clad in a long blue cloak, his mood had changed, and he laughed incongruously. Although he was committed for trial at the assizes, this was a mere formality, because the bench forwarded the necessary certificates to the Home Secretary to implement Richard's admission to the State Criminal Lunatic Asylum, then at Bethlem Hospital, Southwark – the old 'Bedlam'. Here, although there was no cure for his condition, he regained the ability to paint. In 1864, all the 'criminal lunatics' were transferred from Bethlem to the newly-built Broadmoor Hospital. They travelled by rail. What a journey that must have been – a last sight of the world elsewhere! At Broadmoor, with its rhododendron-girt terraces, Richard carried on painting – strange, magical pictures which are now eagerly sought by collectors. And there he died, on 8 January 1886, at the age of sixty-eight, of tuberculosis. His grave in the asylum cemetery was only marked by a numbered stone, but his phoenix paintings live on.

A Reader's Revenge

A caricature of
Fitzhugh Coyle
Goldsborough

David Graham
Phillips

Lamb and a Slaughter

A water colour by G.F. Joseph, ARA *British Library Print Room*

A Reader's Revenge

Albert Borowitz

IN THE SALMAN RUSHDIE affair, a 'death sentence' has been imposed to punish an author for a book that gave offence that he did not intend or foresee. This is a remarkable chapter in the history of revenge, but not without precedent. When the twentieth century was little more than a decade old, the American novelist David Graham Phillips was assassinated by one of his readers; the killer was a madman who imagined that his sister had been defamed by the writer's fictional portrait of a frivolous daughter of Washington's high society.

Phillips, forty-three years old, was a man of regular habits: so regular that they could be easily monitored by a secret enemy. It was the novelist's unbroken custom to work at his desk until the early morning hours, producing manuscripts at the rate of six thousand words a day; he had once boasted, 'If I were to die tomorrow, I would be six years ahead of the game.' Phillips, in fact, praised work and sleep as life's greatest joys, since only they, he said, brought full unconsciousness. This is, of course, a benefit that is also bestowed by death.

On Monday, 23 January 1911, the ruggedly handsome Graham Phillips rose as late as usual and dressed his tall figure in the dandified style which he had affected. In the afternoon, he put on his black, rather crumpled, alpine hat and left his apartment (shared with his adored sister, Mrs Carolyn Frevert, after her separation from her husband) in the National Arts Club on the south side of Gramercy Park, a fashionable gated square in Manhattan. Skirting Gramercy Park, Phillips headed for the Princeton Club, on the northern side of the square, to collect his mail; the club was the former residence of the famed architect Stanford White. As he walked eastward on Twenty-First Street towards the club, the novelist may have given little more than fleeting attention to a man leaning against the iron railing of a house a few doors before the club entrance.

Suddenly the man blocked his path, and in rapid succession fired six shots from a .32 calibre automatic pistol. As Phillips staggered back towards the railing, a florist, John Jacoby, was near enough to prevent him from falling. Two club members, Newton James and Frank Davis, who had witnessed the scene in disbelief, heard the assailant cry something like: 'There you are! I guess that does for you.' The man then pointed the gun to his own head, adding, 'I'll finish the job now.' Walking to the curb, he fired again and fell dead.

James and Davis helped Jacoby carry Phillips into the clubhouse and laid him on a settee in the foyer not far from where Stanford White's coffin had stood five years earlier. Summoned by telephone, his private physician, Eugene Fuller, soon arrived at the club to superintend his removal by ambulance to Bellevue Hospital. There the surgeons confirmed that the first bullet fired had caused the most dangerous wound; it had entered the upper part of Phillips's chest between the first and second rib, passed through the right lung and come out at the back under the left shoulder-blade. Another bullet had passed through the right side of the abdominal wall without penetrating the intestines. The remaining shots had wounded Phillips in the left forearm, both thighs, and the right hip. The doctors removed from the muscles of his hip the only bullet that remained lodged in his body, and issued an optimistic bulletin, identifying as their main concern the risk of septic pneumonia in the injured lung.

The stricken novelist was visited in the hospital by Mrs Frevert and his brother, Harrison C. Phillips, a Denver newspaper man, who by chance had come to New York unannounced almost at the very hour of the shooting. When questioned by James at the club, Graham Phillips had said he did not know his attacker, but at Bellevue he told his sister that during the past few months he had been receiving anonymous threatening letters and telephone calls. Shortly before the shooting, he had received a message signed in his own name; it menaced, 'This is your last day'. A detective from police headquarters told reporters that Phillips had complained about the threats; in the policeman's view, 'that crank has got him'.

On Tuesday evening, 24 January, Phillips's condition took a turn for the worse. He was unable to retain any food, even a little beef broth served at about nine. Soon afterwards, internal haemorrhages began from both his stomach and the punctured lung. As he steadily became weaker with the loss of blood, Phillips himself saw that the efforts of the doctors were futile. Shortly before he lapsed into unconsciousness, the surgeons bending over him heard him murmur: 'I could have won against two bullets, but not against six.'

The news of Phillips's death, coming so soon after the first hopeful reports, shocked the journalistic and literary world and the public at large. Phillips was born in Madison, Indiana, and was educated at DePauw University in his home-state and at Princeton. After his graduation from Princeton, he began his career as a journalist at Cincinnati and in 1890 moved to New York, where he joined the staff of the *Sun*. In 1893, the tyrannical Joseph Pulitzer hired him as London correspondent for the *New York World*, and four years later he became an editorial writer for the newspaper. An uncompromising enemy of economic and political privilege, Phillips climaxed his journalistic career in 1906 by attacking the servility of the United States Senate to big business in his series, 'The Treason of the Senate', in William Randolph Hearst's *Cosmopolitan* (long before the days of Helen Gurley Brown). These articles inspired President Theodore Roosevelt to brand Phillips and other reform-minded journalists, including Lincoln Steffens, as 'muckrakers'.

Beginning in 1901, Phillips also began to turn his acid-dipped pen to fiction. The development of characters was not his strong point or major interest as a novelist, for in his stories he trained his guns against the same targets he had incessantly attacked in his columns: the 'extravagance of the wealthy classes, the abuse of political power, and the oppression of the poor'. As time went on, he took a special interest in exposing the superficiality of America's leisured classes and particularly of their women. One of his later caricatures was Margaret Severence, the female protagonist of *The Fashionable Adventures of Joshua Craig* (1909), described by Phillips as one of the 'fashionable noddle-heads' in Washington society. 'Like the others of her class,' Phillips wrote, 'she left the care of her mind to chance . . . Her person was her real care. To her luxurious, sensuous nature every kind of pleasurable physical sensation made keen appeal, and she strove in every way to make it keener.' To Margaret Severence, 'health meant beauty', and to make sure she had not neglected any muscle, she even engaged in daily yawning exercises. Phillips was frequently criticized for basing his characters on people he had met, but readers generally did not identify Margaret Severence with a real person. One reader, however, thought otherwise. That was Fitzhugh Coyle Goldsborough, Phillips's assassin.

The murderer's identity and address were discovered from an envelope in his pocket. A detective and reporters immediately proceeded to his lodgings, a top-floor rear-hall room rented for $3 a week at the Rand School of Social Science on East Nineteenth Street. The Rand School propagated an idiosyncratic brew of Christian socialism, a circumstance that led the *New York Times* to editorialize prematurely about the irony of a muckraking novelist being struck down by a socialist. The facts as they emerged from the police enquiries were infinitely stranger. Goldsborough, known by fellow lodgers to be an impecunious and unsociable music teacher, had never been to the Rand School lectures; had shown not the slightest interest in socialism. He had taken a room at the school for quite a different reason: its location afforded him an excellent vantage point for spying on the movements of Graham Phillips.

The police learned that Goldsborough was a member of a prominent family of the Eastern Shore of Maryland, which included a famous Civil War admiral. Fitzhugh, thirty-one years old, had been born in Washington, where his father Edmund was a well-known physician. He had early shown a musical talent, and was active in musical circles at Harvard, which he attended for three years. After studying and performing as a violinist in Vienna and Berlin, young Goldsborough joined the Pittsburgh Orchestra as a first violinist. However, about 1910 he left Pittsburgh in mid-season, leaving behind the message: 'The Pittsburgh smoke has driven me crazy. You will never see me again.' Although Goldsborough had established his musical credentials, his real passions lay elsewhere. He prided himself on his poetic gifts, and according to William T. Mossman, manager of the Pittsburgh Orchestra, 'insisted on inflicting his home-made poetry and epigrams on all who would listen'. Goldsborough would rush into the manager's office 'waving a new bit of poetry of his own making and insist on reading it to the whole office, and then would want to know what we all thought of it'. Goldsborough's captive audience judged his looks to be 'those of a man we didn't care to tell the truth to about his compositions, and we would always praise his works'. The caution displayed by Mossman and his colleagues seems to have been well-advised. Otto Kegel, a trumpeter in the orchestra, was also compelled by Goldsborough to listen to some of the poet's verses. When the trumpeter candidly remarked that it was the worst poetry he had ever heard, Goldsborough broke a $400 violin over his head, fled screaming from his house and was not seen for three days and nights.

Apart from his devotion to poetry, Goldsborough nourished a second passion of comparable intensity: like Graham Phillips, he was strongly attached to a sister. The violinist's frustrated literary aspirations and wounded family feelings were powerful emotional forces that, working in combination, were to prove fatal to Graham Phillips.

Phillips's family was convinced that the murderer was the author of the anonymous messages he had been receiving. Harrison Phillips concluded that it was the novel *The Fashionable Adventures of Joshua Craig* that had 'inflamed' Goldsborough's mind; the murderer thought he saw himself in the portrayal of Craig, an ambitious politician, and that his adored sister had been lampooned as Margaret Severence. Mayor William J. Gaynor's office was able to provide some support for this theory, and also revealed Goldsborough's belief that 'he was being shadowed by detectives or some persons seeking to do him an injury'. In the early summer of 1910, the distraught violinist had paid a visit to the mayor's office to render a complaint, but had been shunted aside to Gaynor's secretary Robert Adamson. After stating that he was being followed by two private detectives without cause, Goldsborough asked the patient functionary: 'Do you know David Graham Phillips?' When Adamson replied that he did, his odd visitor continued: 'Well, he has written up me and my family in one of his books, *The Fashionable Adventures of Joshua Craig.*'

Adamson got the impression that the reference to Phillips and his book reflected appreciation rather than resentment. However, the depth of the murderer's antipathy to Phillips was revealed by examination of a notebook and diary, which had dropped from his pocket as he fell in Gramercy Park, and from numerous writings discovered in his room.

Goldsborough appeared to be strongly affected by George Sylvester Viereck's 1907 novel, *The House of the Vampire*, a dramatic version of which had recently run at a New York theatre. The principal character in Viereck's fantasy was 'an intellectual vampire who absorbed the genius of all those with whom he came in contact'. Goldsborough formed the obsession that Phillips was a literary vampire who had sucked his ideas from Goldsborough's brain and had stolen his characters from the violinist's family. His diary entries contained many references to vampires, including the following note:

> To create characters with real blood in their veins, beyond the powers of many writers. Much easier to take them from real life – to utilize their actual flesh and blood by the easy, distinguished, legalized, and lucrative method of literary vampirism.

As a safeguard against being guilty of vampirism, the diarist proposed 'brotherly love'.

The search of Goldsborough's papers confirmed his preoccupations with his own name and with the career of the enemy he believed to be feeding on his life's blood. The solitary lodger 'had the habit of writing his name on little slips of paper torn from book margins, flyleaves, or anywhere else that best suited his convenience'. Sometimes he wrote his name five times to form a star, but if he had enough space on the paper he made a big wheel, with his name, many times repeated, as the spokes.

To reporters these autographs were evidence of the 'exaggerated ego' to which Goldsborough referred in his diary.

The name of Graham Phillips also loomed large in the papers the suicide left behind in his room. The police found a clipping of a newspaper interview with Phillips, published on the very day Goldsborough had moved into the Rand School building, 2 November 1910; the portion dealing with the novelist's reported views on standards of morality was heavily underscored.

It was the diary, however, that disclosed the full extent of the murderer's preoccupation with his enemy. In the first entries, Goldsborough wrote of a woman he saw through a window in the second storey of the National Arts Club building (in which Phillips resided on another floor). At first the violinist thought she was flirting with him, since she 'smiled over at [him] in a pointed manner, and on first catching sight of [him] lifted her hand and waved it'. But he revised his opinion when a man appeared behind her, half in sight near the window. Goldsborough thought this was Phillips, but was by no means sure. Ultimately he concluded that the woman was not attempting a flirtation but must be a friend of Phillips, plotting with the novelist to spread the story that Goldsborough was making advances.

Later Goldsborough found stronger evidence of the conspiracy when he was himself 'shadowed by a man who, by fixed staring at [him] in an impertinent manner on the street and rattling the spoon in his coffee cup when he came in a ten-cent restaurant, evidently wished to arouse [him] into belligerency'. On one occasion the man on his trail seemed to bear a 'good family likeness' to Mr Adamson, Mayor Gaynor's secretary – but 'his clothing was worn and second-hand looking'. In another entry, Goldsborough mentioned passing a man in Central Park who looked very much like Phillips, walking with a girl. He noted yearningly his wish that he could have been introduced to him some time before.

The diary recorded Goldsborough's efforts to communicate with Phillips as early as the previous June. He wrote that he 'called last night again on Phillips' but was told he had gone to Pittsfield, Massachusetts. Reluctantly Goldsborough concluded that the information must be true since it was separately confirmed by two bellboys. In any event, he was furious that Phillips had ignored his letters (a pardonable offence if they were indeed anonymous, as Phillips had told Carolyn Frevert). Nevertheless, to Goldsborough's mind the failure to respond was an acknowledgment of the vampire's guilt:

> At any rate P.'s ignoring my last letter and twice excusing himself after it, is in itself a confession of guilt of a sort. A man who has done no wrong will listen to one who claims he has; moreover the tone of that letter showed my intentions to be as amicable as he would let them be.

Despite his fancied slight at the hands of Phillips, Goldsborough continued to write to him; and the letters assumed a threatening tone. He signed the last of the letters 'David Graham Phillips', showing that his identification with his enemy was complete. As he waited for Phillips in Gramercy Park on the afternoon of Monday, 23 January, he was preparing to shoot his own double.

The funerals of victim and murderer provided a study in contrast. The arrangements for Phillips's service were made by Senator Albert J. Beveridge of Indiana, his college roommate at DePauw and life-long friend, from whom he had learned the gospel of the strenuous life. Pallbearers included Senator Beveridge and the novelist Robert Chambers, who was best known among lovers of fantasy fiction for his *The King in Yellow*. The author was lauded by Hildegarde Hawthorne in the *New York Times* for his 'vivid interest in the trend of American life, both in its public and private aspects'.

The service for Goldsborough was conducted in private and in as much obscurity as his prominent relatives could manage. Shortly before, they were embarrassed by the disclosure that a younger brother of the murderer had been in a sanatorium near Washington for the past couple of months, under treatment for mental troubles.

Despite the ample documentary evidence of Goldsborough's insanity, the crime and the subsequent suicide remained bewildering. In an editorial on 26 January, the *Times* searched for a logical explanation for Goldsborough's having taken his own life. The insane, the newspaper argued, 'differ from the sane by being more, not less, logical in passing from premise to conclusion, and they are weak, not in reasoning power, but in the power to select and judge the data from which they reason'. The special mark of a man like Goldsborough, with an 'exaggerated ego', was the lack of a sense of proportion; this defect, according to the *Times*, tended to make men murderous but did not drive men to suicide. On the contrary, most murderers with an oversized ego and a delusion of persecution (like Harry Thaw and Charles Guiteau, the murderer of President Garfield) were 'confident that everybody would admit the rightness of [their acts]'. Ergo, said the *Times*, the accomplishment of Goldsborough's long-meditated crime 'was followed by a lucid interval in which he appreciated its enormity and punished it'. If the *Times* was right, the lucid interval must have followed with blinding speed on the shooting of David Graham Phillips.

The family of the late Fitzhugh Coyle Goldsborough had a far simpler explanation. They accounted for both the murder and the suicide with the fact that Goldsborough had been suffering from a bad attack of flu.

Lamb and a Slaughter

Jonathan Goodman

IN COMMON WITH several of his literary contemporaries, Charles Lamb (1775–1834) took an interest in crime and punishment – particularly, and perhaps peculiarly, in the subject of survival after hanging.[1]

In January 1829, hearing of the marriage of his friend, Louisa Holcroft, to Dr J. Badams, Lamb wrote to Bryan Waller Proctor[2] from his home on the Chase at Enfield, a few miles north of London:

> Who is Badman, or Bed'em? . . . I hear he is a great chymist. I am sometimes chymical myself. A thought strikes me with horror. Pray heaven he may not have done it for the sake of trying chymical experiments upon her, – young female subjects are so scarce! Louisa would make a capital shot. An't you glad about Burke's case? We may set off the Scotch murders against the Scotch novels – Hare, the Great Un-hanged.

(You will no doubt have gathered that Lamb was speaking of Messrs Burke and Hare, who, early in 1828, had hit on the idea of *making* corpses – 'shots', they came to call them – for sale as 'subjects' for dissection at Dr Robert Knox's school of

---

1 See his *Reflector* essay, 'On the Inconveniences of Being Hanged'; also his farce, *The Pawnbroker's Daughter*.
2 A minor poet under the pen-name of Barry Cornwall; he was living at 38 Harley Street, in the West End of London.

anatomy in Surgeons' Square, Edinburgh; after 'burking' – smothering – at least fifteen persons, they were arrested; Hare turned King's evidence, and Burke, found guilty on Christmas Day, 1828, was hanged a day or so after Lamb wrote to Proctor. The last joke in Lamb's letter was apropos of the fact that when the Waverley Novels first appeared, the anonymous author – actually, Walter Scott – was called 'the Great Unknown'.)

In December 1832, Lamb's interest in crime became more than scholarly – indeed, it seems that for a short while he was actually under suspicion of being an accessory to murder.[1] On the nineteenth, a young man named Benjamin Couch Danby, who had just returned from India and was thought to have money about him, spent the evening at the Crown & Horseshoe, Enfield, in the company of William Johnson, John Cooper, and Samuel Fare. At closing-time, the three men took Danby up Holt White's Hill, where they robbed and murdered him. The crime was versified in a broadsheet ballad:

Give ear ye tender Christians all and listen unto me,
While I relate a deed of blood and great barbarity;
A murder of the blackest dye I now repeat in rhyme,
Committed on Benjamin Danby, a young man in his prime.

This young man was a sailor, and just returned from sea,
And down to Enfield Chase he went, his cousin for to see,
With money in his pocket, so jolly and so free,
But little did he dream of such a dismal destiny.

'Twas on a Wednesday ev'ning he call'ed at the Horseshoe,
And there he drank so freely, as sailors mostly do;
Some ruffians in the company whom he did treat most kind,
To rob and murder him that night most wickedly designed.

---

1 In 1796, Lamb's elder sister Mary, over-work and anxiety affecting her mind, had become so irritated with a young home-help that she had chased the girl round the sitting-room with a knife, and then, further irritated by the efforts of her own mother – an invalid, not quite right in the head – to hinder her efforts to catch the girl, had stabbed her mother to death. Found by a coroner's jury to be temporarily insane, Mary had been given into the custody of Charles, then just of age, who had undertaken to be her guardian.

They threw him on the ground and then stabbed him with a knife;
He cried out, 'Do not murder me! – O do not take my life!'
But heedless of his piteous cries, his throat they cut quite deep,
And turn'd the gully in his throat as butchers kill their sheep.

Then in a ditch they threw his corpse, mangled with ghastly wounds,
Where early the next morning the body it was found.
Now Cooper, Fare and Johnson are committed for this crime,
And will be tried at Newgate all in a little time.

Lamb explained his involvement in the case in a letter to
Louisa Badams, written on New Year's Eve, 1832:

. . . I have been not a little disconcerted.

On the night of our murder (an hour or two before it), the maid
being busy, I went out to order an additional pint of porter for
Moxon [Edward Moxon, Lamb's friend and publisher] who had
surprised us with a late visit. Now I never go out quite disinterested
upon such occasions. And I begged a half-pint of ale at the bar
which our sweet-faced landlady good-humouredly complied with,
asking me into the parlour, but a side door was just open that
disclosed a more cheerful blaze, and I entered where four people
were engaged over Dominoes. One of them, Fare, invited me to
join in it, partly out of impudence, I believe; however, not to balk a
Christmas frolic, I complied, and played with Danby, but soon
gave over, having forgot the game. I was surprised with D.
challenging me as having known me in the Temple. He must have
been a child then. I did not recognise him, but perfectly remembered his father, who was a hairdresser in the Temple. This was all
that passed, as I went away with my beer. Judge my surprise when
the next morning I was summoned before Dr Creswell to say what I
knew of the transaction. My examination was conducted with all
delicacy, and of course I was soon dismissed. I was afraid of getting
into the papers, but I was pleased to find myself only noticed as a
'gentleman whose name we could not gather'.

Poor D.! the few words I spoke to him were to remind him of a
trick Jem White played upon his father. The boy was too young to
know anything about it. In the *Morning Post* appeared this paragraph: 'Yesterday morning, Mr Danby, the respectable Hairdresser in Pump Court in the Temple, in a fit of delirium threw

himself out of a 2 pair stairs window, looking into the passage that leads to Fig-tree Court, and his head was literally smashed to atoms.' White went to D.'s to see how it operated, and found D. quietly weaving wigs, and the shop full of lawyers that had come to enquire particulars. D. was a man much respected. Indeed hairdressers in the Inns of Court are a superior race of tradesmen. They generally leave off rich, as D. did.

Well, poor D. [Junior] had never heard the story or probably forgotten it – and his company looked on me a little suspiciously, as they do in alehouses when a rather better drest person than themselves attempts to join 'em – (it never answers, – at least it seemed so to me when I heard of the murder) – I went away. One often fancies things afterwards that did not perhaps strike one at the time. However, after all, I have felt queer ever since. It has almost sickened me of the Crown and Horseshoe, and I sha'n't hastily go into the taproom again.

As soon as he had recovered from the 'feeling of queerness', Lamb invited Moxon to Enfield, telling him that 'Johnson and Fare's sheets have been wash'd – unless you prefer Danby's *last* bed – at the Horseshoe'.

At the trial at the Old Bailey in January, Cooper turned King's evidence and Fare was acquitted, but Johnson was convicted and sentenced to death. Lamb wrote to Louisa Badams on 15 February 1833:

Thanks for your remembrance of your old fellow-prisoners at murderous Enfield. By the way, Cooper, who turned King's evidence, is come back again Whitewash'd, has resumed his seat at chapel, and took his sister (a fact!) up the Holt White's lane to shew her the topography of the deed. I intend asking him to supper. They say he's pleasant in conversation. Will you come and meet him?

So far as is known, Louisa turned down that invitation.

Acknowledgments and Sources

In addition to those given in the text: 'Pen, Pencil, and Poison' was first published in Frank Harris's *Fortnightly Review*, January 1889, and then became a chapter in *Intentions*, of which there have been several editions (eg by the Unicorn Press, London, 1945); 'The Immortal Trooper', which first appeared in the *Police Review*, is published by permission of the author; 'The Murderous Brush-Work of William Hepper' is published by permission of the author; 'The Sportsman and the Scholar: A Family Secret' is published by permission of the author; 'Salieri and the "Murder" of Mozart', a revised version of a chapter in *Innocence and Arsenic* (Harper & Row, New York, 1977), is published by permission of the author; 'Bloody and Bowed: The Brief Life of a Playwright' is published by permission of the author; the commentating parts of 'Architect of a Murder' are published by permission of the author; 'A Literate Killer', extracts from *French Crime in the Romantic Age* (Hamish Hamilton, London, 1970), is published by permission of Margaret Heppenstall; there are several editions of John Addington Symonds's translation of *The Autobiography of Benvenuto Cellini*, from which 'Revenge in Rome' is taken (eg by Phaidon, Oxford, 1983); 'In the Name of Love', a revised version of an essay that first appeared in *Cleveland* magazine, is published by permission of the author; 'Artist With a Razor' is published by permission of the author; 'A Reader's Revenge' is published by permission of the author; 'Lamb and a

Slaughter', an entry in *Bloody Versicles: The Rhymes of Crime* (2nd, revised edition: Hallmark Books, Penarth, 1990), is published by permission of the author.